04/07

Happy Endings

DARK HORSE MAVERICK™

editor
DIANA SCHUTZ

assistant editor
JEREMY BARLOW

book design
CARY GRAZZINI

digital production
JASON HVAM

publisher
MIKE RICHARDSON

Published by
Dark Horse Comics, Inc.
10956 SE Main Street
Milwaukie, Oregon 97222

First edition: September 2002
ISBN 1-56971-820-2

10 9 8 7 6 5 4 3 2 1

PRINTED IN CANADA

GRAPH
HAPPY

Table of Contents

Cover art by **Frank Miller**
Cover color by **Lynn Varley**

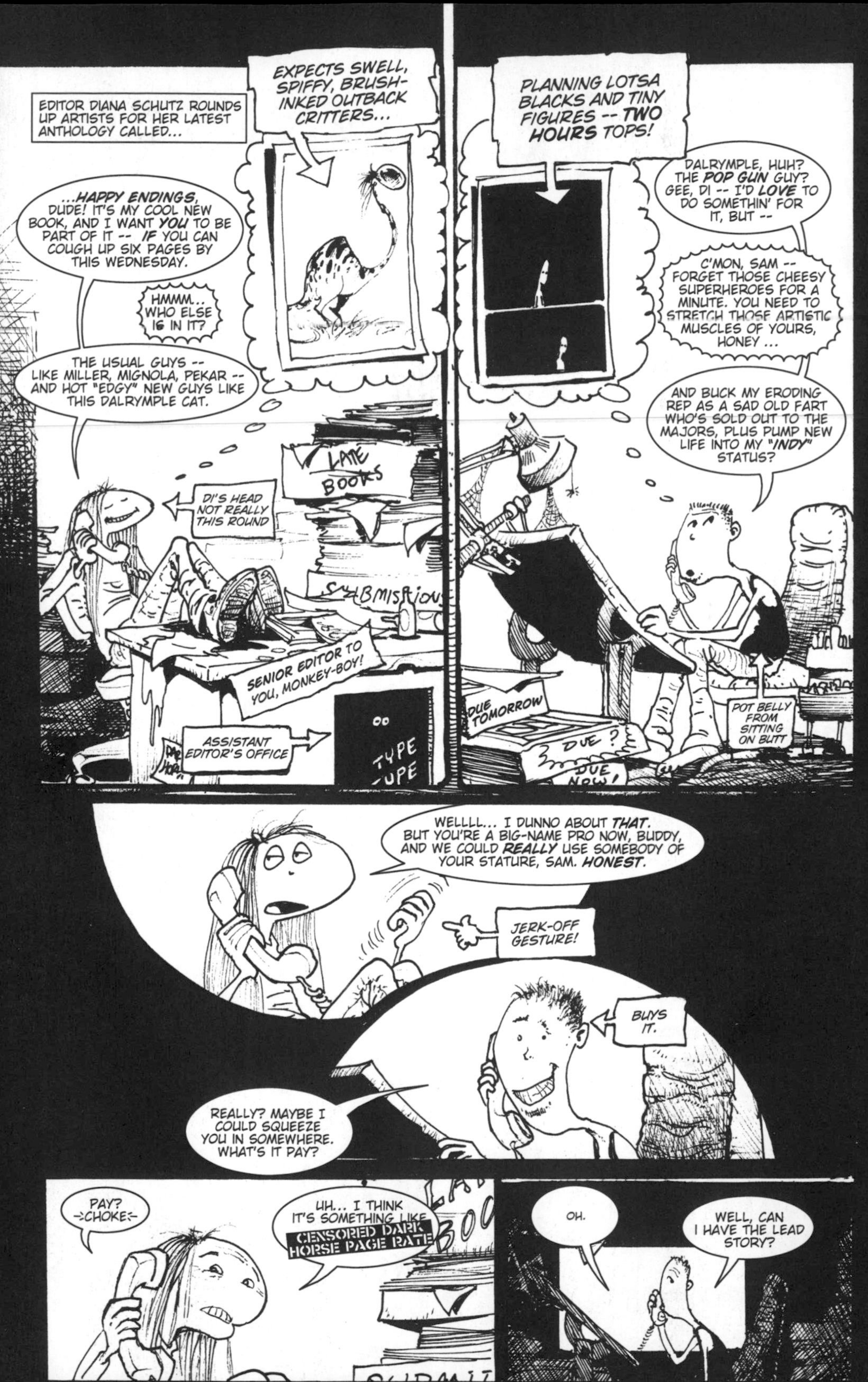
EDITOR DIANA SCHUTZ ROUNDS UP ARTISTS FOR HER LATEST ANTHOLOGY CALLED...
...HAPPY ENDINGS, DUDE! IT'S MY COOL NEW BOOK, AND I WANT YOU TO BE PART OF IT -- IF YOU CAN COUGH UP SIX PAGES BY THIS WEDNESDAY.
HMMM... WHO ELSE IS IN IT?
THE USUAL GUYS -- LIKE MILLER, MIGNOLA, PEKAR -- AND HOT "EDGY" NEW GUYS LIKE THIS DALRYMPLE CAT.
EXPECTS SWELL, SPIFFY, BRUSH-INKED OUTBACK CRITTERS...
LATE BOOKS
SUBMISSIONS
DI'S HEAD NOT REALLY THIS ROUND
SENIOR EDITOR TO YOU, MONKEY-BOY!
ASSISTANT EDITOR'S OFFICE
TYPE TYPE
PLANNING LOTSA BLACKS AND TINY FIGURES -- TWO HOURS TOPS!
DALRYMPLE, HUH? THE POP GUN GUY? GEE, DI -- I'D LOVE TO DO SOMETHIN' FOR IT, BUT --
C'MON, SAM -- FORGET THOSE CHEESY SUPERHEROES FOR A MINUTE. YOU NEED TO STRETCH THOSE ARTISTIC MUSCLES OF YOURS, HONEY ...
AND BUCK MY ERODING REP AS A SAD OLD FART WHO'S SOLD OUT TO THE MAJORS, PLUS PUMP NEW LIFE INTO MY "INDY" STATUS?
DUE TOMORROW
DUE?
DUE NOW!
POT BELLY FROM SITTING ON BUTT
WELLLL... I DUNNO ABOUT THAT. BUT YOU'RE A BIG-NAME PRO NOW, BUDDY, AND WE COULD REALLY USE SOMEBODY OF YOUR STATURE, SAM. HONEST.
JERK-OFF GESTURE!
BUYS IT.
REALLY? MAYBE I COULD SQUEEZE YOU IN SOMEWHERE. WHAT'S IT PAY?
PAY? -:CHOKE:-
UH... I THINK IT'S SOMETHING LIKE CENSORED DARK HORSE PAGE RATE
OH.
WELL, CAN I HAVE THE LEAD STORY?

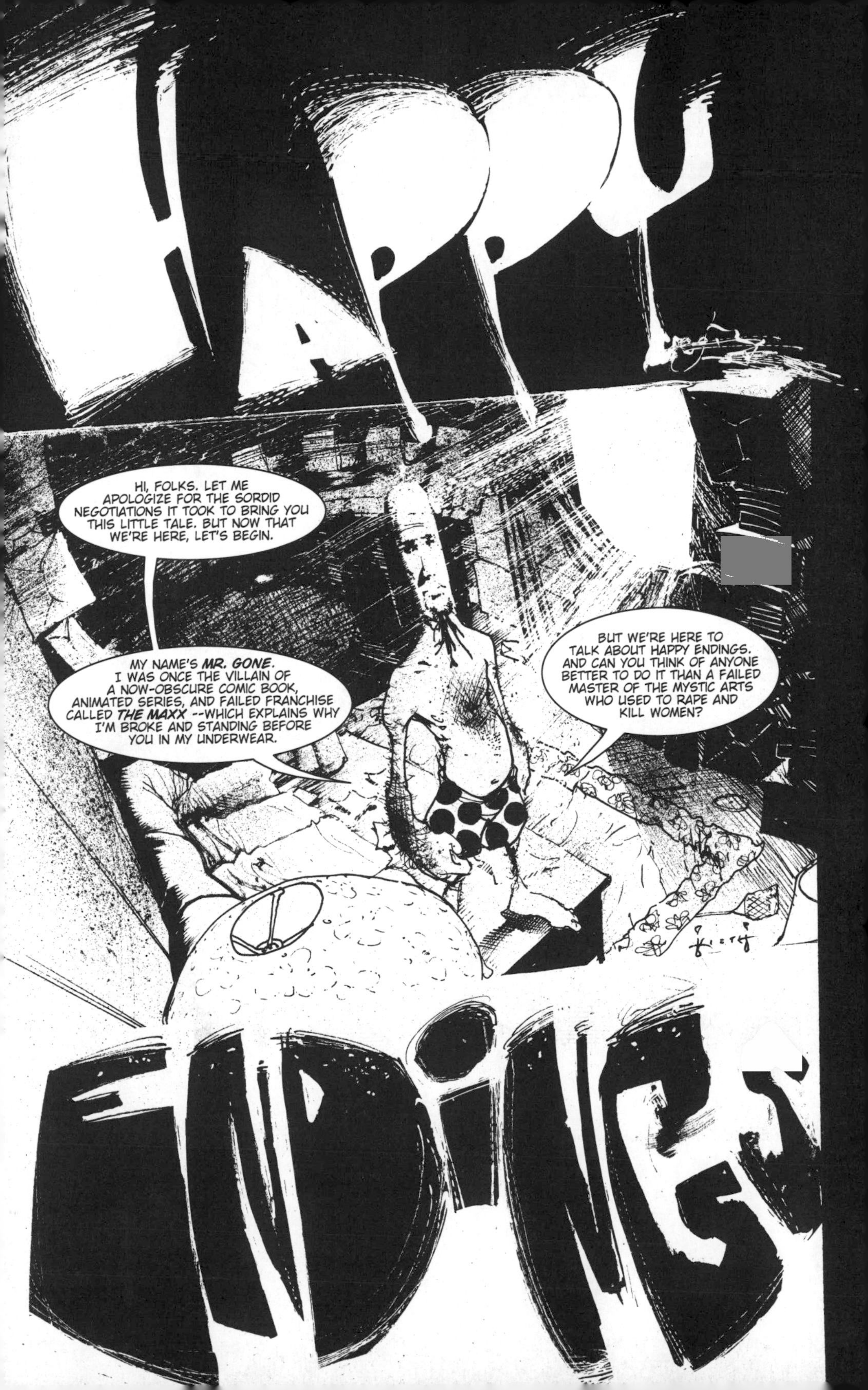
HAPPY
HI, FOLKS. LET ME APOLOGIZE FOR THE SORDID NEGOTIATIONS IT TOOK TO BRING YOU THIS LITTLE TALE. BUT NOW THAT WE'RE HERE, LET'S BEGIN.
MY NAME'S **MR. GONE.** I WAS ONCE THE VILLAIN OF A NOW-OBSCURE COMIC BOOK, ANIMATED SERIES, AND FAILED FRANCHISE CALLED ***THE MAXX*** --WHICH EXPLAINS WHY I'M BROKE AND STANDING BEFORE YOU IN MY UNDERWEAR.
BUT WE'RE HERE TO TALK ABOUT HAPPY ENDINGS. AND CAN YOU THINK OF ANYONE BETTER TO DO IT THAN A FAILED MASTER OF THE MYSTIC ARTS WHO USED TO RAPE AND KILL WOMEN?
ENDINGS

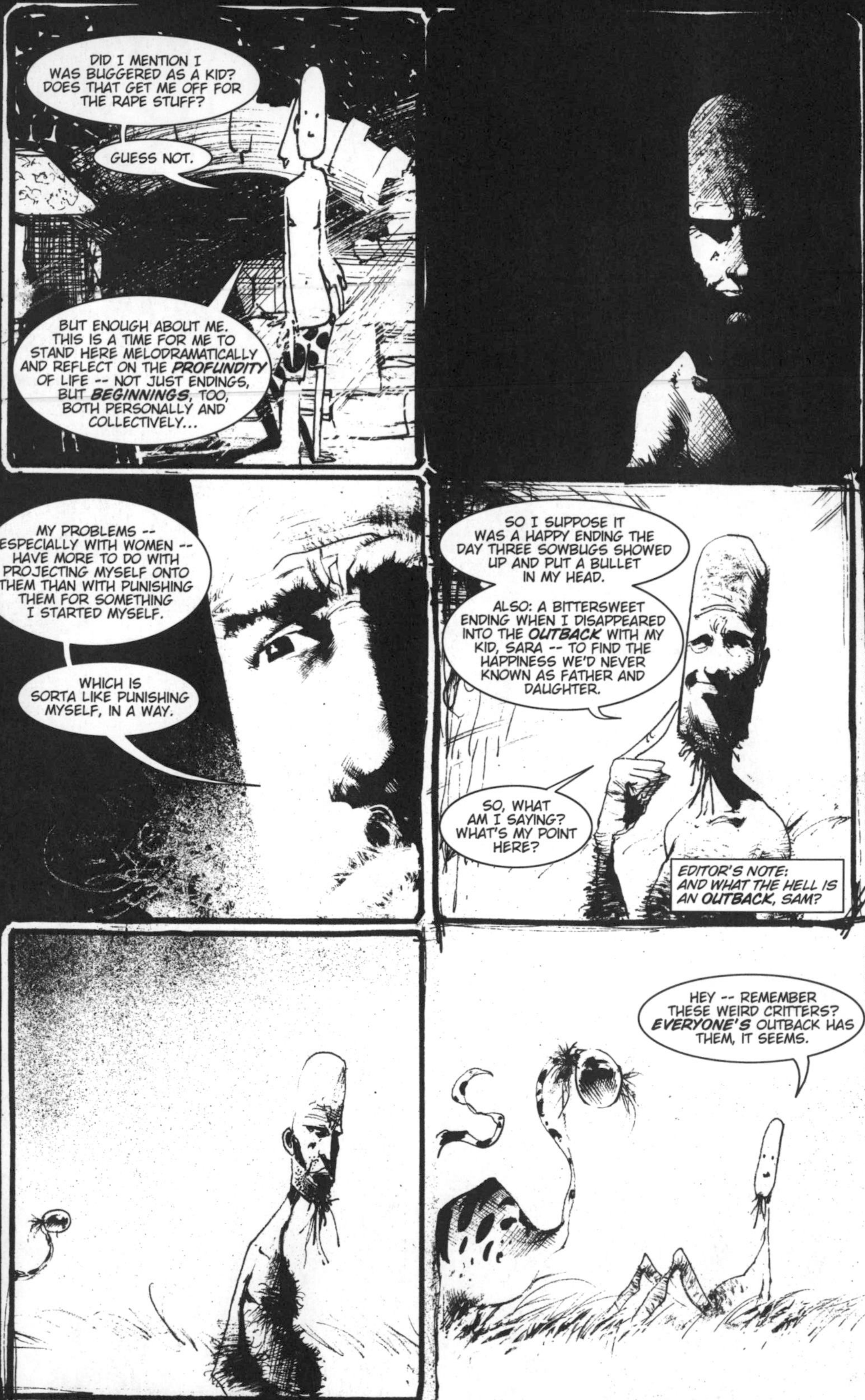
DID I MENTION I WAS BUGGERED AS A KID? DOES THAT GET ME OFF FOR THE RAPE STUFF?
GUESS NOT.
BUT ENOUGH ABOUT ME. THIS IS A TIME FOR ME TO STAND HERE MELODRAMATICALLY AND REFLECT ON THE *PROFUNDITY* OF LIFE -- NOT JUST ENDINGS, BUT *BEGINNINGS*, TOO, BOTH PERSONALLY AND COLLECTIVELY...
MY PROBLEMS -- ESPECIALLY WITH WOMEN -- HAVE MORE TO DO WITH PROJECTING MYSELF ONTO THEM THAN WITH PUNISHING THEM FOR SOMETHING I STARTED MYSELF.
WHICH IS SORTA LIKE PUNISHING MYSELF, IN A WAY.
SO I SUPPOSE IT WAS A HAPPY ENDING THE DAY THREE SOWBUGS SHOWED UP AND PUT A BULLET IN MY HEAD.
ALSO: A BITTERSWEET ENDING WHEN I DISAPPEARED INTO THE *OUTBACK* WITH MY KID, SARA -- TO FIND THE HAPPINESS WE'D NEVER KNOWN AS FATHER AND DAUGHTER.
SO, WHAT AM I SAYING? WHAT'S MY POINT HERE?
EDITOR'S NOTE: AND WHAT THE HELL IS AN OUTBACK, SAM?
HEY -- REMEMBER THESE WEIRD CRITTERS? *EVERYONE'S* OUTBACK HAS THEM, IT SEEMS.

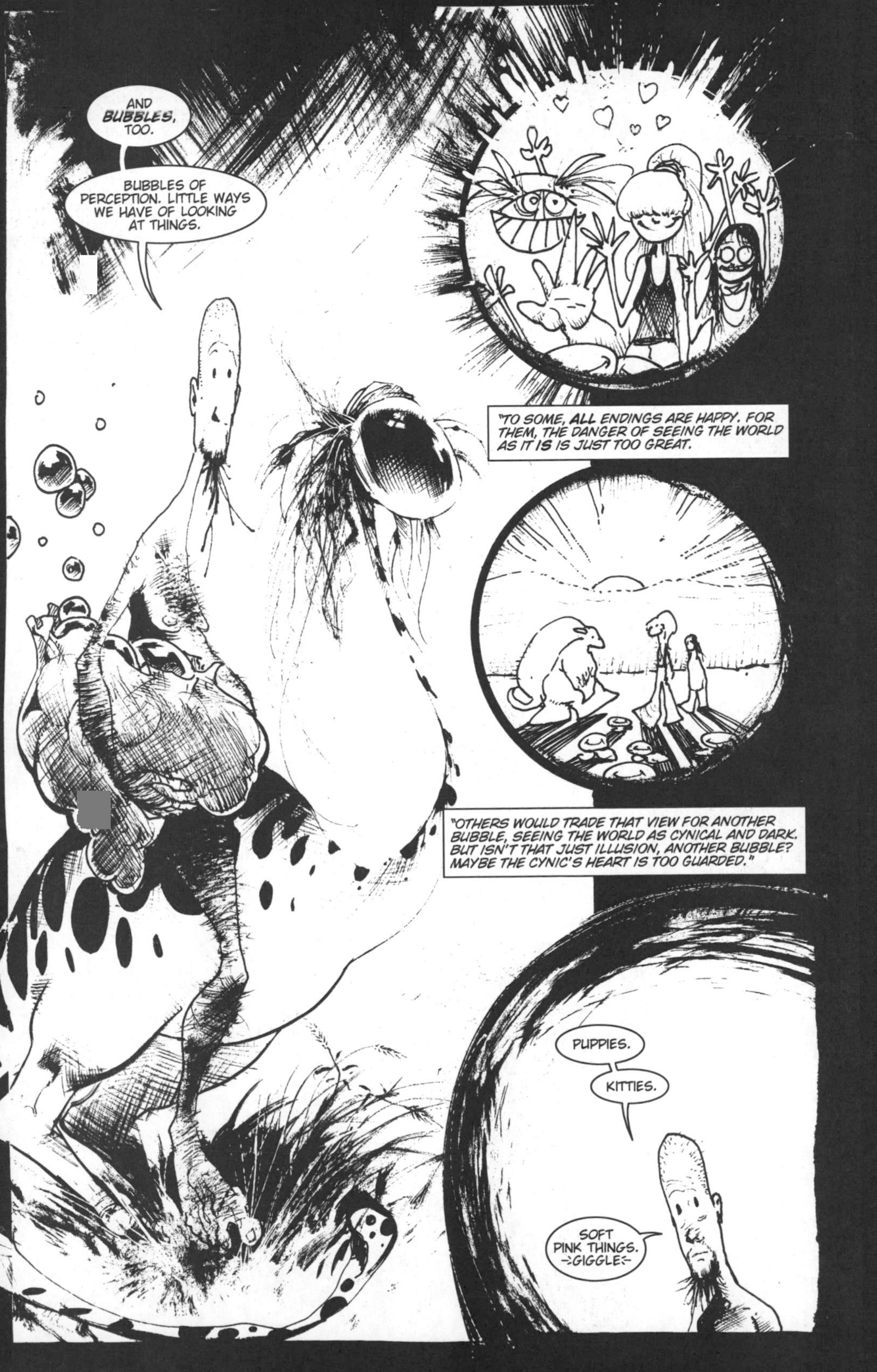
AND BUBBLES, TOO.
BUBBLES OF PERCEPTION. LITTLE WAYS WE HAVE OF LOOKING AT THINGS.
"TO SOME, ALL ENDINGS ARE HAPPY. FOR THEM, THE DANGER OF SEEING THE WORLD AS IT IS IS JUST TOO GREAT.
"OTHERS WOULD TRADE THAT VIEW FOR ANOTHER BUBBLE, SEEING THE WORLD AS CYNICAL AND DARK. BUT ISN'T THAT JUST ILLUSION, ANOTHER BUBBLE? MAYBE THE CYNIC'S HEART IS TOO GUARDED."
PUPPIES.
KITTIES.
SOFT PINK THINGS. *GIGGLE*

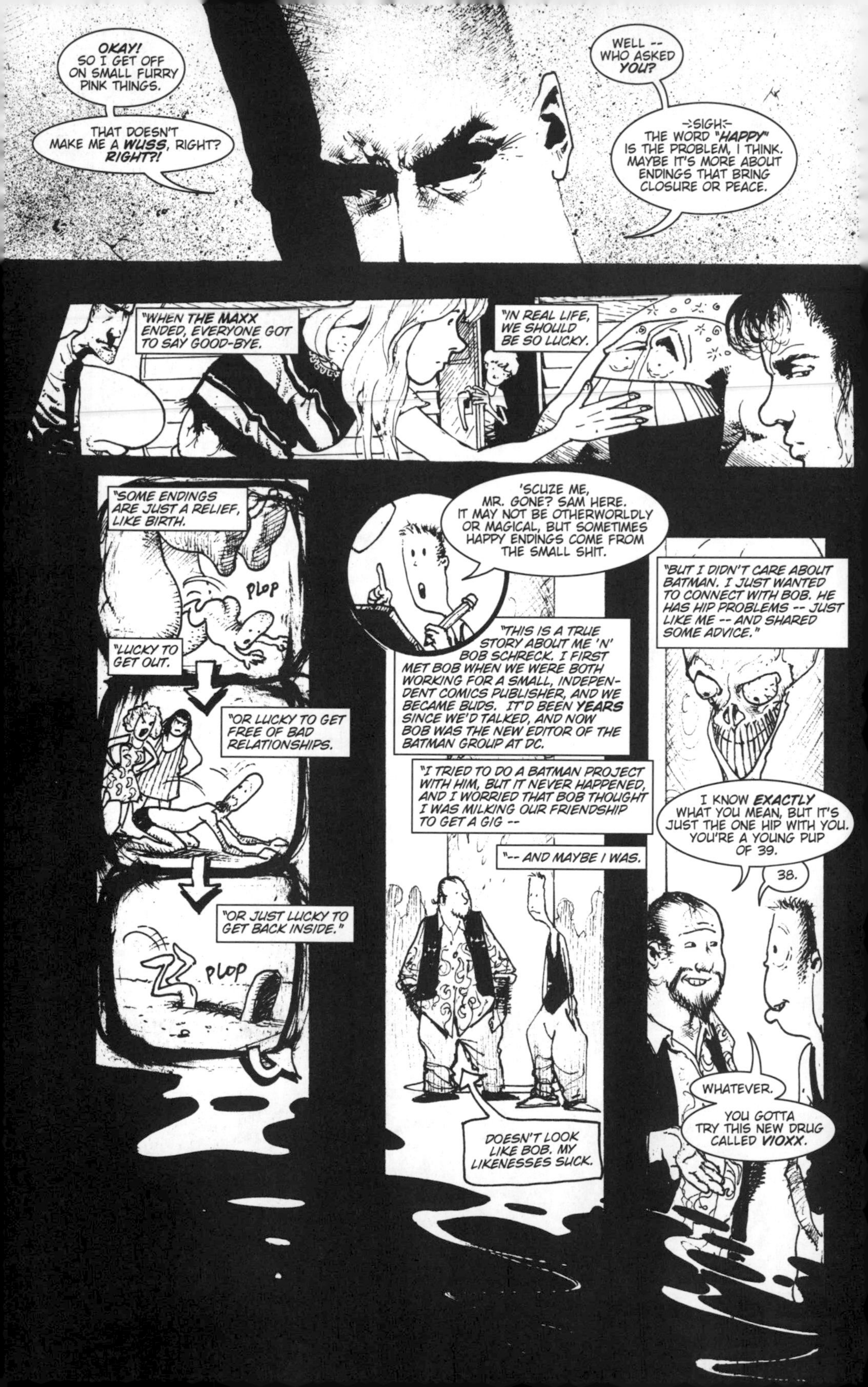
OKAY! SO I GET OFF ON SMALL FURRY PINK THINGS.
THAT DOESN'T MAKE ME A WUSS, RIGHT? RIGHT?!
WELL -- WHO ASKED YOU?
-SIGH- THE WORD "HAPPY" IS THE PROBLEM, I THINK. MAYBE IT'S MORE ABOUT ENDINGS THAT BRING CLOSURE OR PEACE.
"WHEN THE MAXX ENDED, EVERYONE GOT TO SAY GOOD-BYE.
"IN REAL LIFE, WE SHOULD BE SO LUCKY.
"SOME ENDINGS ARE JUST A RELIEF, LIKE BIRTH.
PLOP
"LUCKY TO GET OUT.
"OR LUCKY TO GET FREE OF BAD RELATIONSHIPS.
"OR JUST LUCKY TO GET BACK INSIDE."
PLOP
'SCUZE ME, MR. GONE? SAM HERE. IT MAY NOT BE OTHERWORLDLY OR MAGICAL, BUT SOMETIMES HAPPY ENDINGS COME FROM THE SMALL SHIT.
"THIS IS A TRUE STORY ABOUT ME 'N' BOB SCHRECK. I FIRST MET BOB WHEN WE WERE BOTH WORKING FOR A SMALL, INDEPENDENT COMICS PUBLISHER, AND WE BECAME BUDS. IT'D BEEN YEARS SINCE WE'D TALKED, AND NOW BOB WAS THE NEW EDITOR OF THE BATMAN GROUP AT DC.
"I TRIED TO DO A BATMAN PROJECT WITH HIM, BUT IT NEVER HAPPENED, AND I WORRIED THAT BOB THOUGHT I WAS MILKING OUR FRIENDSHIP TO GET A GIG --
"-- AND MAYBE I WAS.
DOESN'T LOOK LIKE BOB. MY LIKENESSES SUCK.
"BUT I DIDN'T CARE ABOUT BATMAN. I JUST WANTED TO CONNECT WITH BOB. HE HAS HIP PROBLEMS -- JUST LIKE ME -- AND SHARED SOME ADVICE."
I KNOW EXACTLY WHAT YOU MEAN, BUT IT'S JUST THE ONE HIP WITH YOU. YOU'RE A YOUNG PUP OF 39.
38.
WHATEVER.
YOU GOTTA TRY THIS NEW DRUG CALLED VIOXX.

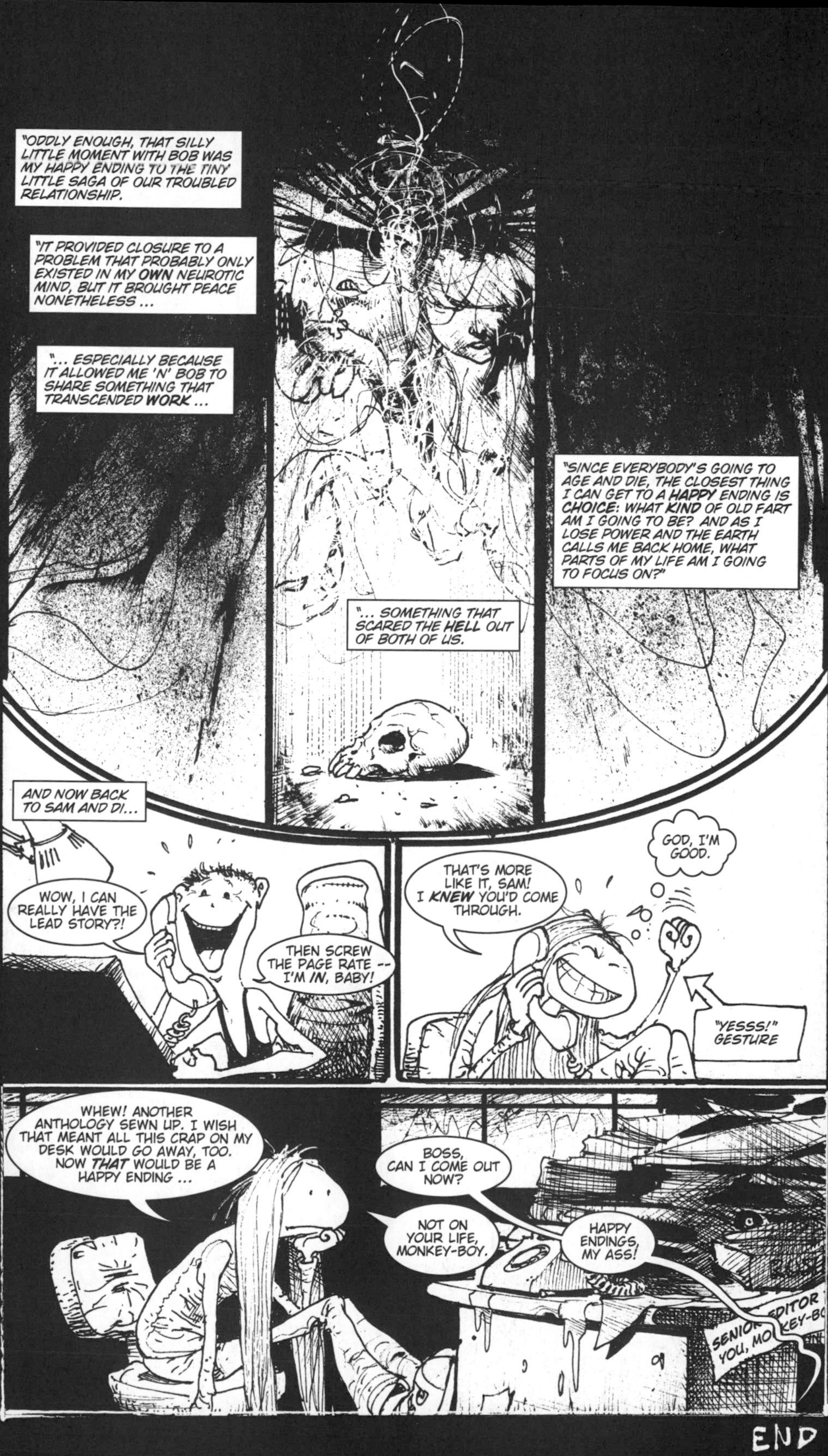
"ODDLY ENOUGH, THAT SILLY LITTLE MOMENT WITH BOB WAS MY HAPPY ENDING TO THE TINY LITTLE SAGA OF OUR TROUBLED RELATIONSHIP.
"IT PROVIDED CLOSURE TO A PROBLEM THAT PROBABLY ONLY EXISTED IN MY OWN NEUROTIC MIND, BUT IT BROUGHT PEACE NONETHELESS ...
"... ESPECIALLY BECAUSE IT ALLOWED ME 'N' BOB TO SHARE SOMETHING THAT TRANSCENDED WORK ...
"... SOMETHING THAT SCARED THE HELL OUT OF BOTH OF US.
"SINCE EVERYBODY'S GOING TO AGE AND DIE, THE CLOSEST THING I CAN GET TO A HAPPY ENDING IS CHOICE: WHAT KIND OF OLD FART AM I GOING TO BE? AND AS I LOSE POWER AND THE EARTH CALLS ME BACK HOME, WHAT PARTS OF MY LIFE AM I GOING TO FOCUS ON?"
AND NOW BACK TO SAM AND DI...
WOW, I CAN REALLY HAVE THE LEAD STORY?!
THEN SCREW THE PAGE RATE -- I'M IN, BABY!
THAT'S MORE LIKE IT, SAM! I KNEW YOU'D COME THROUGH.
GOD, I'M GOOD.
"YESSS!" GESTURE
WHEW! ANOTHER ANTHOLOGY SEWN UP. I WISH THAT MEANT ALL THIS CRAP ON MY DESK WOULD GO AWAY, TOO. NOW THAT WOULD BE A HAPPY ENDING ...
BOSS, CAN I COME OUT NOW?
NOT ON YOUR LIFE, MONKEY-BOY.
HAPPY ENDINGS, MY ASS!
END

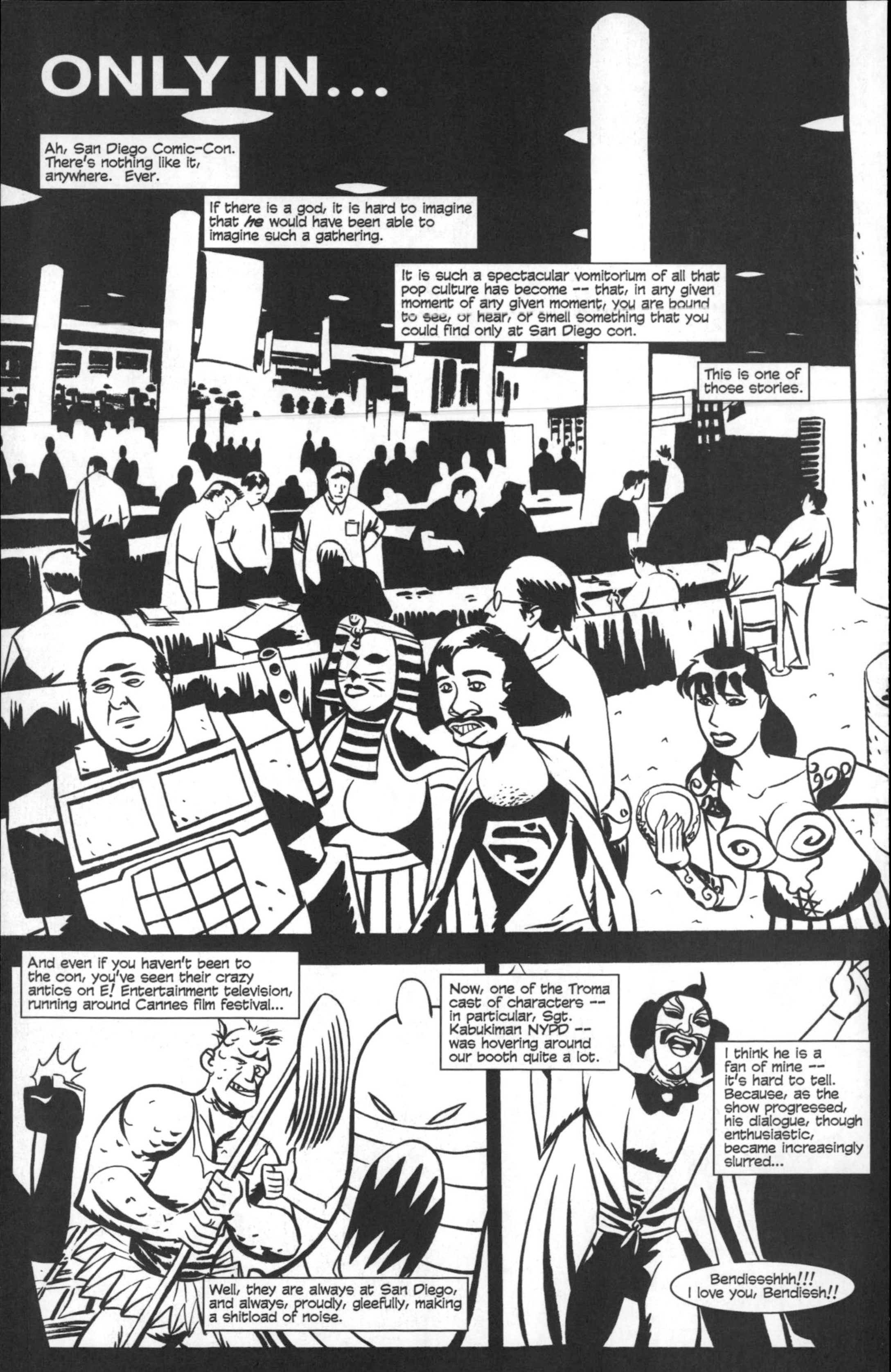
ONLY IN...
Ah, San Diego Comic-Con. There's nothing like it, anywhere. Ever.
If there is a god, it is hard to imagine that *he* would have been able to imagine such a gathering.
It is such a spectacular vomitorium of all that pop culture has become -- that, in any given moment of any given moment, you are bound to see, or hear, or smell something that you could find only at San Diego con.
This is one of those stories.
And even if you haven't been to the con, you've seen their crazy antics on E! Entertainment television, running around Cannes film festival...
Well, they are always at San Diego, and always, proudly, gleefully, making a shitload of noise.
Now, one of the Troma cast of characters -- in particular, Sgt. Kabukiman NYPD -- was hovering around our booth quite a lot.
I think he is a fan of mine -- it's hard to tell. Because, as the show progressed, his dialogue, though enthusiastic, became increasingly slurred...
Bendissshhh!!! I love you, Bendissh!!

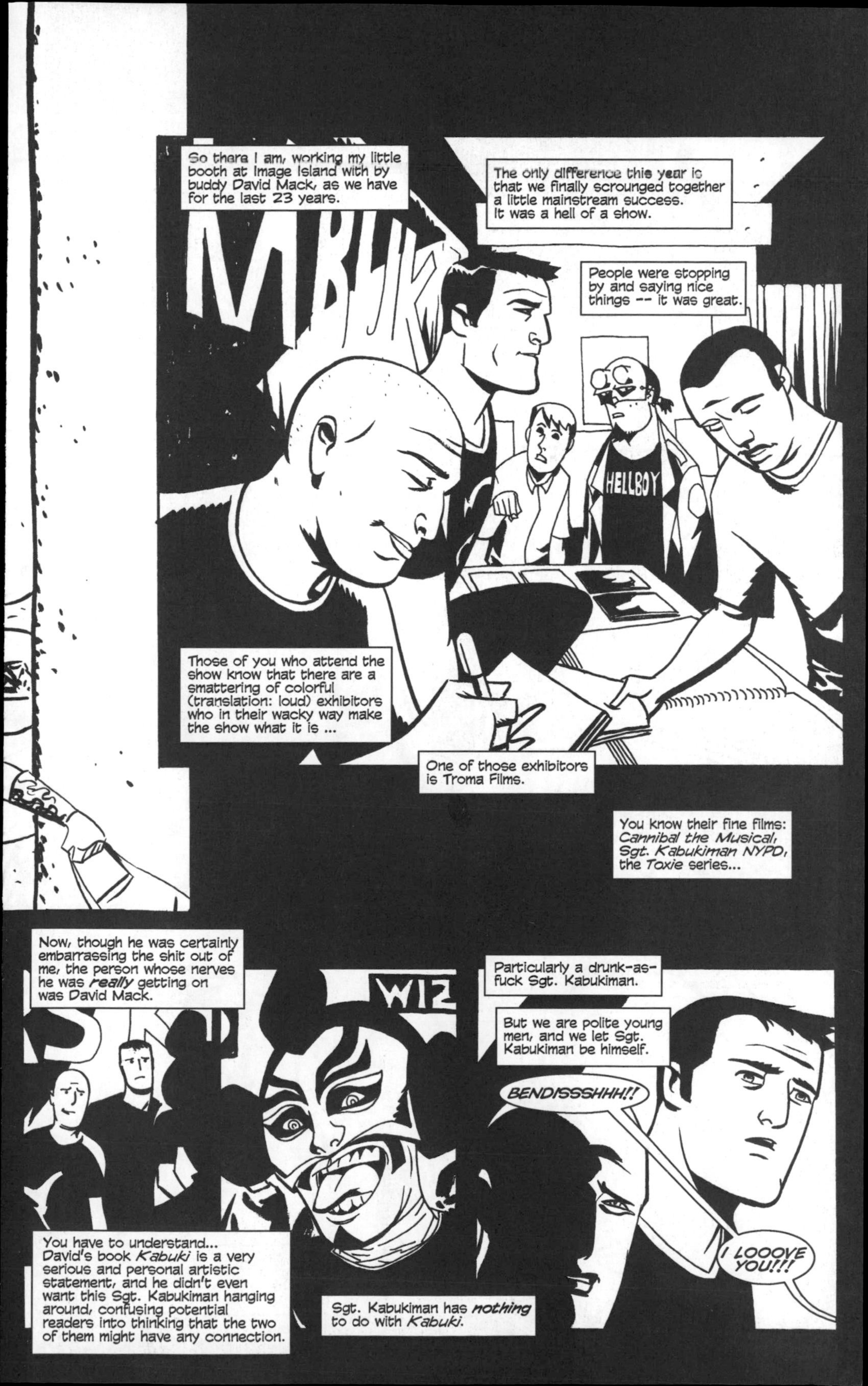

So there I am, working my little booth at Image Island with by buddy David Mack, as we have for the last 23 years.
The only difference this year is that we finally scrounged together a little mainstream success. It was a hell of a show.
People were stopping by and saying nice things -- it was great.
HELLBOY
Those of you who attend the show know that there are a smattering of colorful (translation: loud) exhibitors who in their wacky way make the show what it is ...
One of those exhibitors is Troma Films.
You know their fine films: *Cannibal the Musical, Sgt. Kabukiman NYPD*, the *Toxie* series...
Now, though he was certainly embarrassing the shit out of me, the person whose nerves he was *really* getting on was David Mack.
WIZ
You have to understand... David's book *Kabuki* is a very serious and personal artistic statement, and he didn't even want this Sgt. Kabukiman hanging around, confusing potential readers into thinking that the two of them might have any connection.
Sgt. Kabukiman has *nothing* to do with *Kabuki*.
Particularly a drunk-as-fuck Sgt. Kabukiman.
But we are polite young men, and we let Sgt. Kabukiman be himself.
BENDISSSHHH!!
I LOOOVE YOU!!!

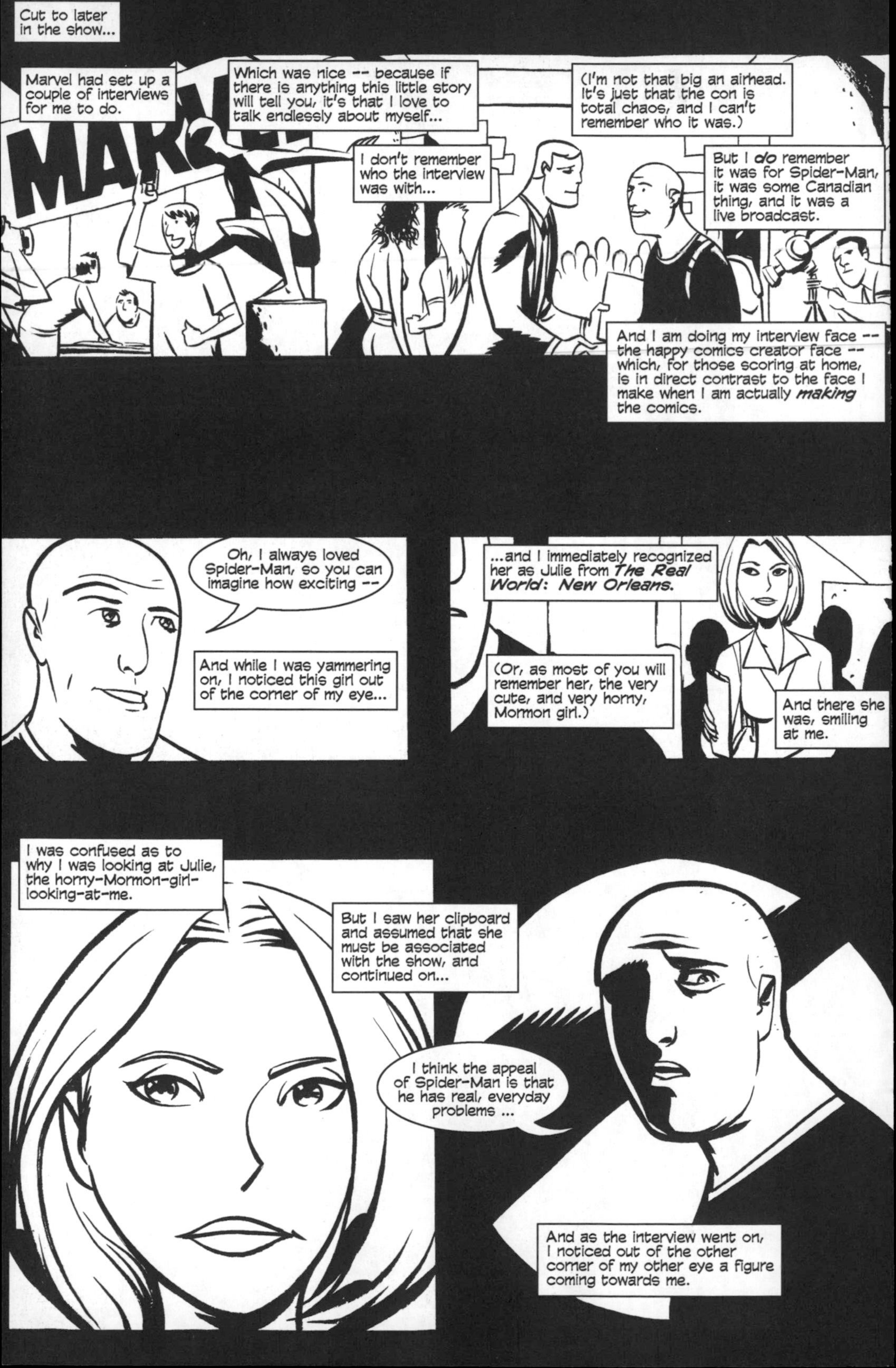
Cut to later in the show...
Marvel had set up a couple of interviews for me to do.
MARVEL
Which was nice -- because if there is anything this little story will tell you, it's that I love to talk endlessly about myself...
(I'm not that big an airhead. It's just that the con is total chaos, and I can't remember who it was.)
I don't remember who the interview was with...
But I *do* remember it was for Spider-Man, it was some Canadian thing, and it was a live broadcast.
And I am doing my interview face -- the happy comics creator face -- which, for those scoring at home, is in direct contrast to the face I make when I am actually *making* the comics.
Oh, I always loved Spider-Man, so you can imagine how exciting --
And while I was yammering on, I noticed this girl out of the corner of my eye...
...and I immediately recognized her as Julie from *The Real World: New Orleans.*
(Or, as most of you will remember her, the very cute, and very horny, Mormon girl.)
And there she was, smiling at me.
I was confused as to why I was looking at Julie, the horny-Mormon-girl-looking-at-me.
But I saw her clipboard and assumed that she must be associated with the show, and continued on...
I think the appeal of Spider-Man is that he has real, everyday problems ...
And as the interview went on, I noticed out of the other corner of my other eye a figure coming towards me.

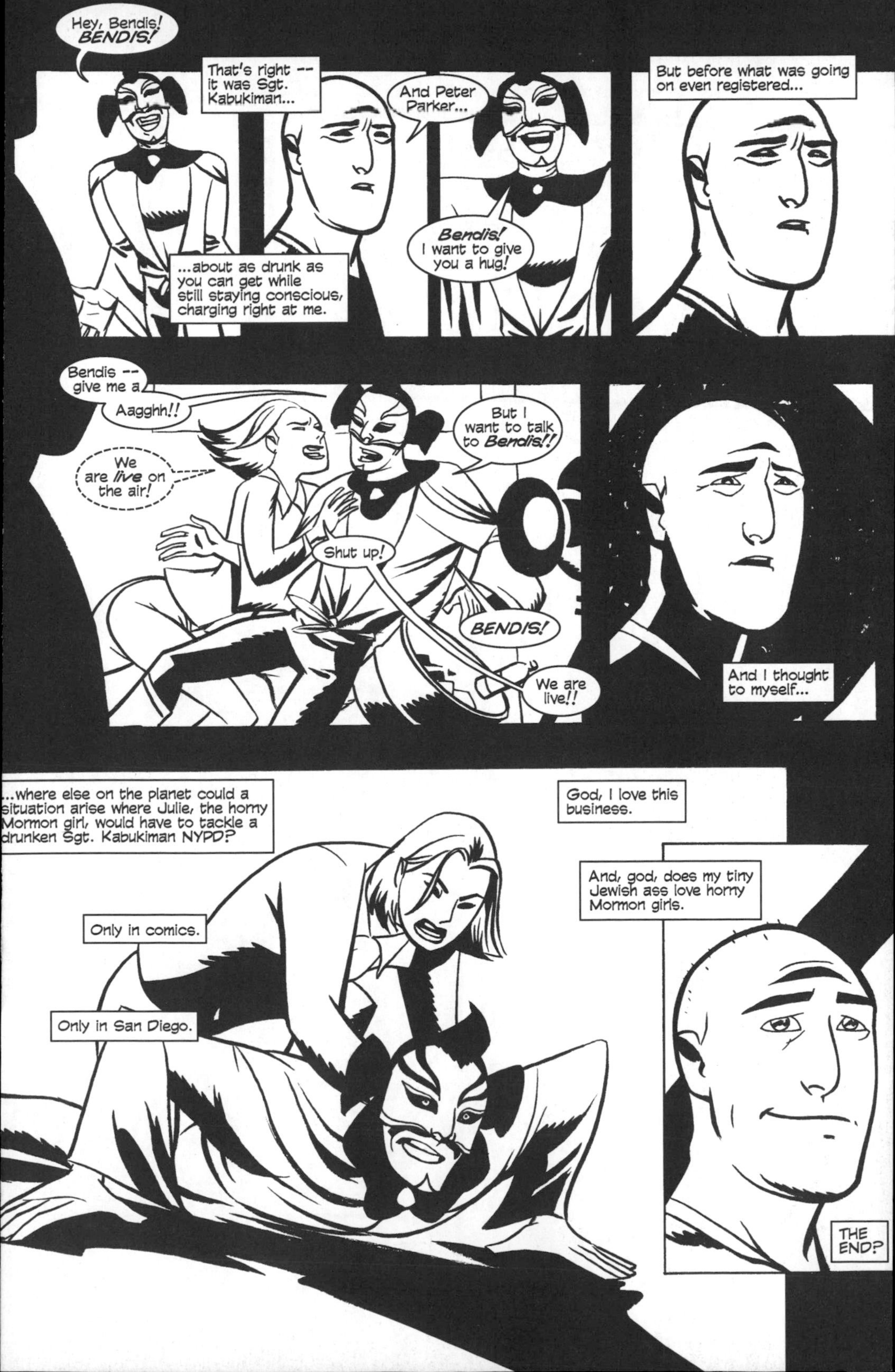
Hey, Bendis! BENDIS!
That's right -- it was Sgt. Kabukiman...
...about as drunk as you can get while still staying conscious, charging right at me.
And Peter Parker...
Bendis! I want to give you a hug!
But before what was going on even registered...
Bendis -- give me a
Aagghh!!
We are live on the air!
But I want to talk to Bendis!!
Shut up!
BENDIS!
We are live!!
And I thought to myself...
...where else on the planet could a situation arise where Julie, the horny Mormon girl, would have to tackle a drunken Sgt. Kabukiman NYPD?
Only in comics.
Only in San Diego.
God, I love this business.
And, god, does my tiny Jewish ass love horny Mormon girls.
THE END?

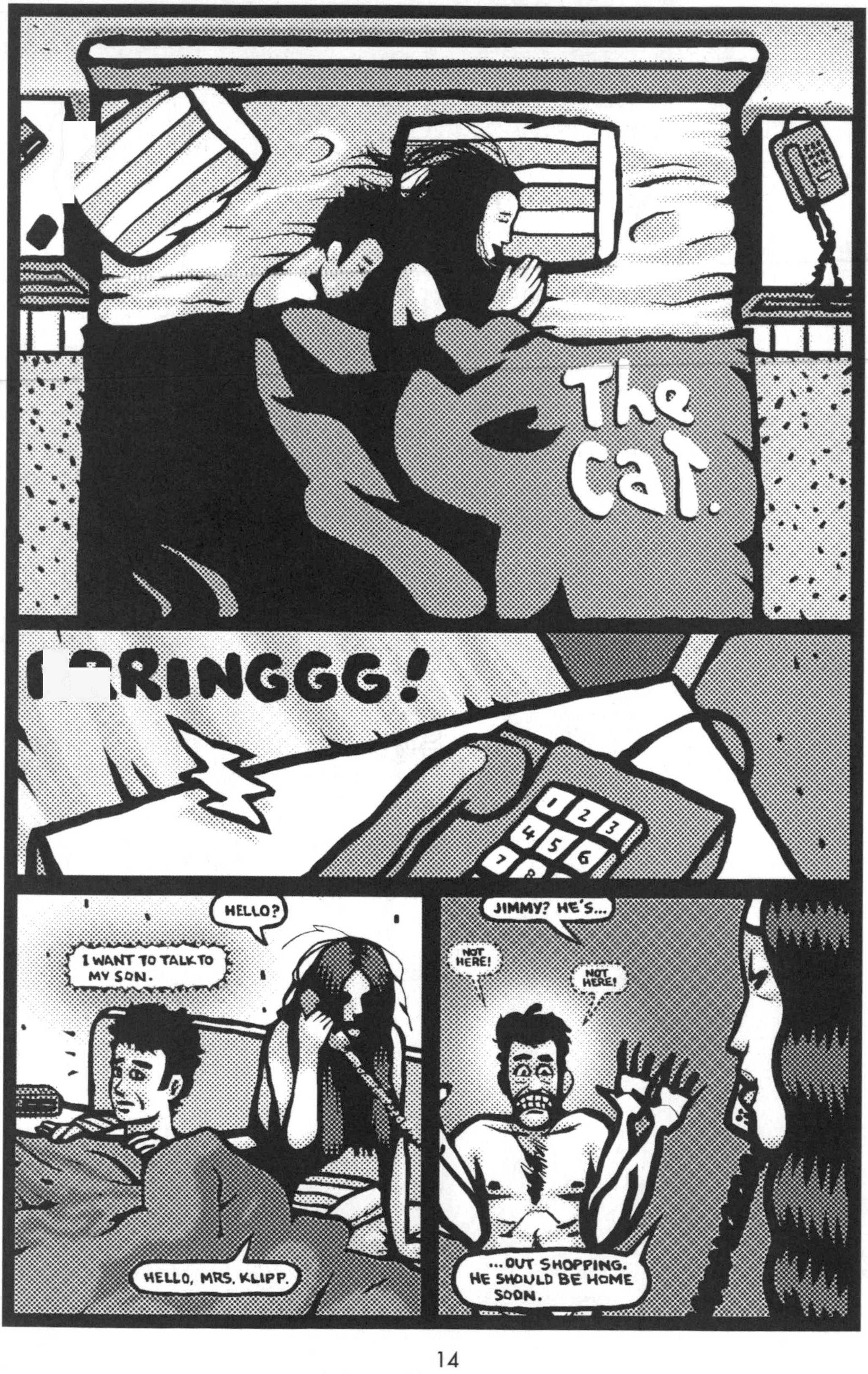

The Cat.
RINGGG!
HELLO?
I WANT TO TALK TO MY SON.
HELLO, MRS. KLIPP.
JIMMY? HE'S...
NOT HERE!
NOT HERE!
...OUT SHOPPING. HE SHOULD BE HOME SOON.

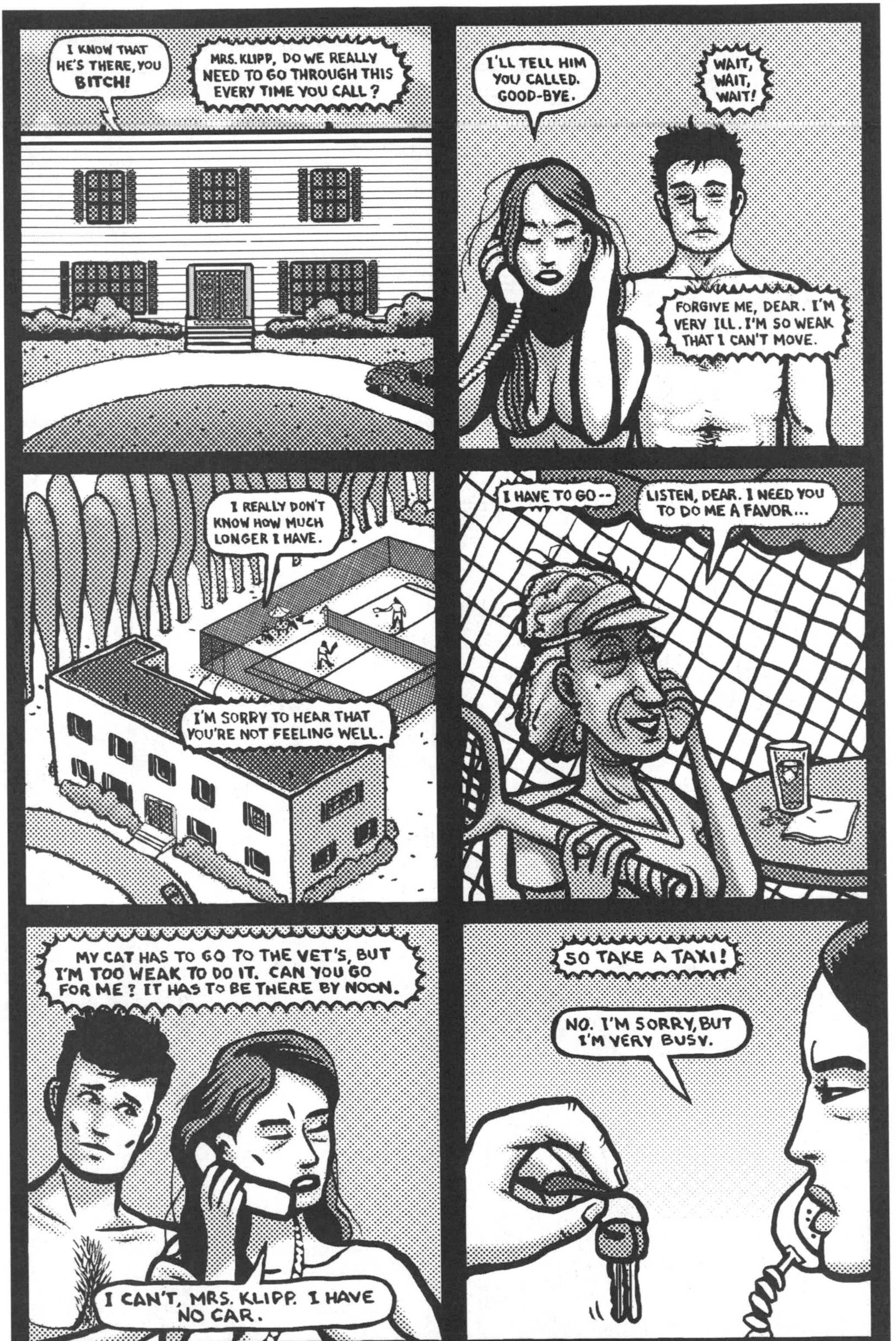
I KNOW THAT HE'S THERE, YOU BITCH!
MRS. KLIPP, DO WE REALLY NEED TO GO THROUGH THIS EVERY TIME YOU CALL?
I'LL TELL HIM YOU CALLED. GOOD-BYE.
WAIT, WAIT, WAIT!
FORGIVE ME, DEAR. I'M VERY ILL. I'M SO WEAK THAT I CAN'T MOVE.
I REALLY DON'T KNOW HOW MUCH LONGER I HAVE.
I'M SORRY TO HEAR THAT YOU'RE NOT FEELING WELL.
I HAVE TO GO--
LISTEN, DEAR. I NEED YOU TO DO ME A FAVOR...
MY CAT HAS TO GO TO THE VET'S, BUT I'M TOO WEAK TO DO IT. CAN YOU GO FOR ME? IT HAS TO BE THERE BY NOON.
I CAN'T, MRS. KLIPP. I HAVE NO CAR.
SO TAKE A TAXI!
NO. I'M SORRY, BUT I'M VERY BUSY.

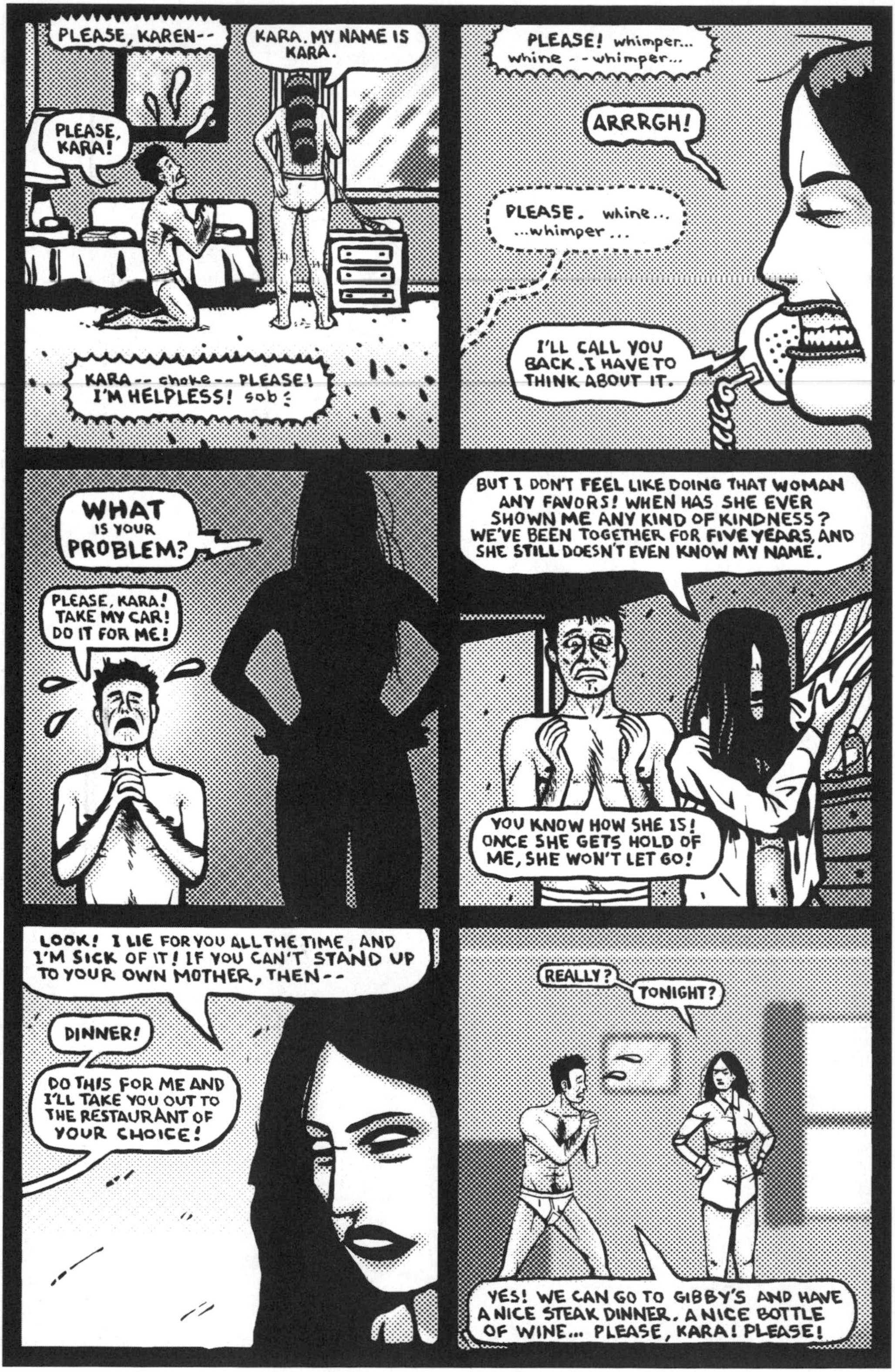
PLEASE, KAREN--
KARA. MY NAME IS KARA.
PLEASE, KARA!
KARA -- choke -- PLEASE! I'M HELPLESS! sob
PLEASE! whimper... whine -- whimper...
ARRRGH!
PLEASE. whine... ...whimper...
I'LL CALL YOU BACK. I HAVE TO THINK ABOUT IT.
WHAT IS YOUR PROBLEM?
PLEASE, KARA! TAKE MY CAR! DO IT FOR ME!
BUT I DON'T FEEL LIKE DOING THAT WOMAN ANY FAVORS! WHEN HAS SHE EVER SHOWN ME ANY KIND OF KINDNESS? WE'VE BEEN TOGETHER FOR FIVE YEARS, AND SHE STILL DOESN'T EVEN KNOW MY NAME.
YOU KNOW HOW SHE IS! ONCE SHE GETS HOLD OF ME, SHE WON'T LET GO!
LOOK! I LIE FOR YOU ALL THE TIME, AND I'M SICK OF IT! IF YOU CAN'T STAND UP TO YOUR OWN MOTHER, THEN--
DINNER!
DO THIS FOR ME AND I'LL TAKE YOU OUT TO THE RESTAURANT OF YOUR CHOICE!
REALLY?
TONIGHT?
YES! WE CAN GO TO GIBBY'S AND HAVE A NICE STEAK DINNER. A NICE BOTTLE OF WINE... PLEASE, KARA! PLEASE!

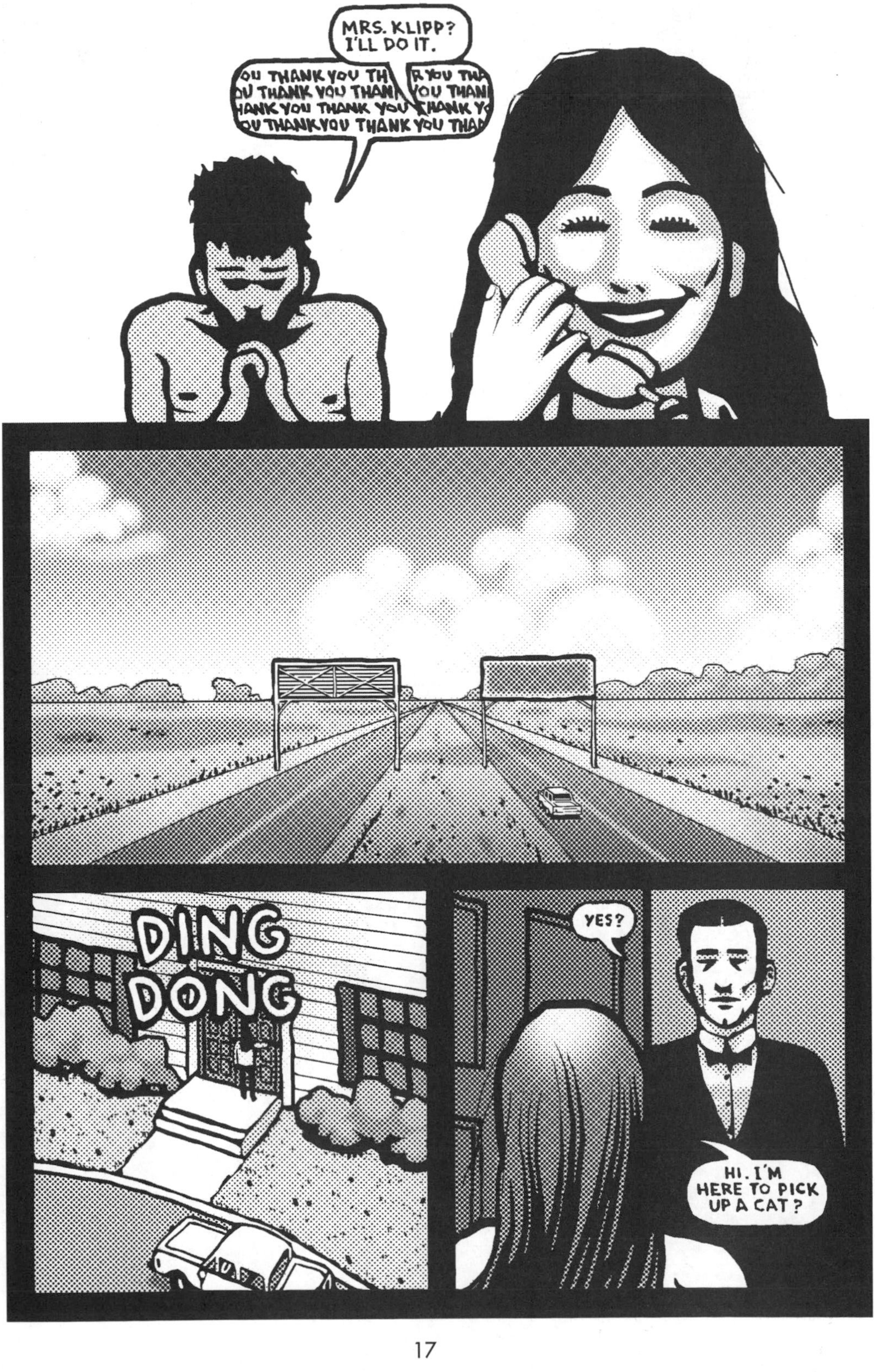
MRS. KLIPP? I'LL DO IT.
OU THANK YOU THANK YOU THANK YOU THANK YOU THANK YOU THANK YOU THANK YOU THANK YOU THANK YOU THANK YOU THANK YOU THANK YOU THA
DING DONG
YES?
HI. I'M HERE TO PICK UP A CAT?

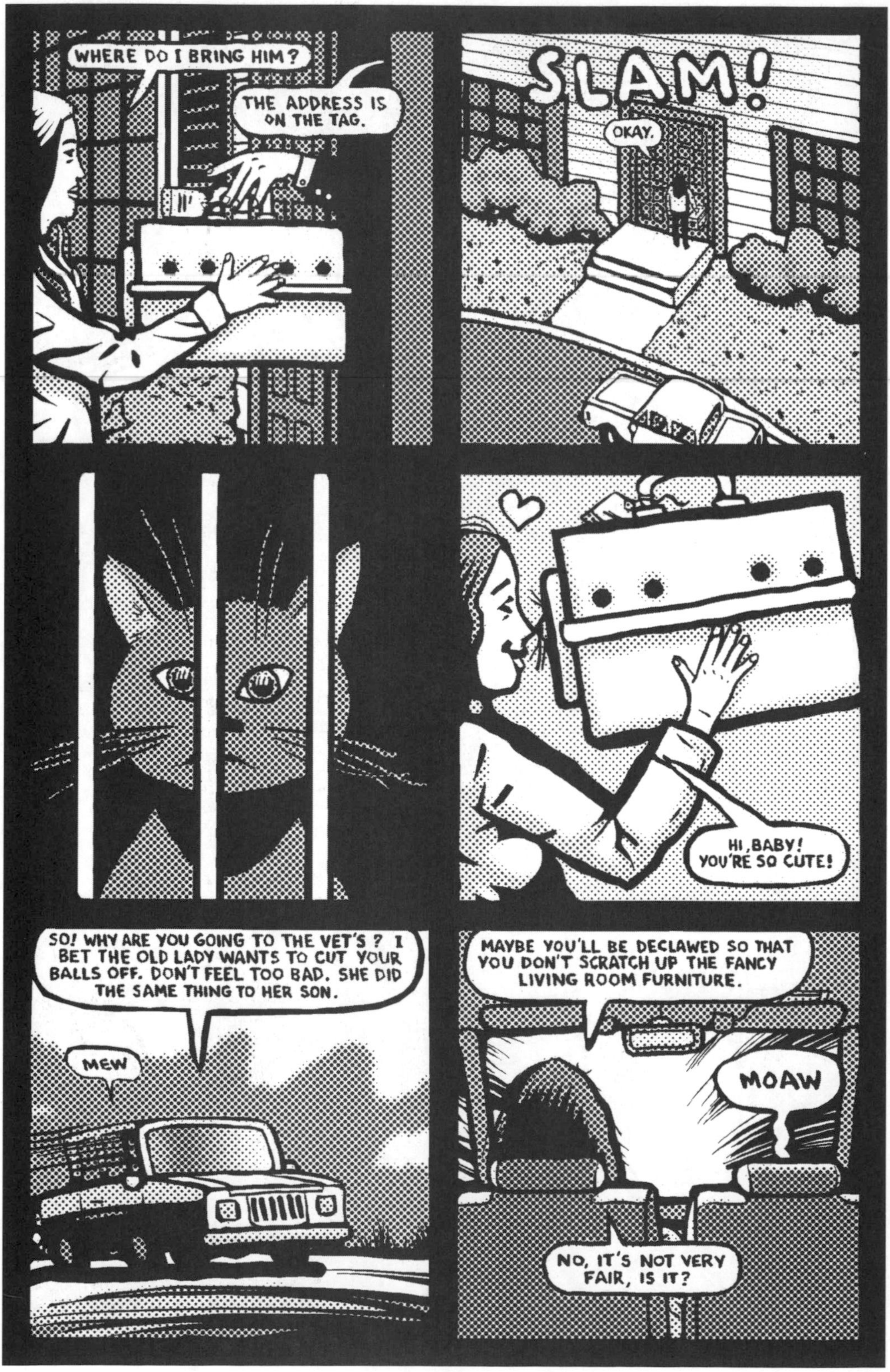
WHERE DO I BRING HIM?
THE ADDRESS IS ON THE TAG.
SLAM!
OKAY.
HI, BABY! YOU'RE SO CUTE!
SO! WHY ARE YOU GOING TO THE VET'S? I BET THE OLD LADY WANTS TO CUT YOUR BALLS OFF. DON'T FEEL TOO BAD. SHE DID THE SAME THING TO HER SON.
MEW
MAYBE YOU'LL BE DECLAWED SO THAT YOU DON'T SCRATCH UP THE FANCY LIVING ROOM FURNITURE.
MOAW
NO, IT'S NOT VERY FAIR, IS IT?

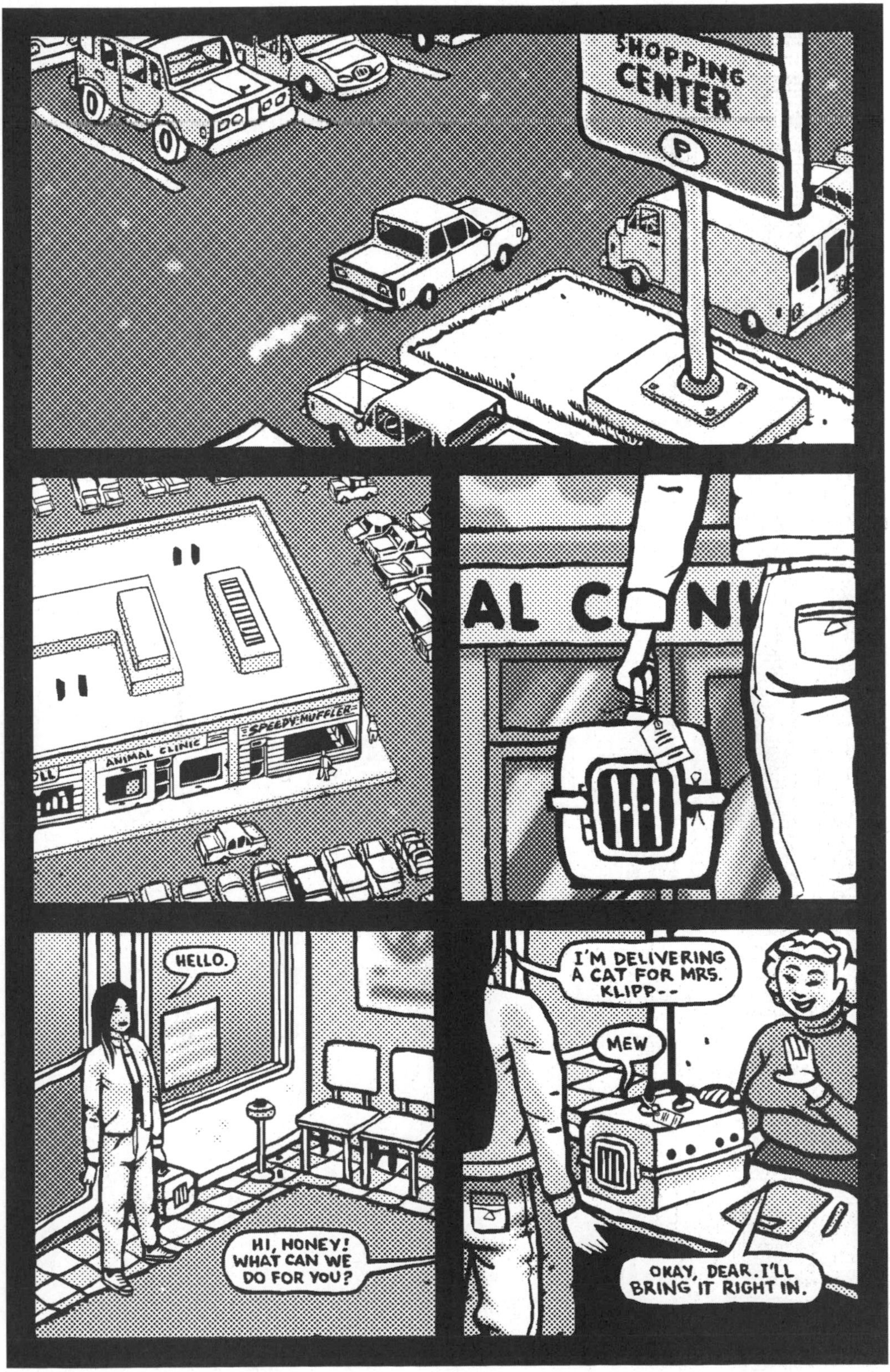
SHOPPING CENTER
P
AL C N
ANIMAL CLINIC
SPEEDY MUFFLER
HELLO.
HI, HONEY! WHAT CAN WE DO FOR YOU?
I'M DELIVERING A CAT FOR MRS. KLIPP--
MEW
OKAY, DEAR. I'LL BRING IT RIGHT IN.

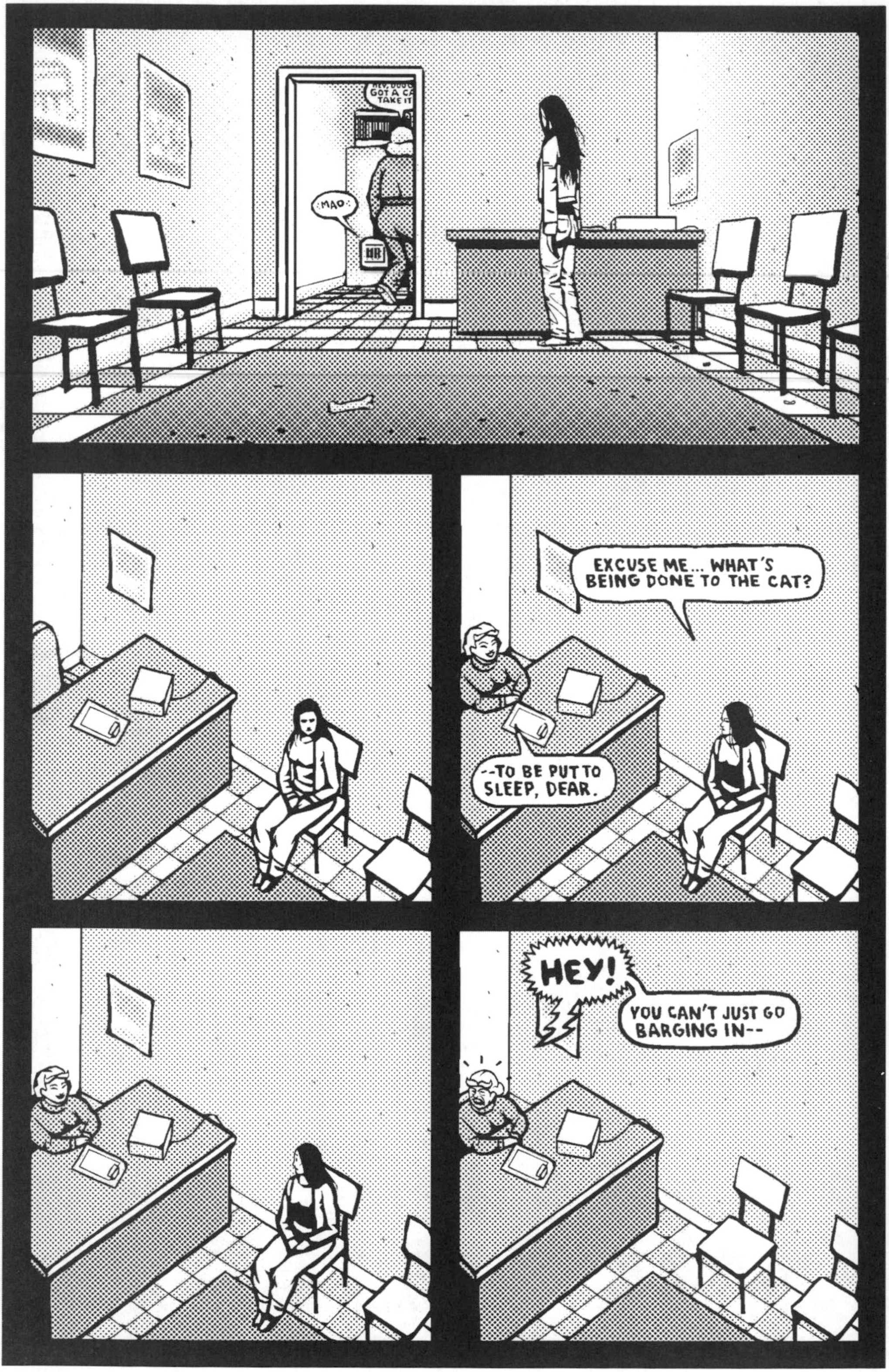

MAO
EXCUSE ME... WHAT'S BEING DONE TO THE CAT?
--TO BE PUT TO SLEEP, DEAR.
HEY!
YOU CAN'T JUST GO BARGING IN--

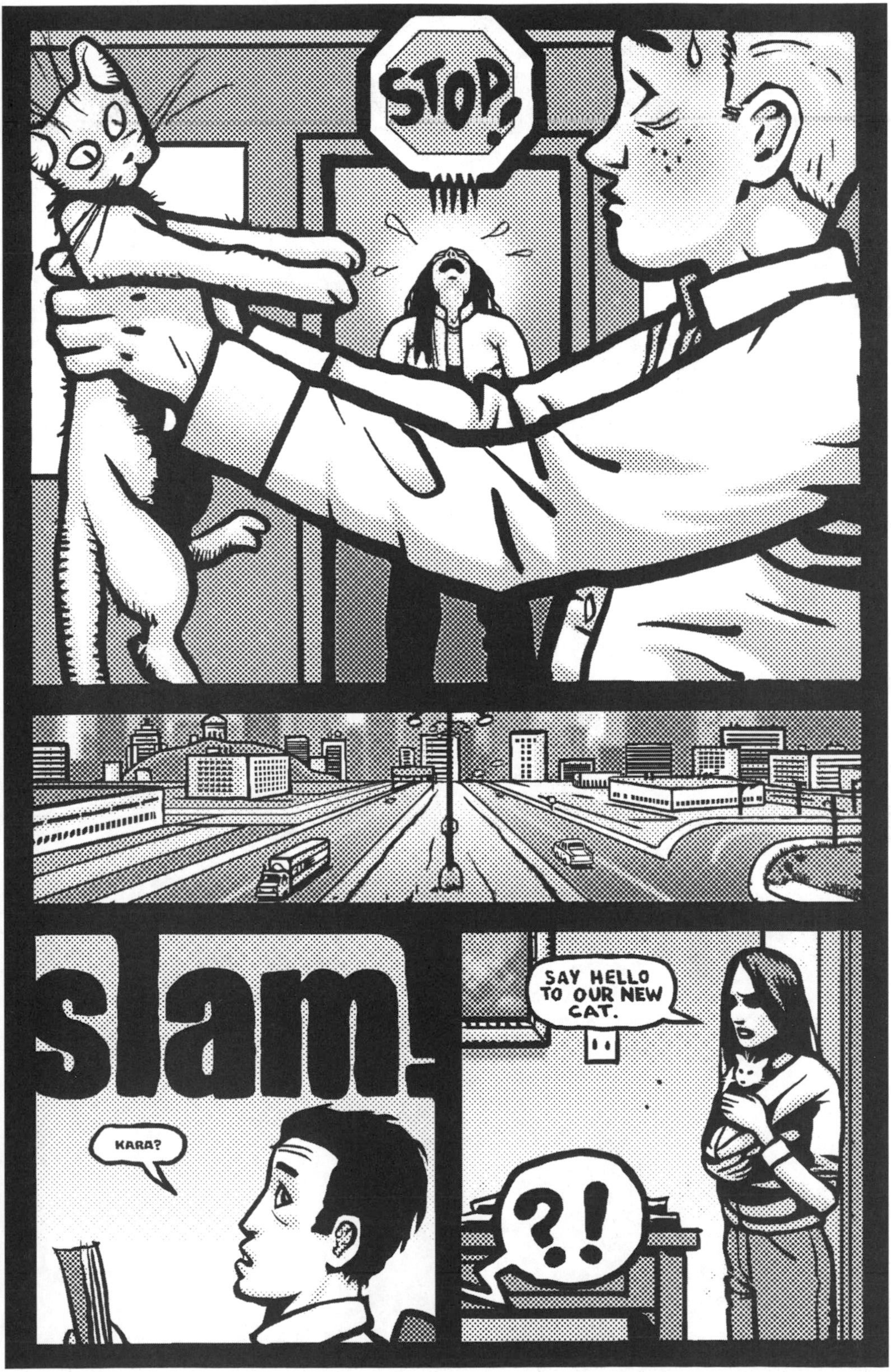
STOP!
slam.
KARA?
SAY HELLO TO OUR NEW CAT.
?!

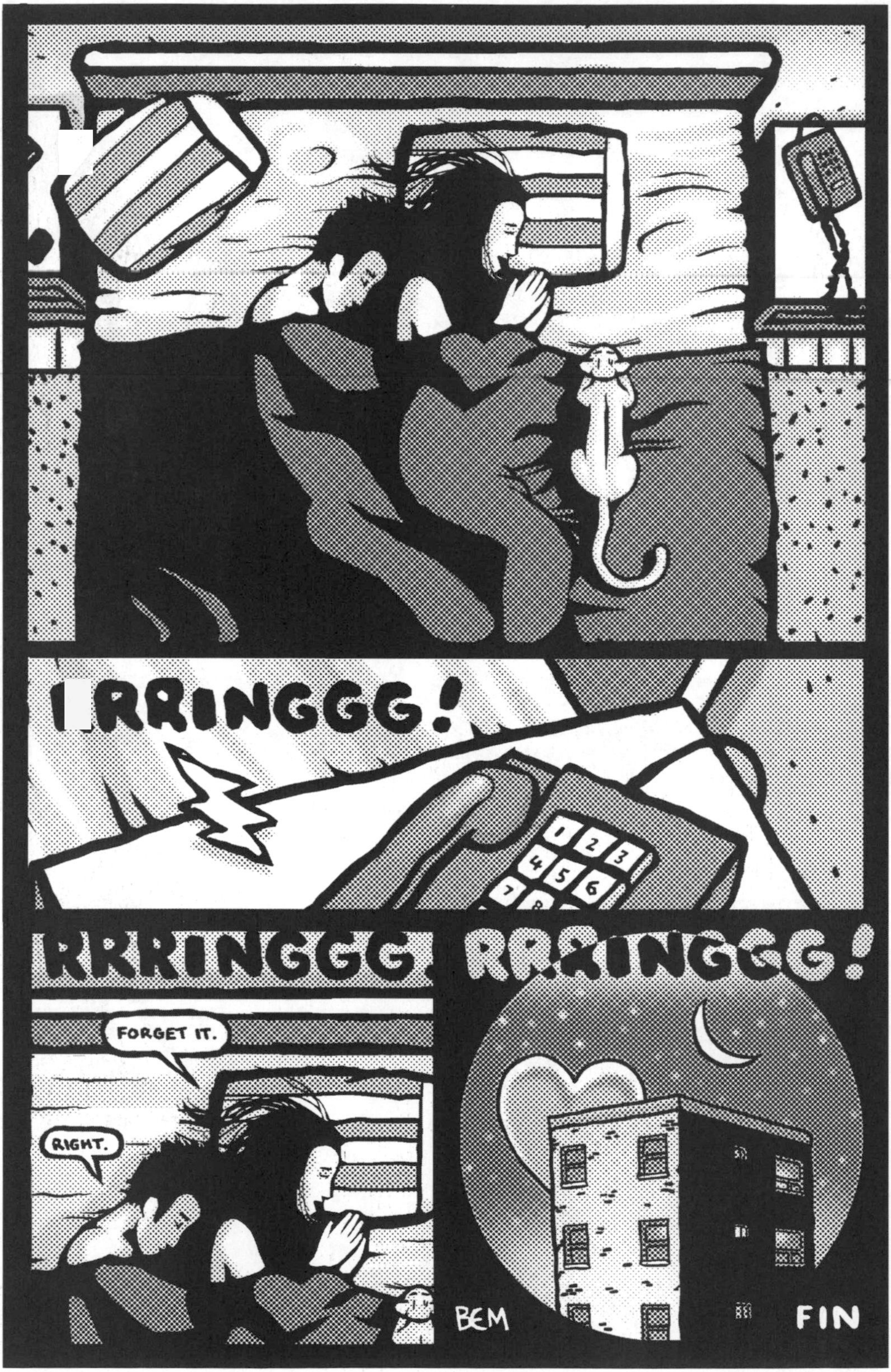
RRINGGG!
RRRINGGG! RRRINGGG!
FORGET IT.
RIGHT.
BEM
FIN

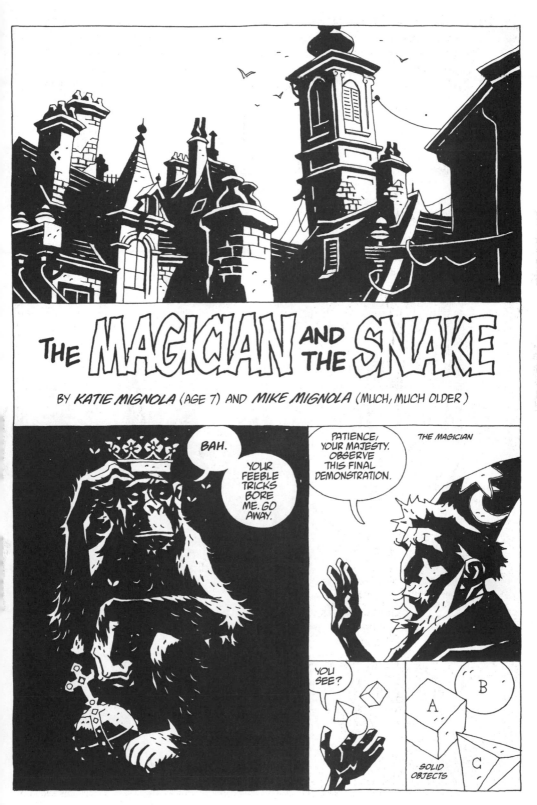

THE MAGICIAN AND THE SNAKE

BY *KATIE MIGNOLA* (AGE 7) AND *MIKE MIGNOLA* (MUCH, MUCH OLDER)

BAH.

YOUR FEEBLE TRICKS BORE ME. GO AWAY.

PATIENCE, YOUR MAJESTY. OBSERVE THIS FINAL DEMONSTRATION.

THE MAGICIAN

YOU SEE?

A

B

C

SOLID OBJECTS

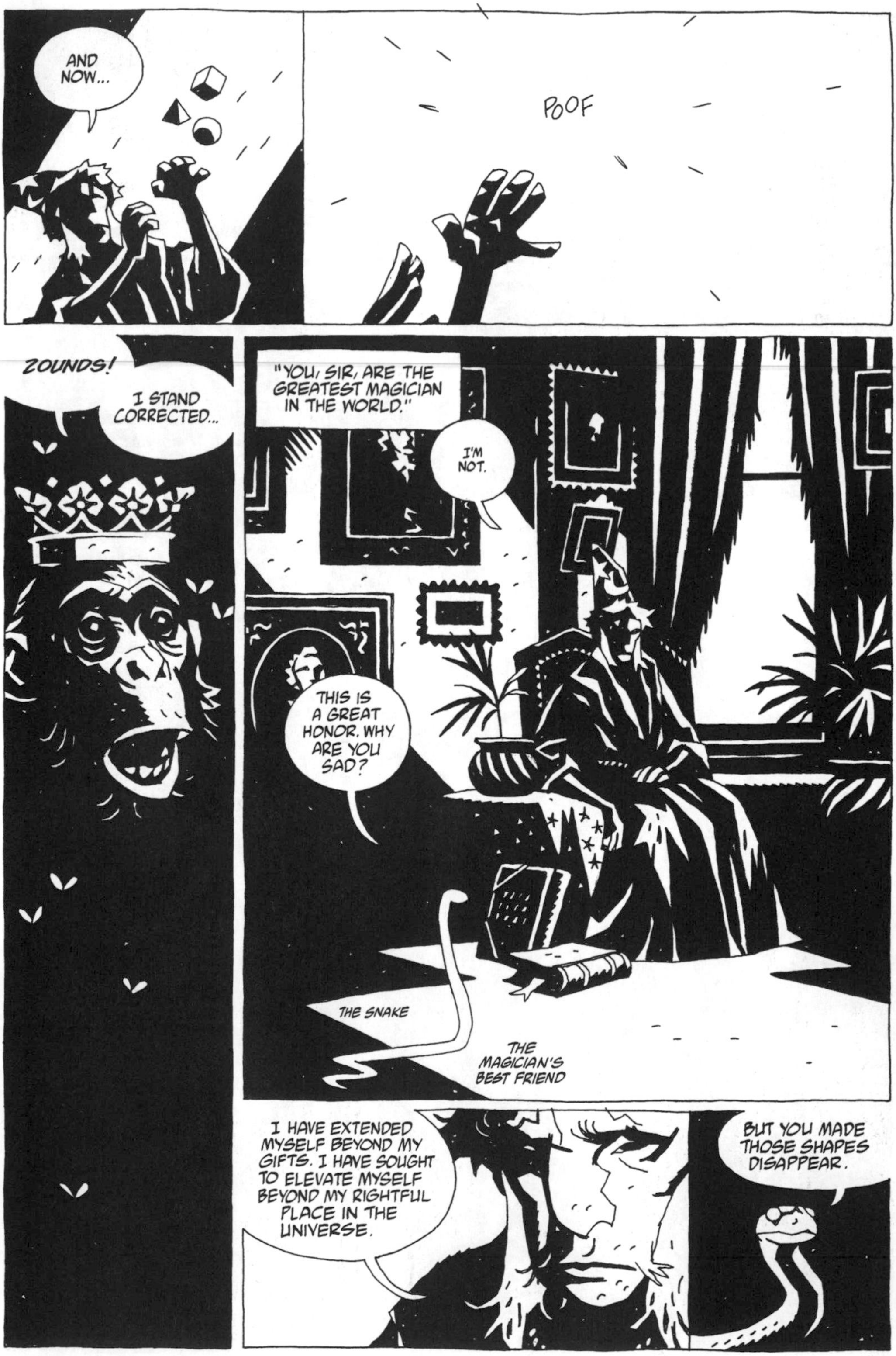
AND NOW...
POOF
ZOUNDS!
I STAND CORRECTED...
"YOU, SIR, ARE THE GREATEST MAGICIAN IN THE WORLD."
I'M NOT.
THIS IS A GREAT HONOR. WHY ARE YOU SAD?
THE SNAKE
THE MAGICIAN'S BEST FRIEND
I HAVE EXTENDED MYSELF BEYOND MY GIFTS. I HAVE SOUGHT TO ELEVATE MYSELF BEYOND MY RIGHTFUL PLACE IN THE UNIVERSE.
BUT YOU MADE THOSE SHAPES DISAPPEAR.

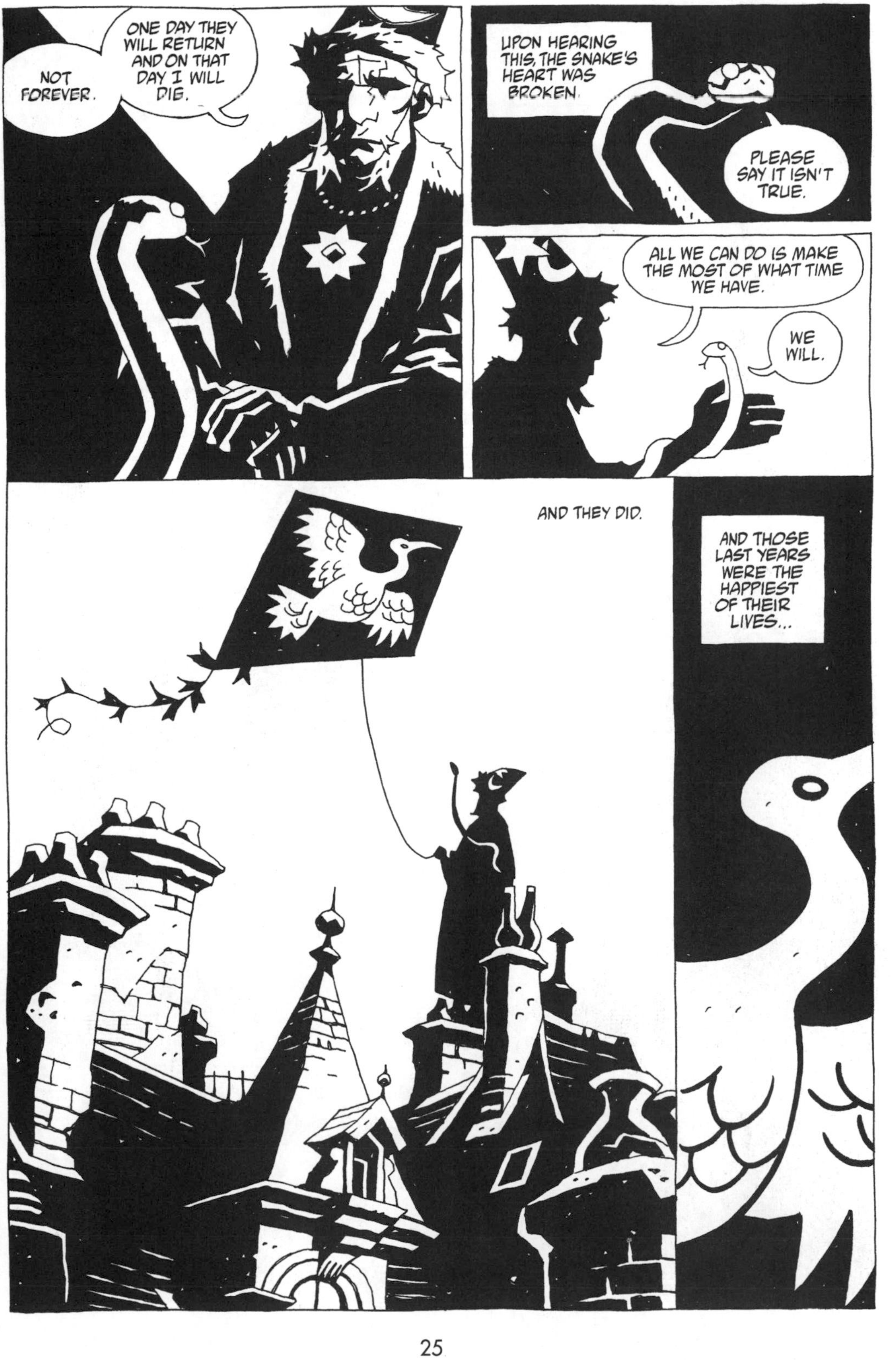
NOT FOREVER.
ONE DAY THEY WILL RETURN AND ON THAT DAY I WILL DIE.
UPON HEARING THIS, THE SNAKE'S HEART WAS BROKEN.
PLEASE SAY IT ISN'T TRUE.
ALL WE CAN DO IS MAKE THE MOST OF WHAT TIME WE HAVE.
WE WILL.
AND THEY DID.
AND THOSE LAST YEARS WERE THE HAPPIEST OF THEIR LIVES...

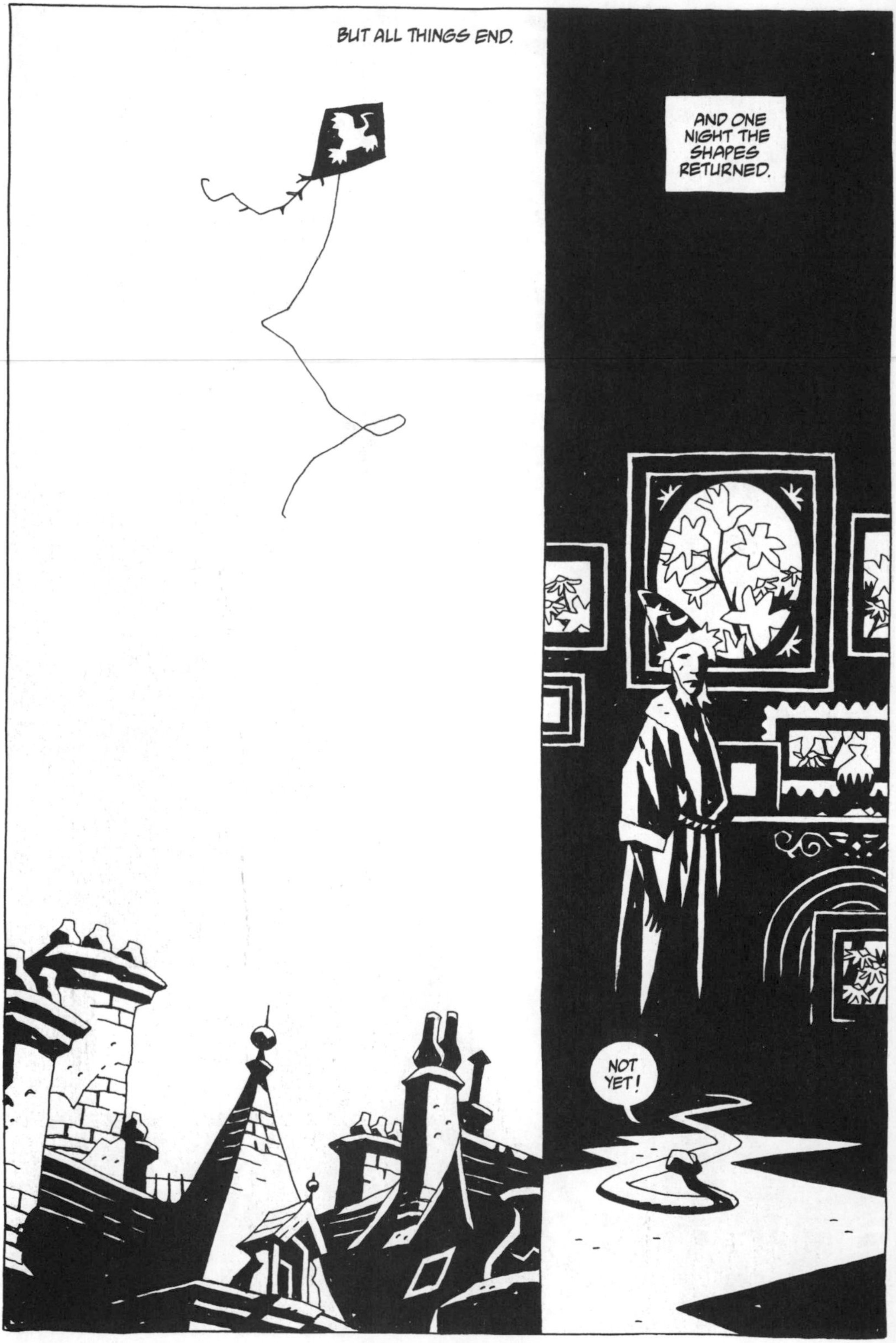
BUT ALL THINGS END.
AND ONE NIGHT THE SHAPES RETURNED.
NOT YET!

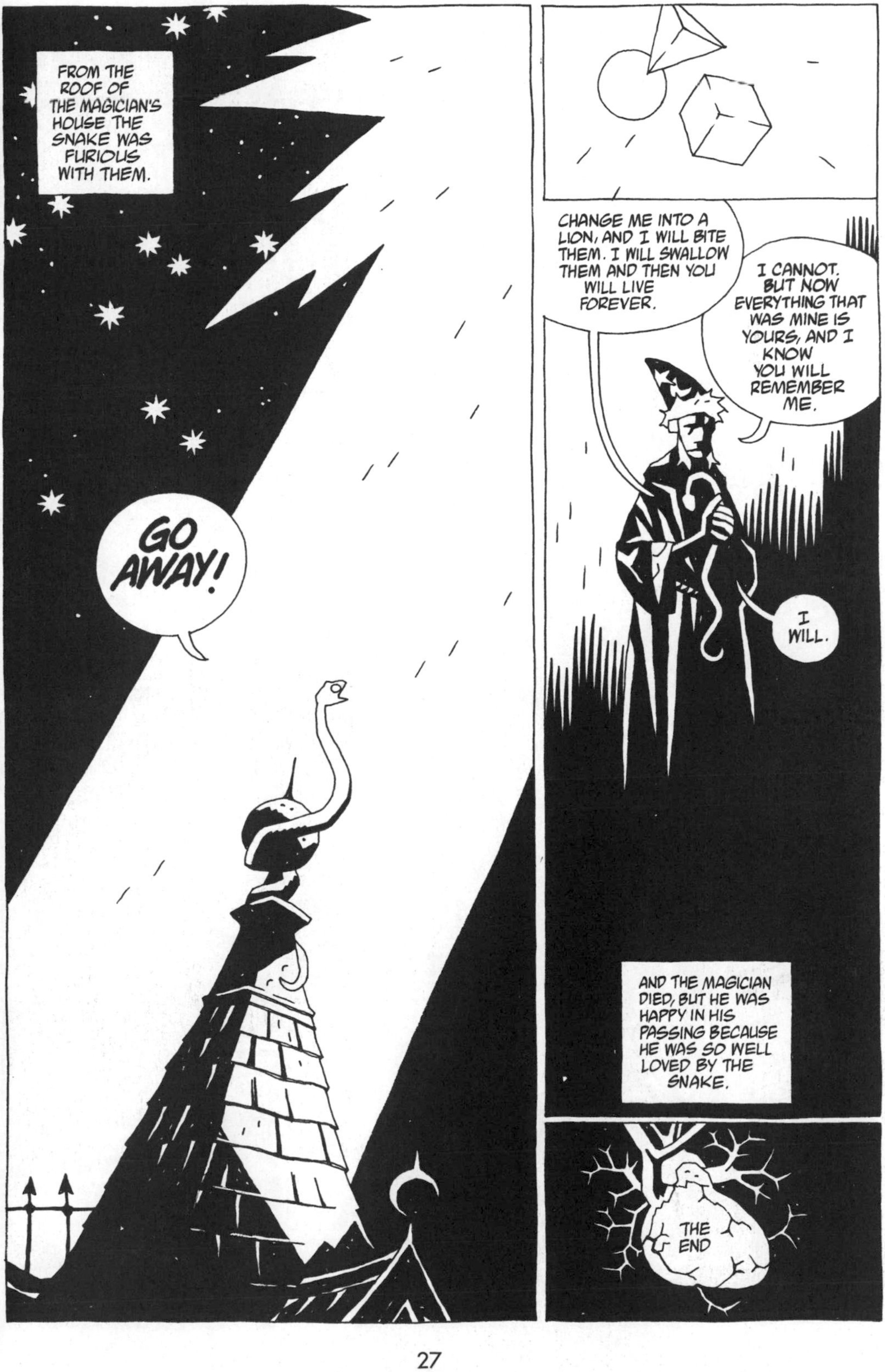
FROM THE ROOF OF THE MAGICIAN'S HOUSE THE SNAKE WAS FURIOUS WITH THEM.
GO AWAY!
CHANGE ME INTO A LION, AND I WILL BITE THEM. I WILL SWALLOW THEM AND THEN YOU WILL LIVE FOREVER.
I CANNOT. BUT NOW EVERYTHING THAT WAS MINE IS YOURS, AND I KNOW YOU WILL REMEMBER ME.
I WILL.
AND THE MAGICIAN DIED, BUT HE WAS HAPPY IN HIS PASSING BECAUSE HE WAS SO WELL LOVED BY THE SNAKE.
THE END

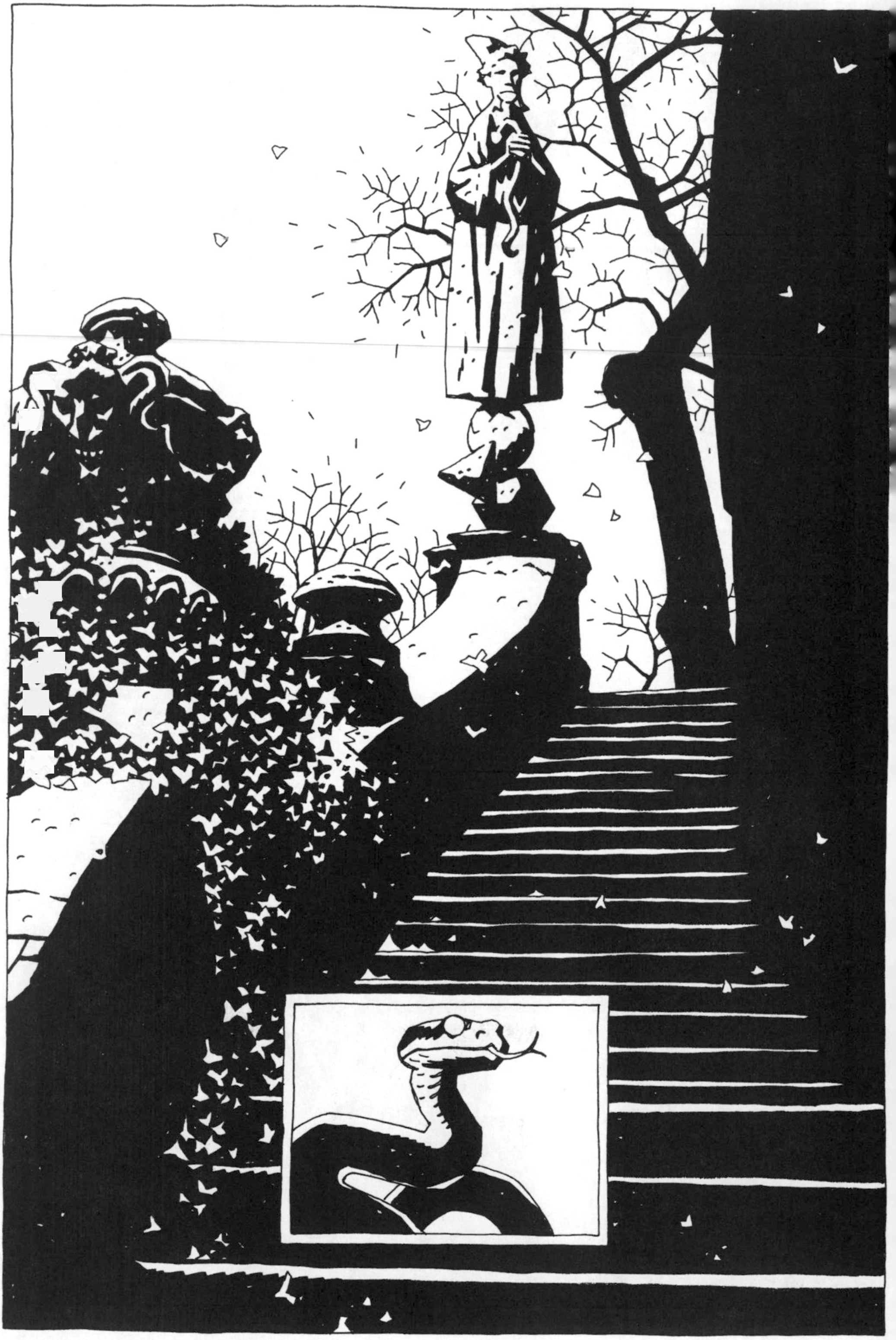

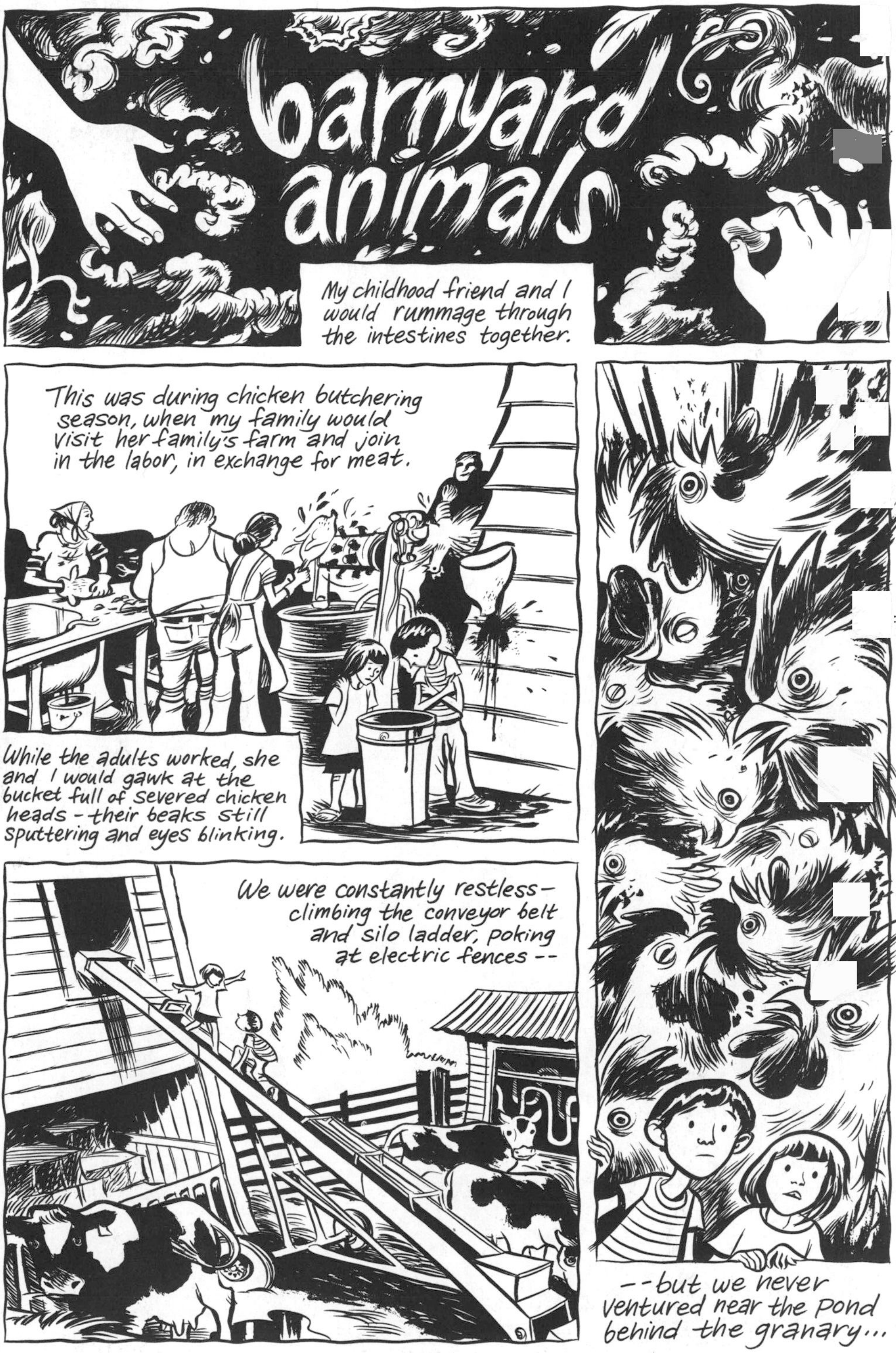
barnyard animals
My childhood friend and I would rummage through the intestines together.
This was during chicken butchering season, when my family would visit her family's farm and join in the labor, in exchange for meat.
While the adults worked, she and I would gawk at the bucket full of severed chicken heads -- their beaks still sputtering and eyes blinking.
We were constantly restless -- climbing the conveyor belt and silo ladder, poking at electric fences --
-- but we never ventured near the pond behind the granary...

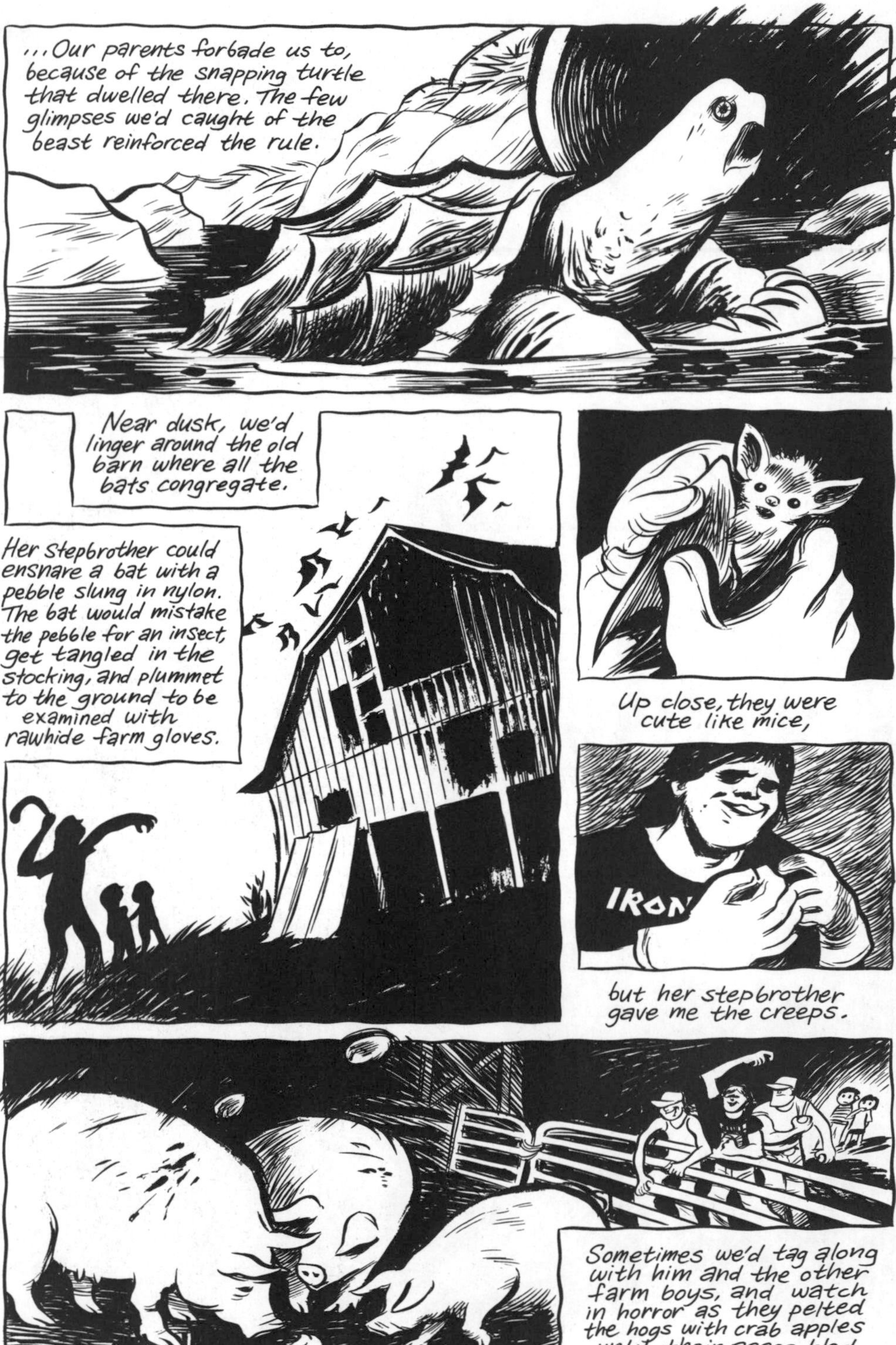
...Our parents forbade us to, because of the snapping turtle that dwelled there. The few glimpses we'd caught of the beast reinforced the rule.
Near dusk, we'd linger around the old barn where all the bats congregate.
Her stepbrother could ensnare a bat with a pebble slung in nylon. The bat would mistake the pebble for an insect, get tangled in the stocking, and plummet to the ground to be examined with rawhide farm gloves.
Up close, they were cute like mice,
IRON
but her stepbrother gave me the creeps.
Sometimes we'd tag along with him and the other farm boys, and watch in horror as they pelted the hogs with crab apples until their asses bled.

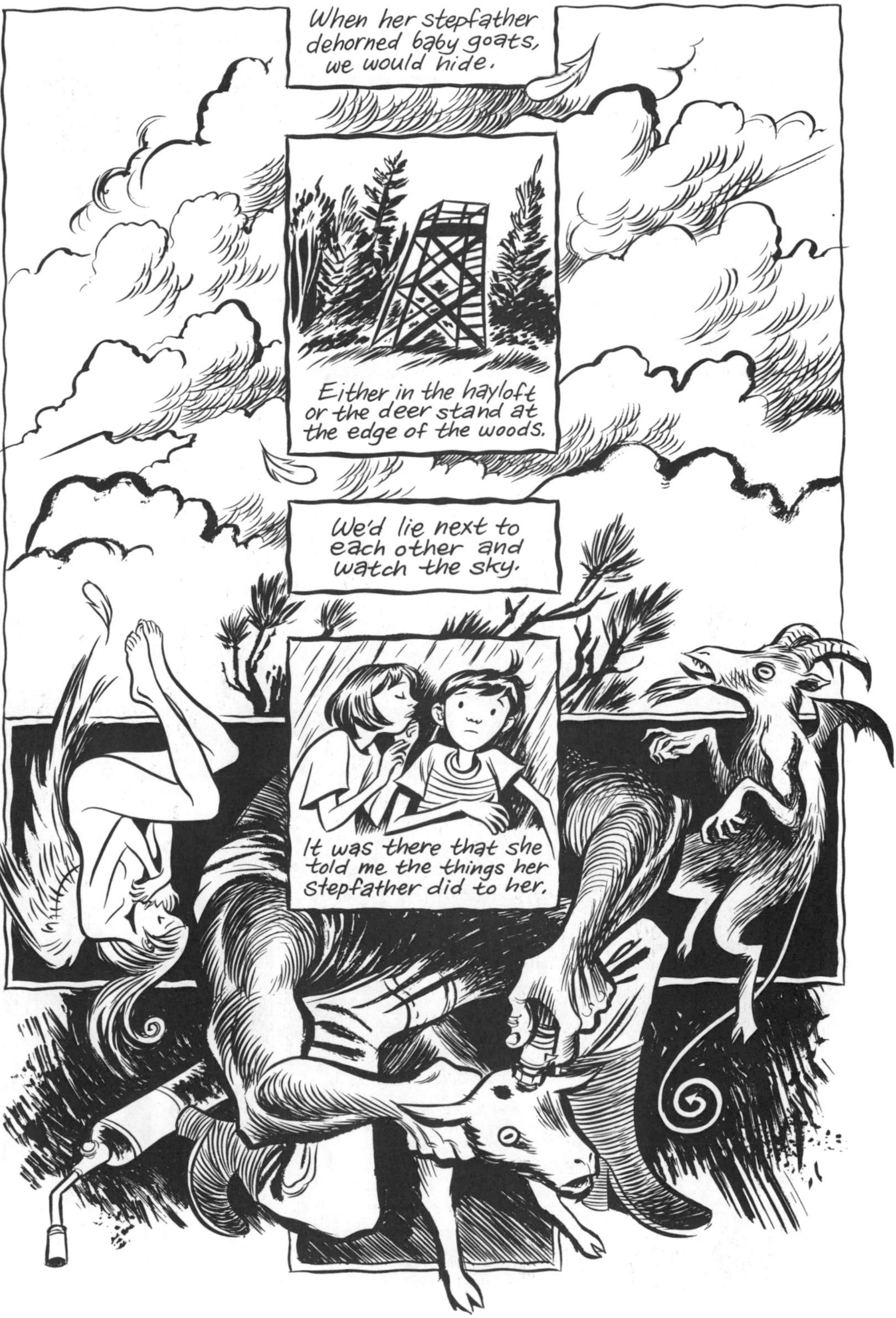
When her stepfather dehorned baby goats, we would hide.
Either in the hayloft or the deer stand at the edge of the woods.
We'd lie next to each other and watch the sky.
It was there that she told me the things her stepfather did to her.

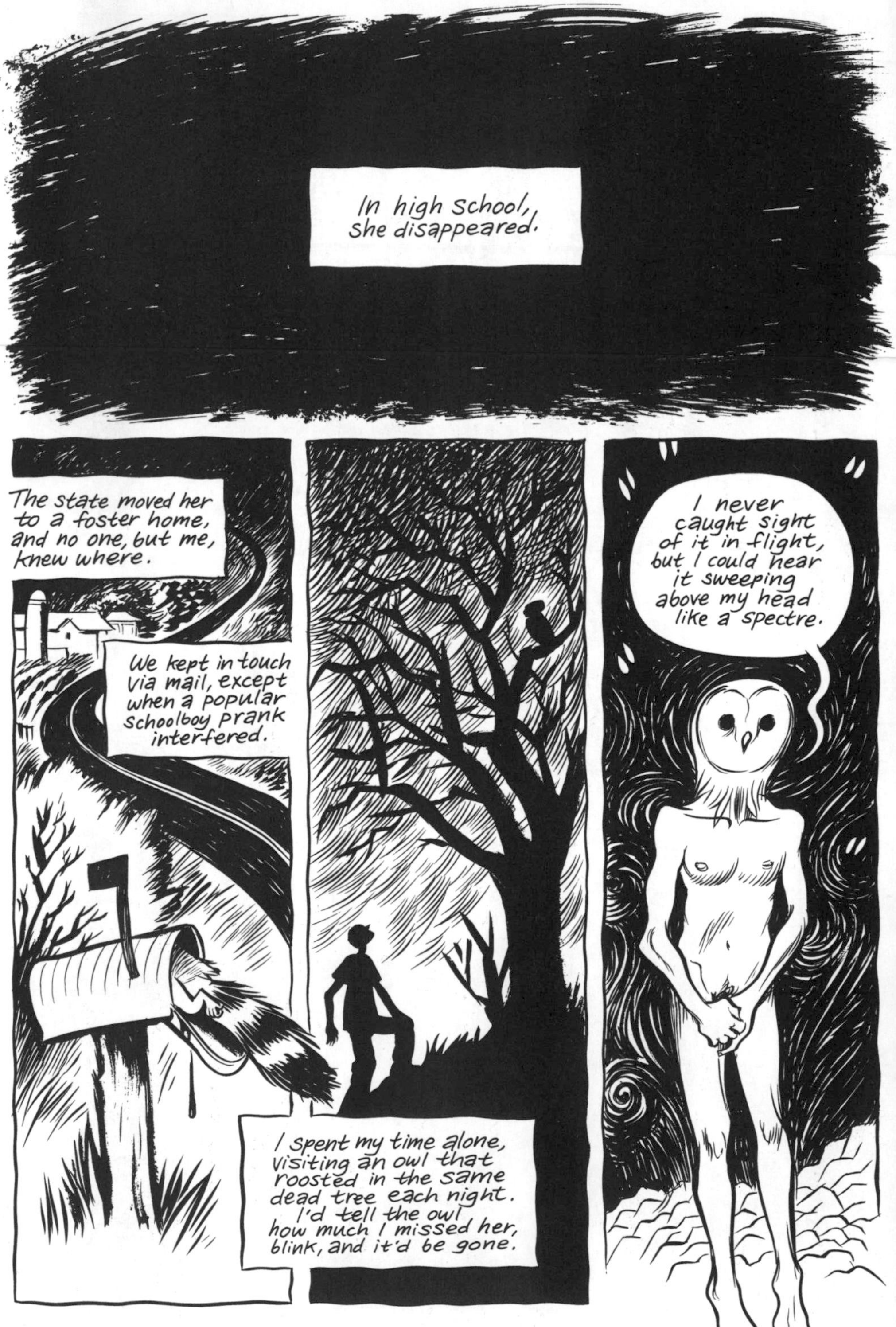
In high school, she disappeared.
The state moved her to a foster home, and no one, but me, knew where.
We kept in touch via mail, except when a popular schoolboy prank interfered.
I spent my time alone, visiting an owl that roosted in the same dead tree each night. I'd tell the owl how much I missed her, blink, and it'd be gone.
I never caught sight of it in flight, but I could hear it sweeping above my head like a spectre.

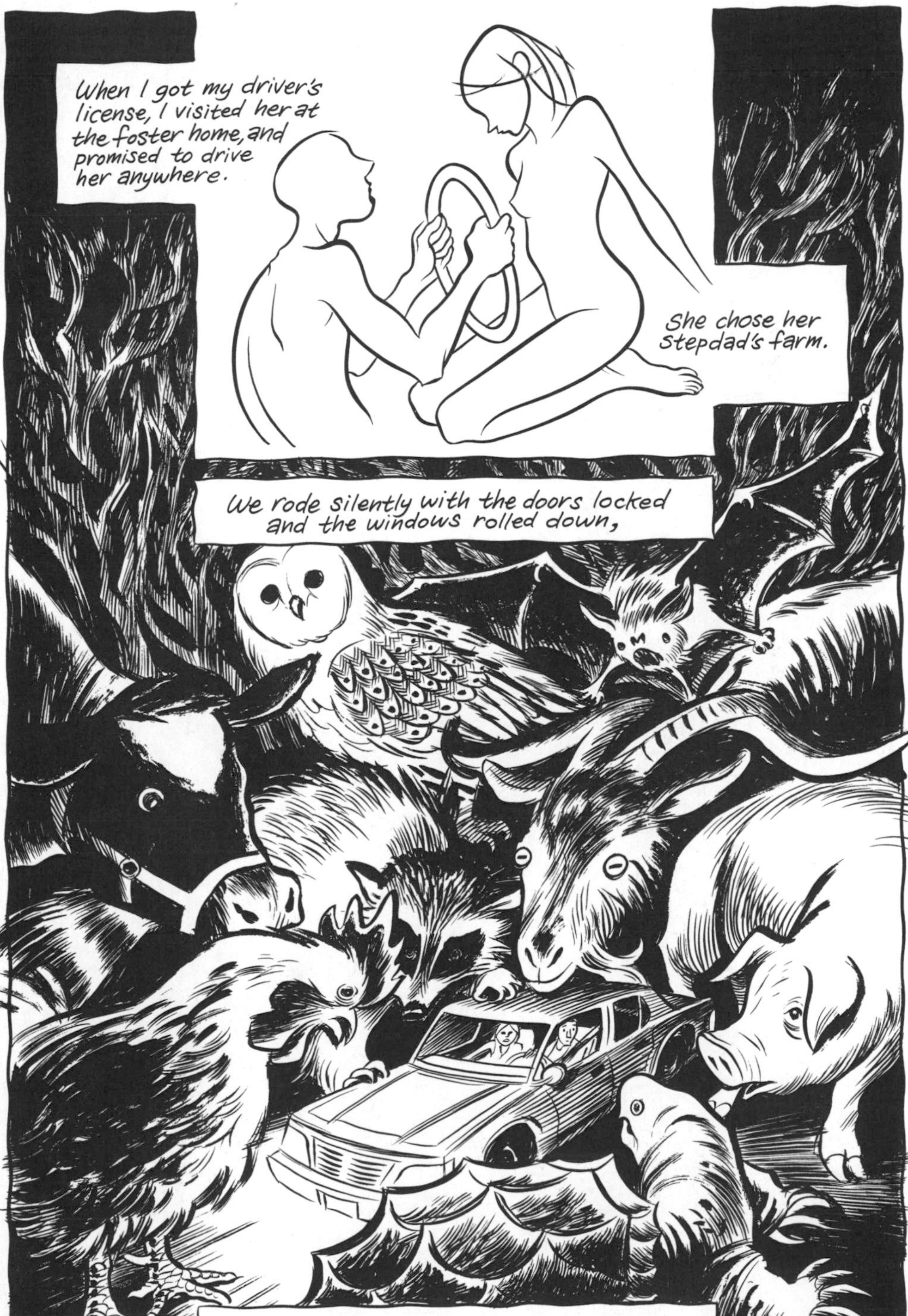
When I got my driver's license, I visited her at the foster home, and promised to drive her anywhere.
She chose her stepdad's farm.
We rode silently with the doors locked and the windows rolled down,
but we never reached our destination.

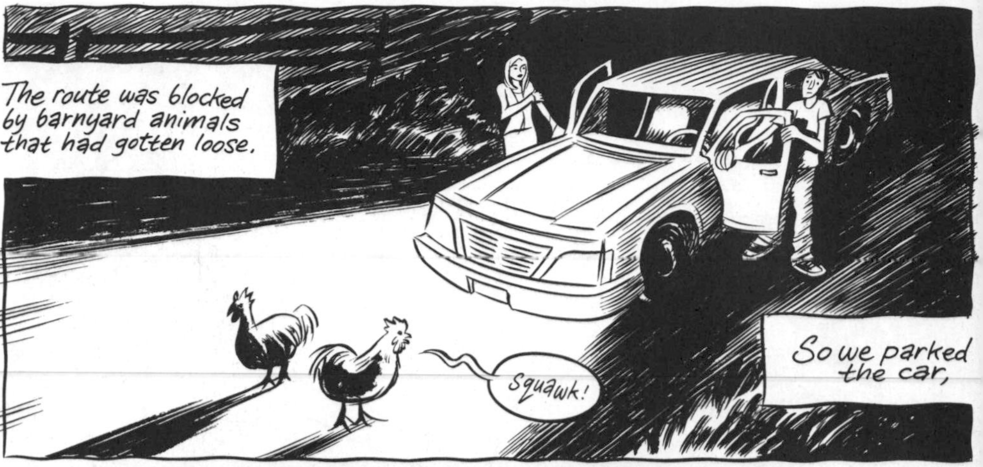
The route was blocked by barnyard animals that had gotten loose.
Squawk!
So we parked the car,

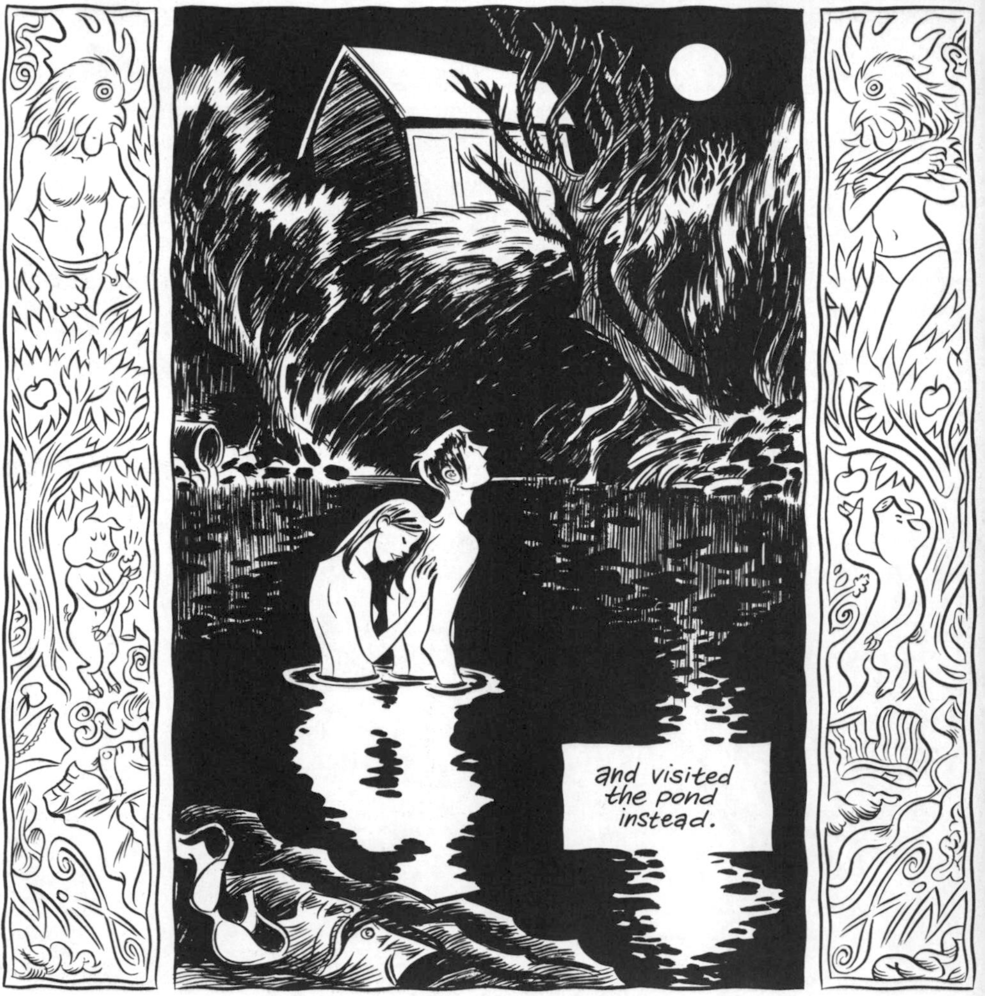
and visited the pond instead.

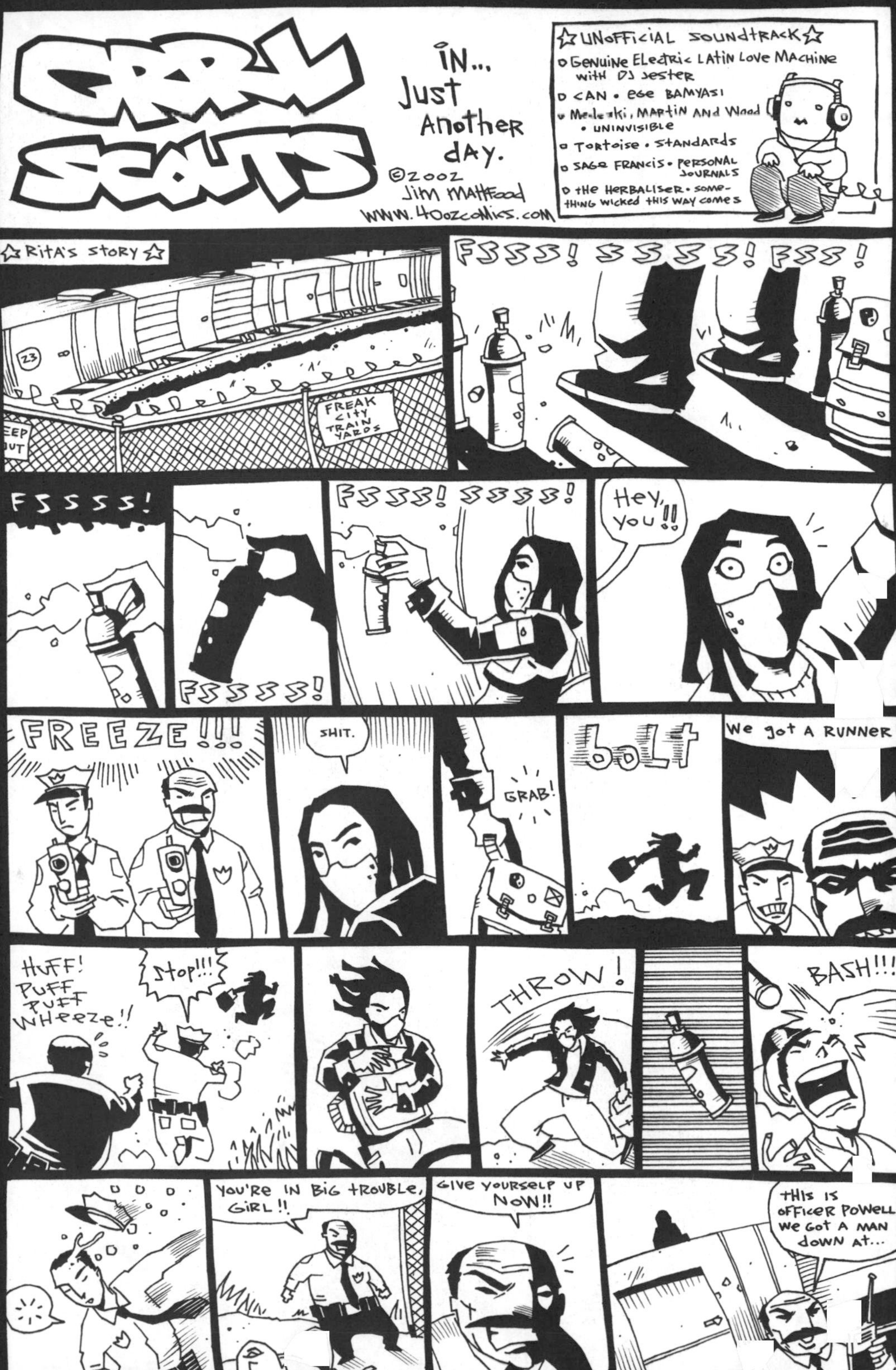
GRRL SCOUTS
IN... Just Another day.
©2002 Jim Mahfood
www.40ozcomics.com
☆UNOFFICIAL SOUNDTRACK☆
Genuine Electric Latin Love Machine with DJ Jester
CAN • Ege Bamyasi
Medeski, Martin And Wood • Uninvisible
Tortoise • Standards
Sage Francis • Personal Journals
The Herbaliser • Something Wicked This Way Comes
☆RITA'S STORY☆
FREAK CITY TRAIN YARDS
FSSS! SSSSS! FSSS!
FSSSS!
FSSSSS!
FSSSS! SSSSS!
Hey, you!!
FREEZE!!!
SHIT.
GRAB!
bolt
We got A RUNNER
HUFF! PUFF PUFF WHEEZE!!
STOP!!!
THROW!
BASH!!!
YOU'RE IN BIG TROUBLE, GIRL!!
GIVE YOURSELF UP NOW!!
THIS IS OFFICER POWELL WE GOT A MAN DOWN AT...

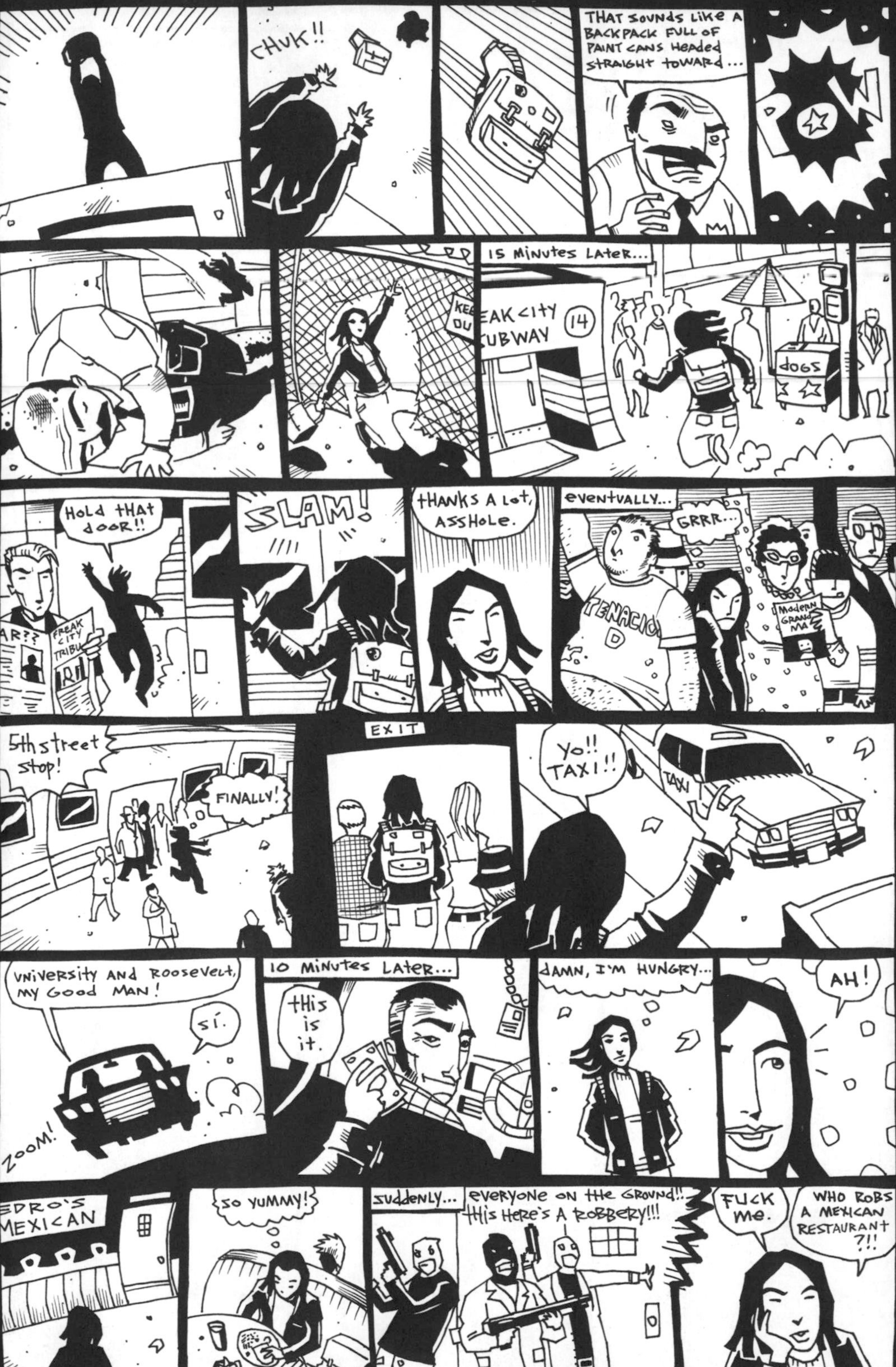
CHUK!!
THAT SOUNDS LIKE A BACKPACK FULL OF PAINT CANS HEADED STRAIGHT TOWARD...
POW
15 MINUTES LATER...
EAK CITY SUBWAY 14
dogs
HOLD THAT DOOR!!
FREAK CITY TRIBU
SLAM!
THANKS A LOT, ASSHOLE.
EVENTUALLY...
GRRR...
TENACIO D
MODERN GRANDMA
5th street stop!
FINALLY!
EXIT
YO!! TAXI!!
TAXI
UNIVERSITY AND ROOSEVELT, MY GOOD MAN!
SÍ.
ZOOM!
10 MINUTES LATER...
THIS IS IT.
DAMN, I'M HUNGRY...
AH!
EDRO'S MEXICAN
SO YUMMY!
SUDDENLY...
EVERYONE ON THE GROUND!! THIS HERE'S A ROBBERY!!!
FUCK ME.
WHO ROBS A MEXICAN RESTAURANT?!!

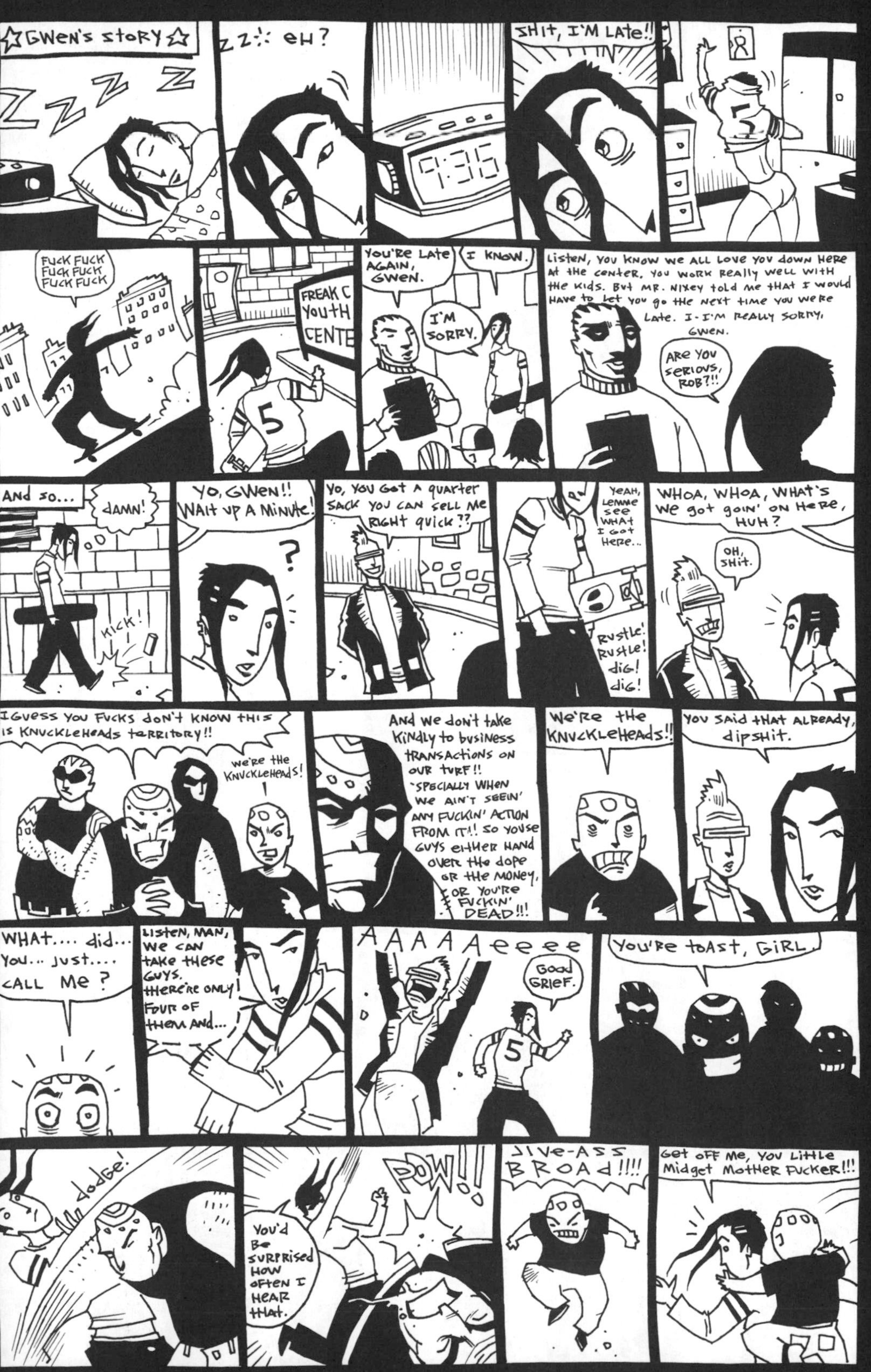
☆GWEN'S STORY☆
ZZZZZ
ZZ?! EH?
SHIT, I'M LATE!!
FUCK FUCK
FUCK FUCK
FUCK FUCK
FREAK C
YOUTH
CENTE
YOU'RE LATE AGAIN, GWEN.
I KNOW.
I'M SORRY.
LISTEN, YOU KNOW WE ALL LOVE YOU DOWN HERE AT THE CENTER. YOU WORK REALLY WELL WITH THE KIDS. BUT MR. NIXEY TOLD ME THAT I WOULD HAVE TO LET YOU GO THE NEXT TIME YOU WERE LATE. I-I'M REALLY SORRY, GWEN.
ARE YOU SERIOUS, ROB?!!
AND SO...
DAMN!
KICK!
YO, GWEN!! WAIT UP A MINUTE!
?
YO, YOU GOT A QUARTER SACK YOU CAN SELL ME RIGHT QUICK??
YEAH, LEMME SEE WHAT I GOT HERE...
RUSTLE! RUSTLE! DIG! DIG!
WHOA, WHOA, WHAT'S WE GOT GOIN' ON HERE, HUH?
OH, SHIT.
I GUESS YOU FUCKS DON'T KNOW THIS IS KNUCKLEHEADS TERRITORY!!
WE'RE THE KNUCKLEHEADS!
AND WE DON'T TAKE KINDLY TO BUSINESS TRANSACTIONS ON OUR TURF!! 'SPECIALLY WHEN WE AIN'T SEEIN' ANY FUCKIN' ACTION FROM IT!! SO YOUSE GUYS EITHER HAND OVER THE DOPE OR THE MONEY, OR YOU'RE FUCKIN' DEAD!!!
WE'RE THE KNUCKLEHEADS!!
YOU SAID THAT ALREADY, DIPSHIT.
WHAT.... DID... YOU... JUST.... CALL ME?
LISTEN, MAN, WE CAN TAKE THESE GUYS. THERE'RE ONLY FOUR OF THEM AND...
AAAAAEEEEE
GOOD GRIEF.
YOU'RE TOAST, GIRL.
DODGE!
POW!!
YOU'D BE SURPRISED HOW OFTEN I HEAR THAT.
JIVE-ASS BROAD!!!!
GET OFF ME, YOU LITTLE MIDGET MOTHER FUCKER!!!

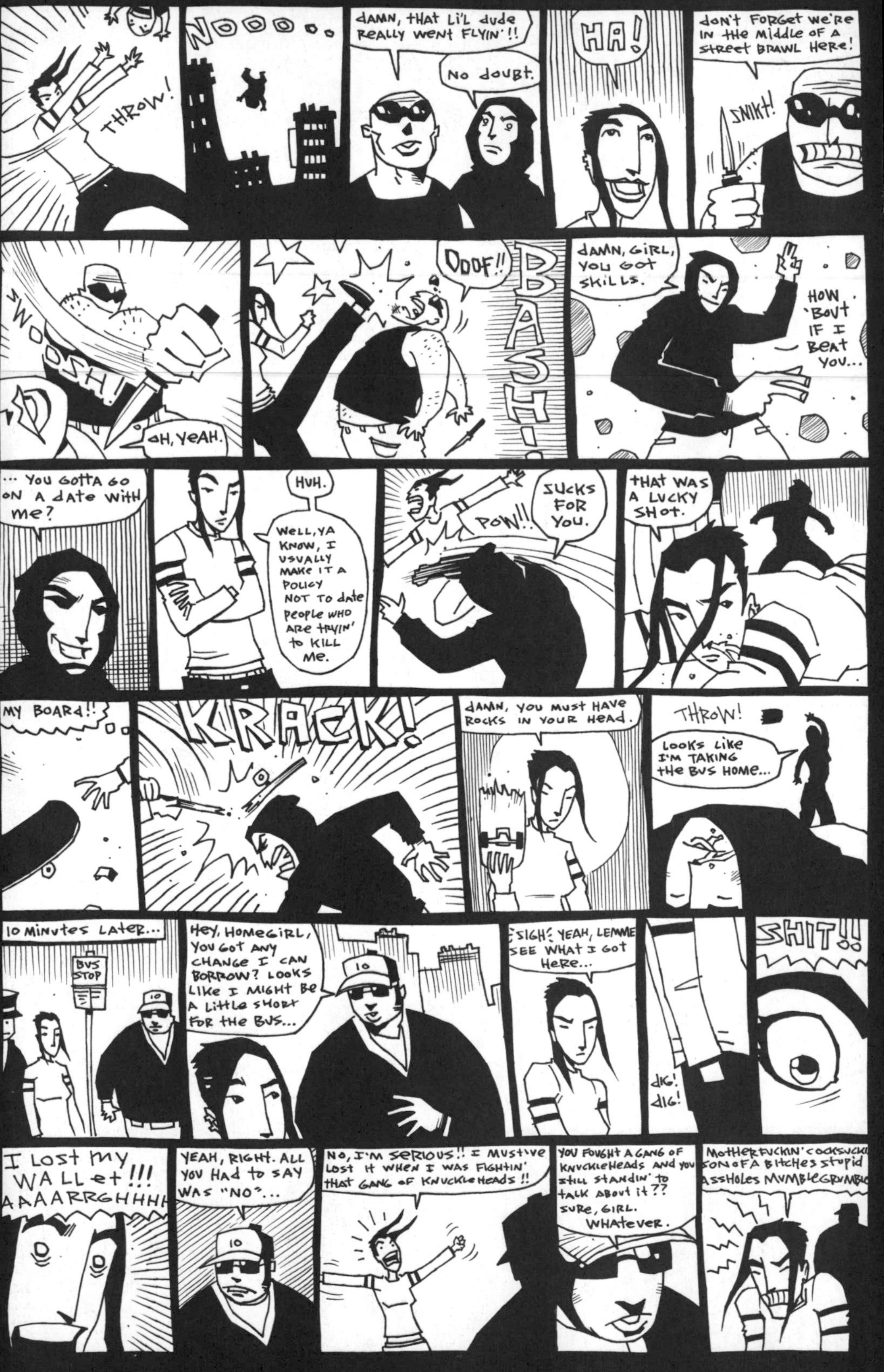
THROW!
NOOOO...
DAMN, THAT LI'L DUDE REALLY WENT FLYIN'!!
NO DOUBT.
HA!
DON'T FORGET WE'RE IN THE MIDDLE OF A STREET BRAWL HERE!
SNIKT!
WOOSH!
OH, YEAH.
OOOF!!
BASH!
DAMN, GIRL, YOU GOT SKILLS.
HOW 'BOUT IF I BEAT YOU...
... YOU GOTTA GO ON A DATE WITH ME?
HUH.
WELL, YA KNOW, I USUALLY MAKE IT A POLICY NOT TO DATE PEOPLE WHO ARE TRYIN' TO KILL ME.
POW!!
SUCKS FOR YOU.
THAT WAS A LUCKY SHOT.
MY BOARD!!
KRACK!
DAMN, YOU MUST HAVE ROCKS IN YOUR HEAD.
THROW!
LOOKS LIKE I'M TAKING THE BUS HOME...
10 MINUTES LATER...
BUS STOP
HEY, HOMEGIRL, YOU GOT ANY CHANGE I CAN BORROW? LOOKS LIKE I MIGHT BE A LITTLE SHORT FOR THE BUS...
SIGH. YEAH, LEMME SEE WHAT I GOT HERE...
DIG! DIG!
SHIT!!
I LOST MY WALLET!!! AAAARRGHHHH
YEAH, RIGHT. ALL YOU HAD TO SAY WAS "NO"...
NO, I'M SERIOUS!! I MUST'VE LOST IT WHEN I WAS FIGHTIN' THAT GANG OF KNUCKLEHEADS!!
YOU FOUGHT A GANG OF KNUCKLEHEADS AND YOU STILL STANDIN' TO TALK ABOUT IT?? SURE, GIRL. WHATEVER.
MOTHERFUCKIN' COCKSUCKI
SON OF A BITCHES STUPID
ASSHOLES MUMBLEGRUMBLE

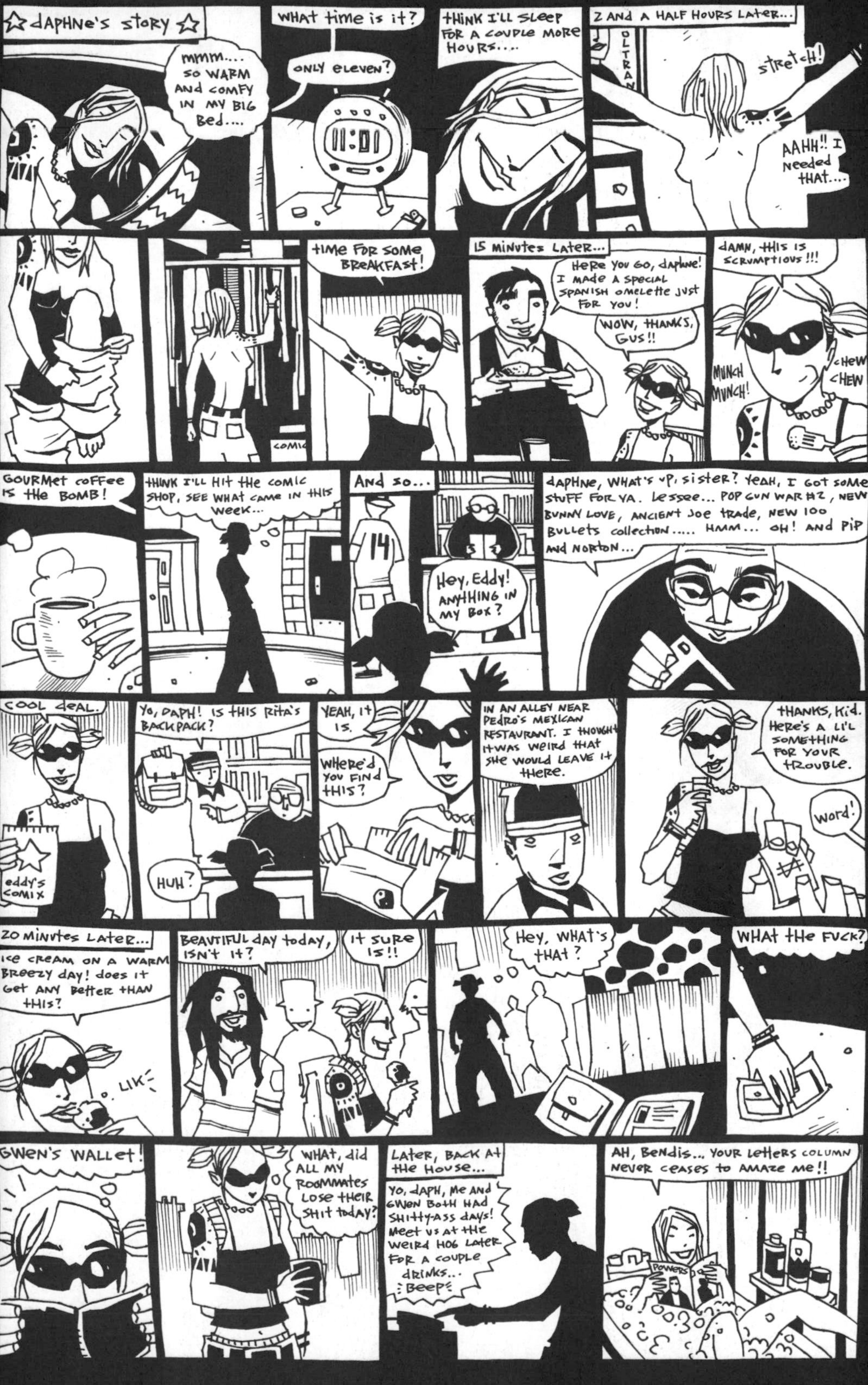
☆ daphne's story ☆
mmm.... so warm and comfy in my big bed....
What time is it?
only eleven?
11:01
think I'll sleep for a couple more hours....
2 and a half hours later...
stretch!
AAHH!! I needed that....
time for some breakfast!
15 minutes later...
Here you go, daphne! I made a special spanish omelette just for you!
Wow, thanks, Gus!!
damn, this is scrumptious!!!
Munch munch!
chew chew
Gourmet coffee is the bomb!
think I'll hit the comic shop, see what came in this week...
And so...
Hey, Eddy! Anything in my box?
daphne, what's up, sister? yeah, I got some stuff for ya. lessee... pop gun war #2, new bunny love, ancient joe trade, new 100 bullets collection..... hmm... oh! and pip and norton...
cool deal.
eddy's comix
Yo, daph! Is this Rita's backpack?
Huh?
Yeah, it is.
Where'd you find this?
In an alley near Pedro's Mexican restaurant. I thought it was weird that she would leave it there.
thanks, kid. Here's a li'l something for your trouble.
word!
20 minutes later...
ice cream on a warm breezy day! does it get any better than this?
lik
Beautiful day today, isn't it?
it sure is!!
Hey, what's that?
What the fuck?
Gwen's wallet!
What, did all my roommates lose their shit today?
Later, back at the house...
Yo, daph, me and Gwen both had shitty-ass days! Meet us at the Weird Hog later for a couple drinks...
Beep
Ah, Bendis... your letters column never ceases to amaze me!!
Powers

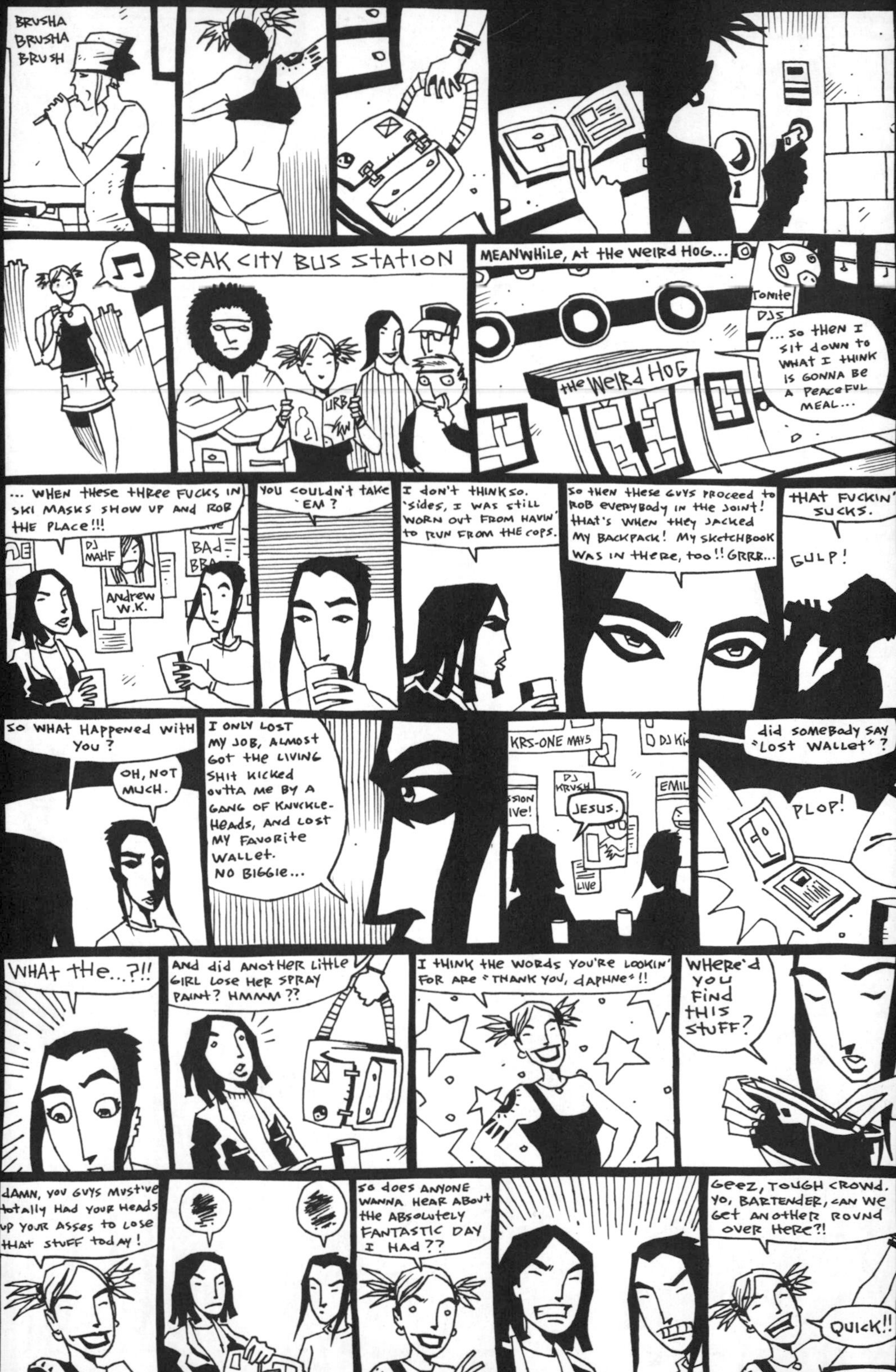
BRUSHA BRUSHA BRUSH
REAK CITY BUS STATION
URB
MEANWHILE, AT THE WEIRD HOG...
TONITE DJS
THE WEIRD HOG
...SO THEN I SIT DOWN TO WHAT I THINK IS GONNA BE A PEACEFUL MEAL...
...WHEN THESE THREE FUCKS IN SKI MASKS SHOW UP AND ROB THE PLACE!!!
DJ MAHF
ANDREW W.K.
YOU COULDN'T TAKE 'EM?
I DON'T THINK SO. 'SIDES, I WAS STILL WORN OUT FROM HAVIN' TO RUN FROM THE COPS.
SO THEN THESE GUYS PROCEED TO ROB EVERYBODY IN THE JOINT! THAT'S WHEN THEY JACKED MY BACKPACK! MY SKETCHBOOK WAS IN THERE, TOO!! GRRR...
THAT FUCKIN' SUCKS.
GULP!
SO WHAT HAPPENED WITH YOU?
OH, NOT MUCH.
I ONLY LOST MY JOB, ALMOST GOT THE LIVING SHIT KICKED OUTTA ME BY A GANG OF KNUCKLE-HEADS, AND LOST MY FAVORITE WALLET. NO BIGGIE...
KRS-ONE MAY 5
DJ KRUSH
JESUS.
DID SOMEBODY SAY "LOST WALLET"?
PLOP!
WHAT THE...?!!
AND DID ANOTHER LITTLE GIRL LOSE HER SPRAY PAINT? HMMM??
I THINK THE WORDS YOU'RE LOOKIN' FOR ARE "THANK YOU, DAPHNE"!!
WHERE'D YOU FIND THIS STUFF?
DAMN, YOU GUYS MUST'VE TOTALLY HAD YOUR HEADS UP YOUR ASSES TO LOSE THAT STUFF TODAY!
SO DOES ANYONE WANNA HEAR ABOUT THE ABSOLUTELY FANTASTIC DAY I HAD??
GEEZ, TOUGH CROWD. YO, BARTENDER, CAN WE GET ANOTHER ROUND OVER HERE?!
QUICK!!
END.

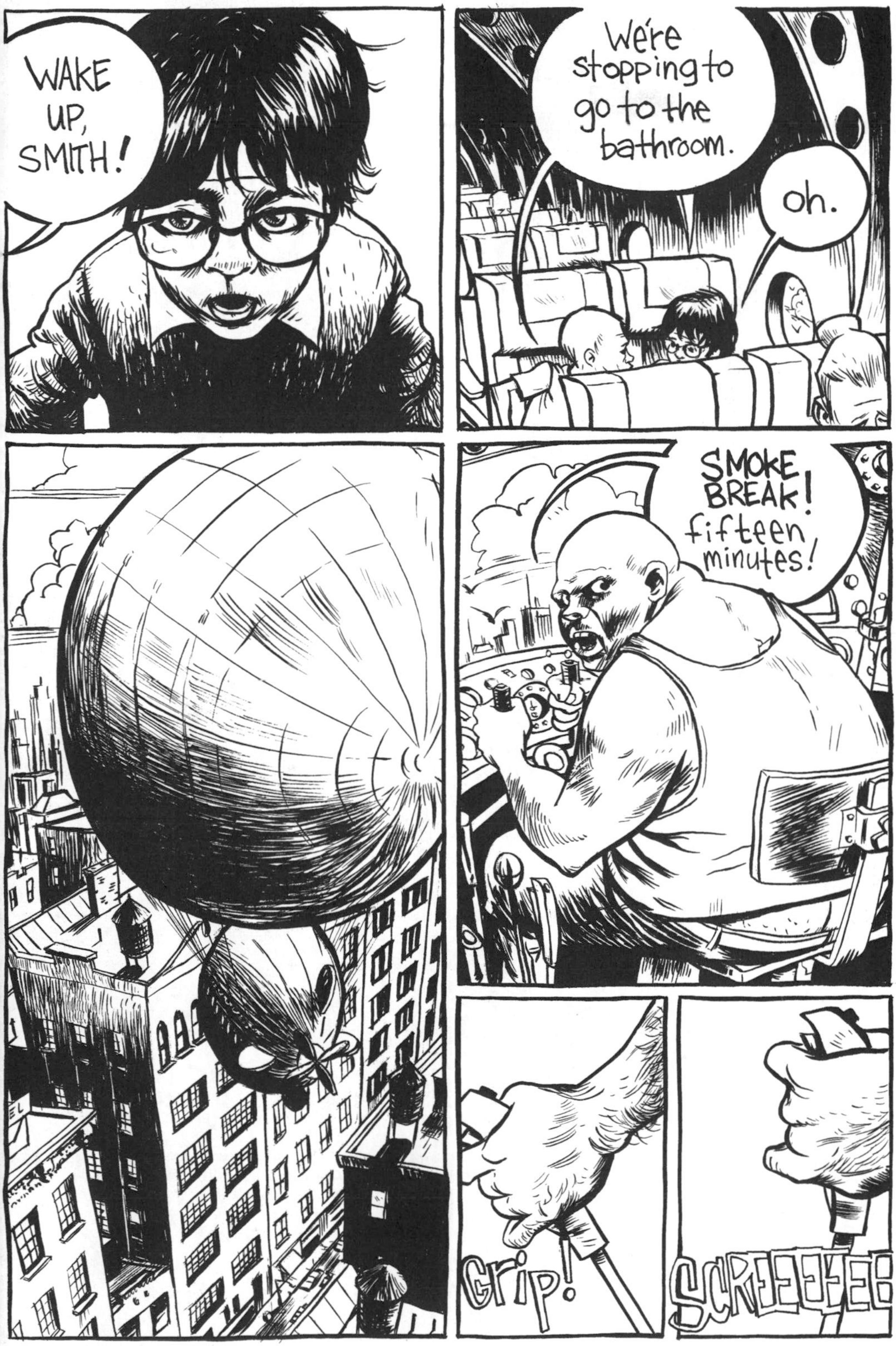
WAKE UP, SMITH!
We're stopping to go to the bathroom.
oh.
SMOKE BREAK! fifteen minutes!
Grip!
SCREEEEE!

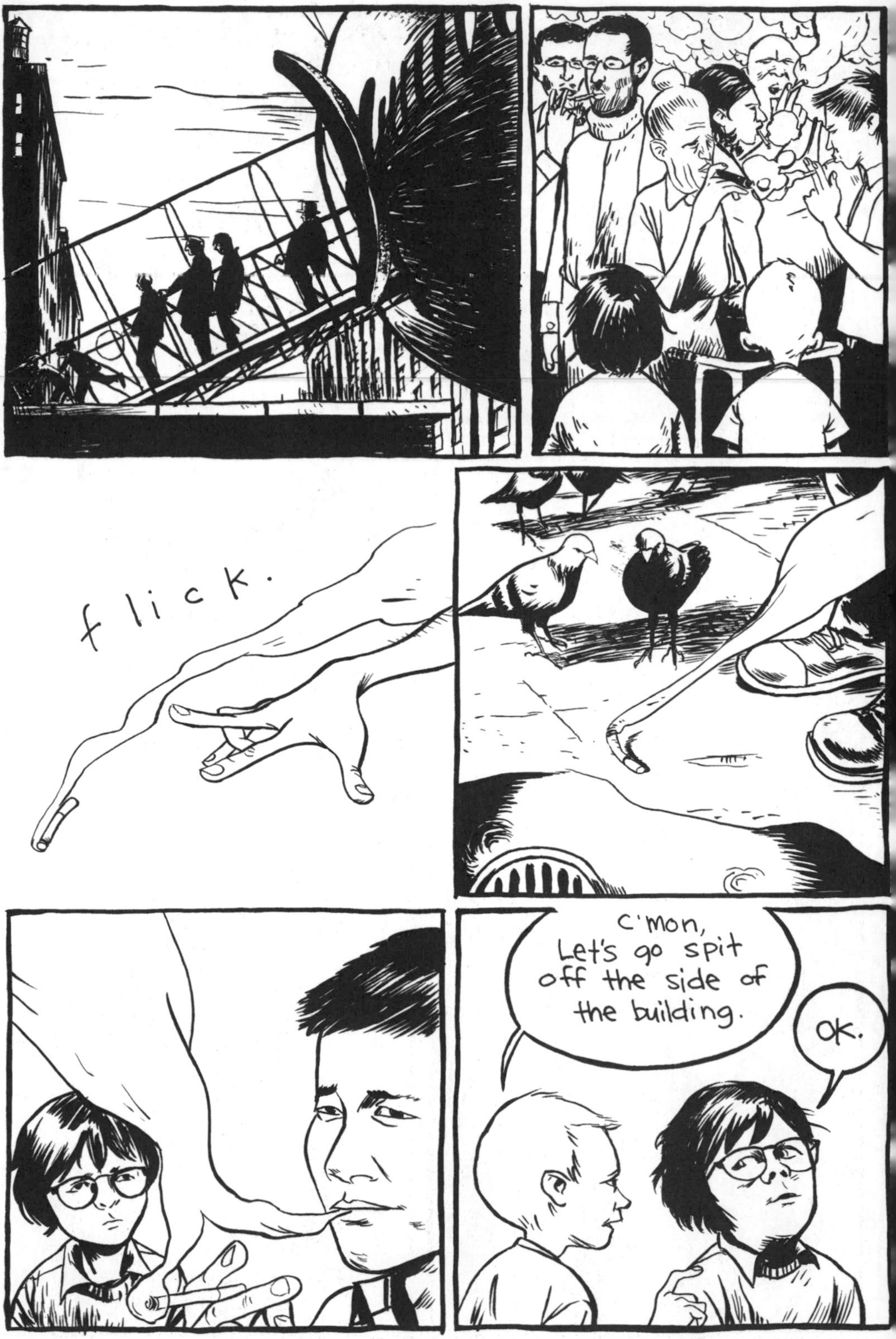
flick.
c'mon, Let's go spit off the side of the building.
OK.

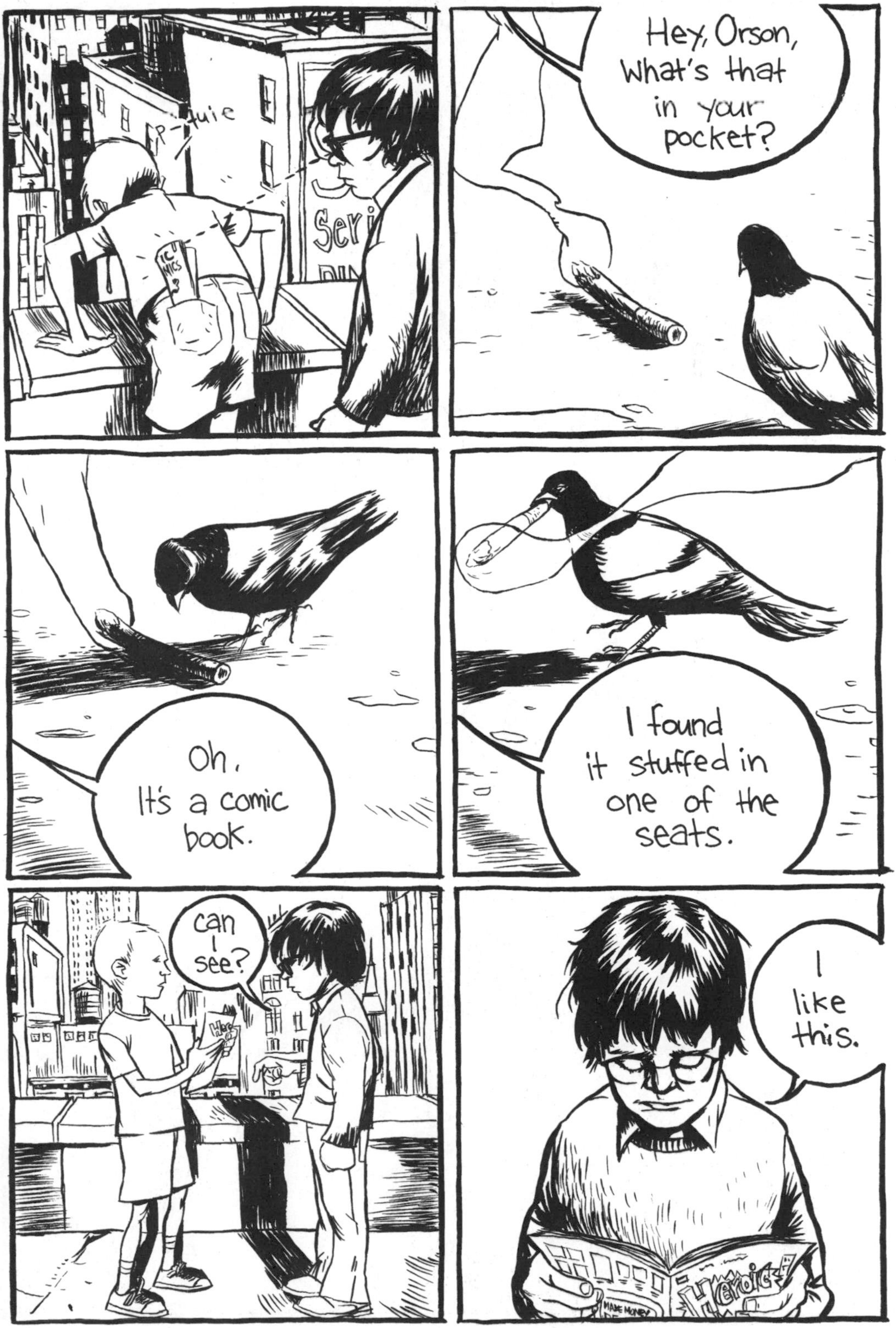
P-tuie
Ser
Hey, Orson, what's that in your pocket?
Oh. It's a comic book.
I found it stuffed in one of the seats.
can I see?
I like this.
Heroic
MAKE MONEY

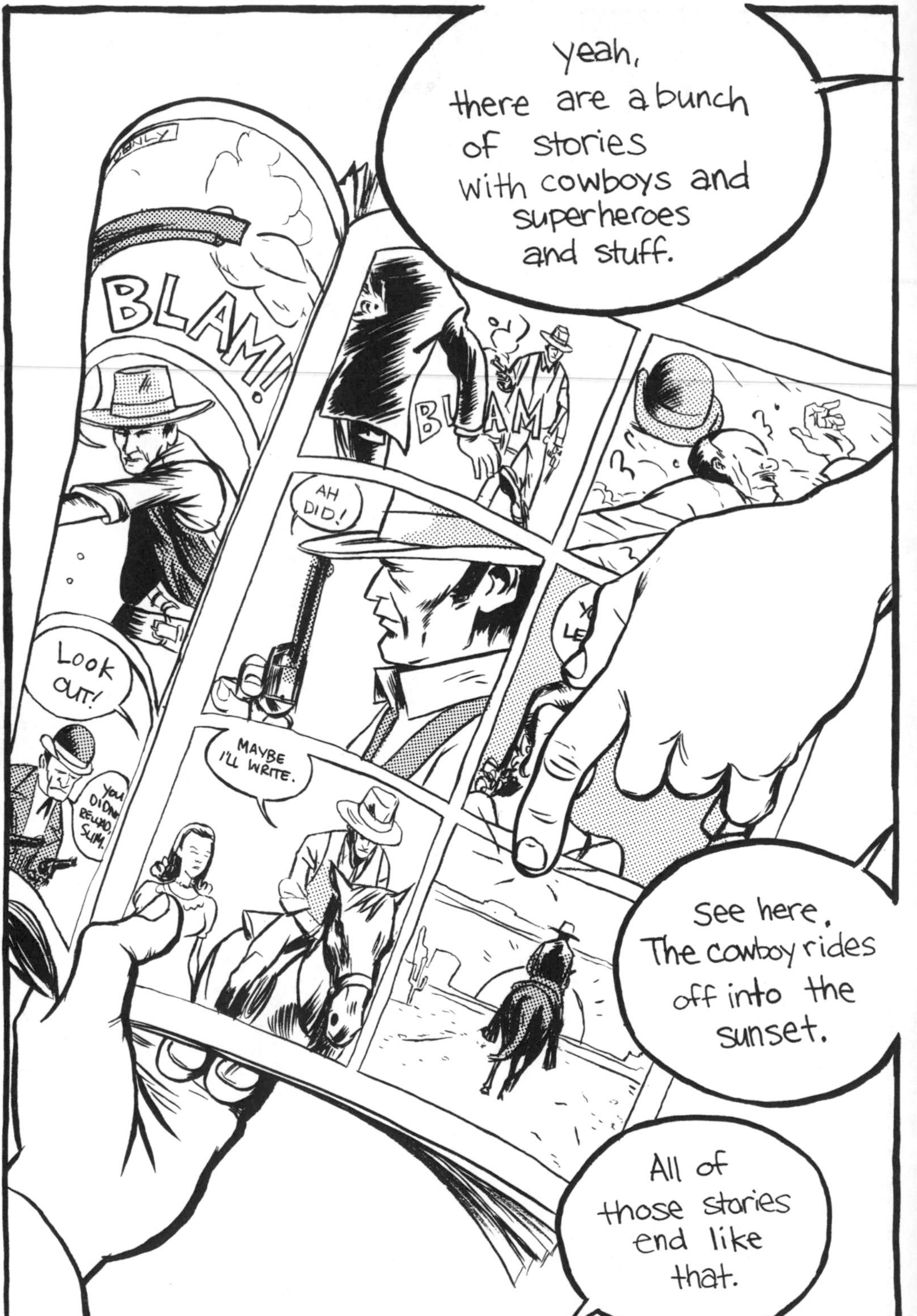
yeah, there are a bunch of stories with cowboys and superheroes and stuff.
BLAM!
Look OUT!
AH DID!
BLAM
MAYBE I'LL WRITE.
See here. The cowboy rides off into the sunset.
All of those stories end like that.

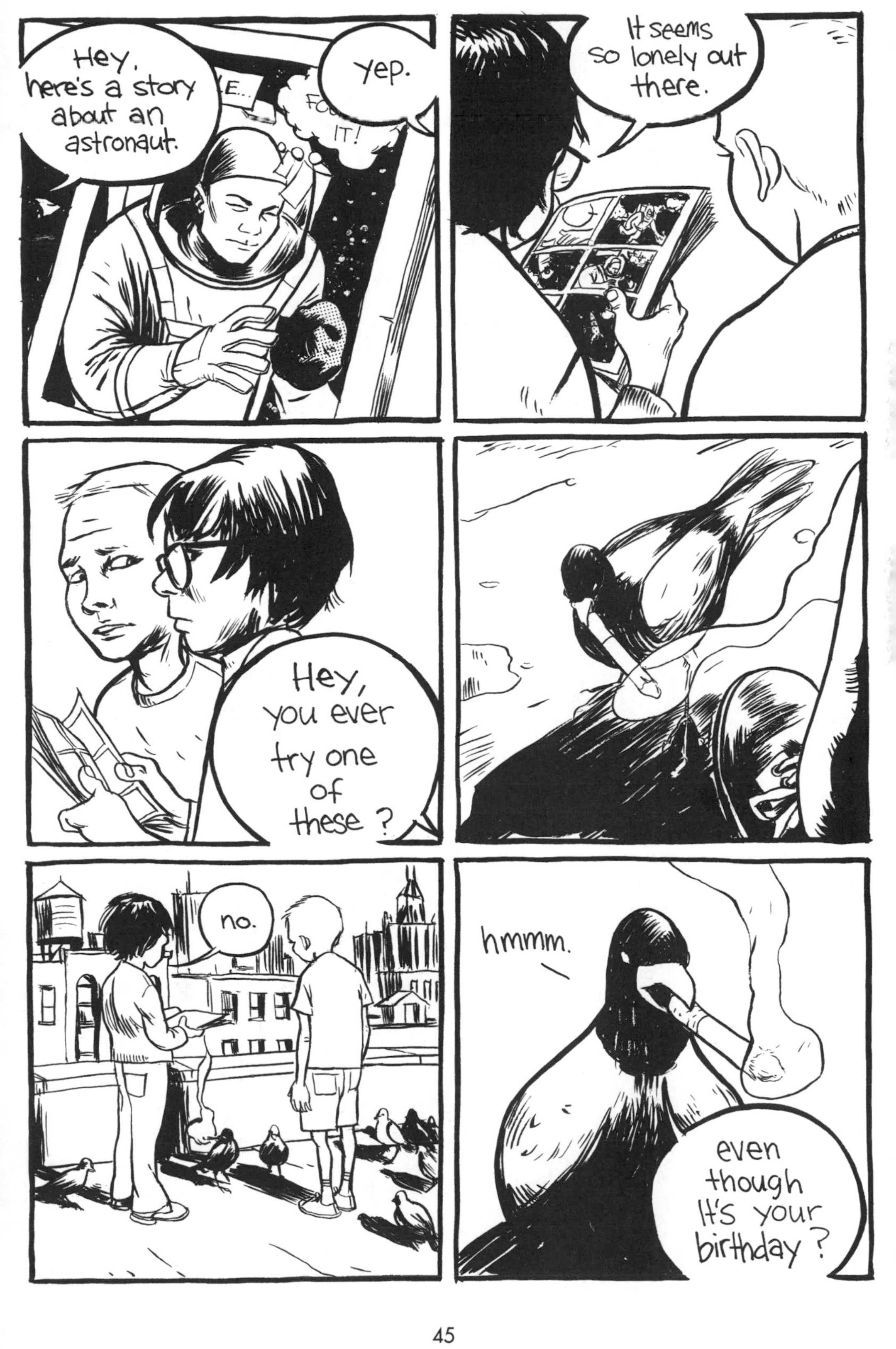
Hey, here's a story about an astronaut.
yep.
It seems so lonely out there.
Hey, you ever try one of these ?
no.
hmmm.
even though It's your birthday ?

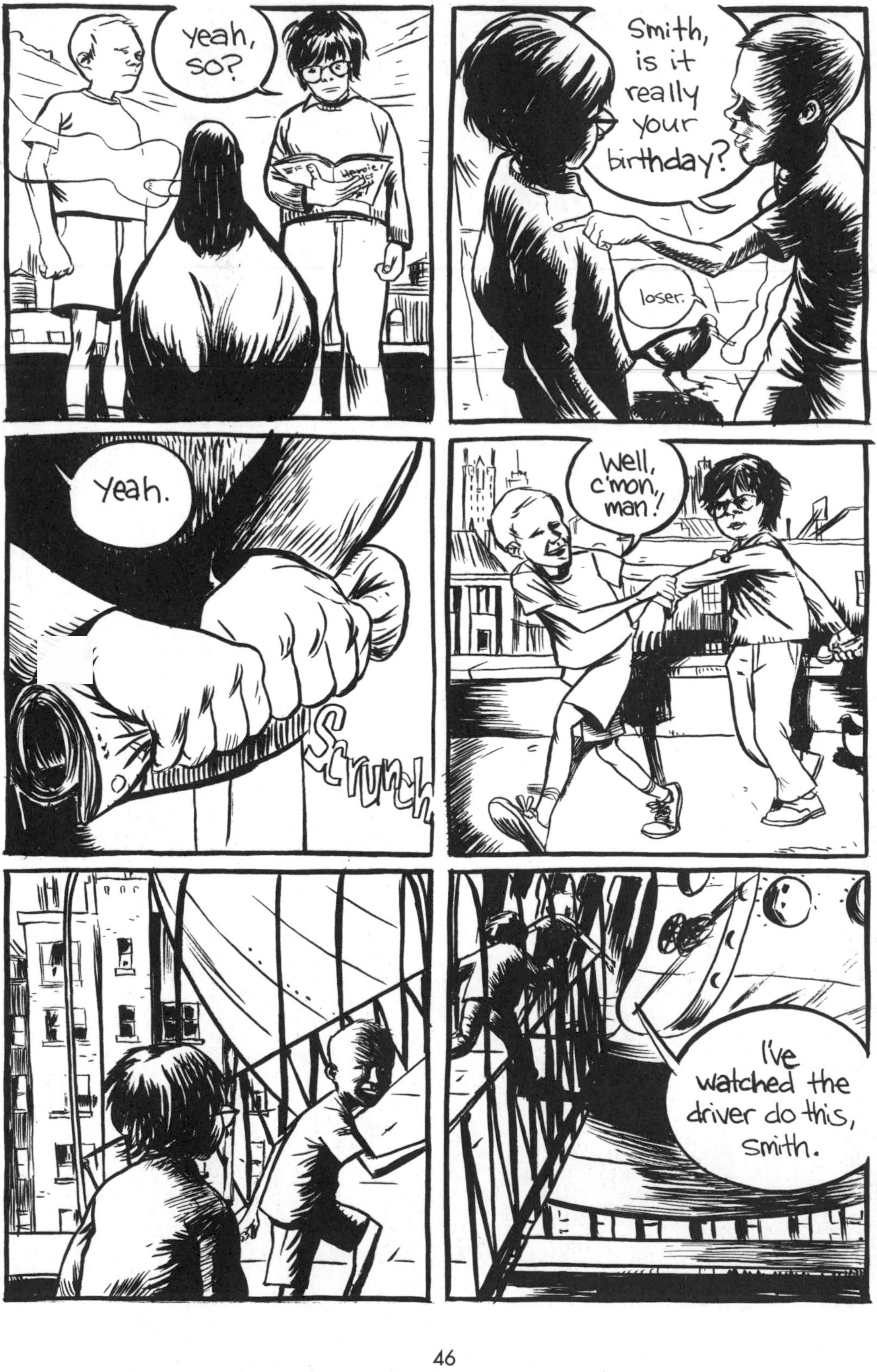
yeah, so?
Smith, is it really your birthday?
loser.
yeah.
Scrunch
Well, c'mon, man!
I've watched the driver do this, smith.

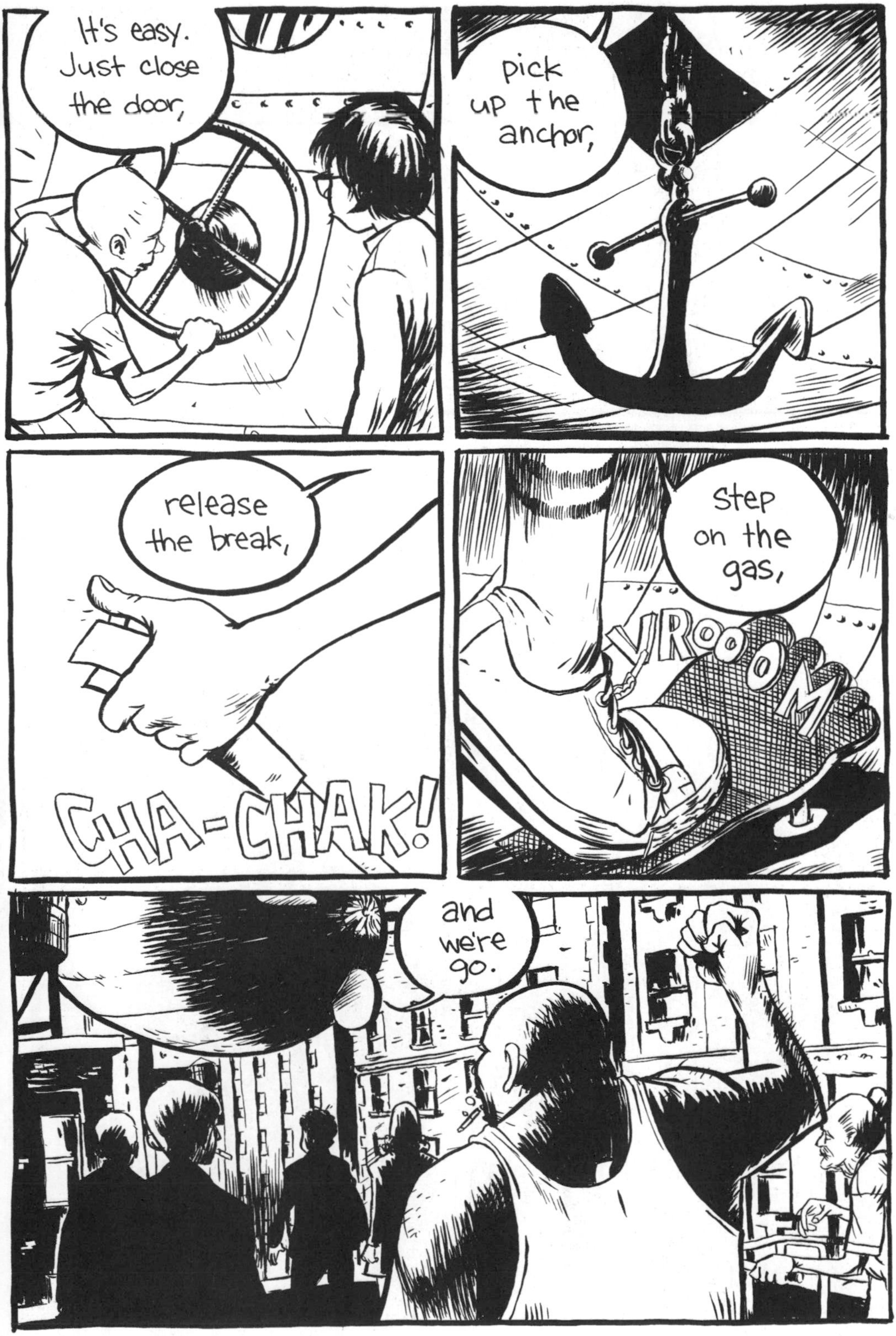
It's easy. Just close the door,
pick up the anchor,
release the break,
CHA-CHAK!
step on the gas,
VROOOM
and we're go.

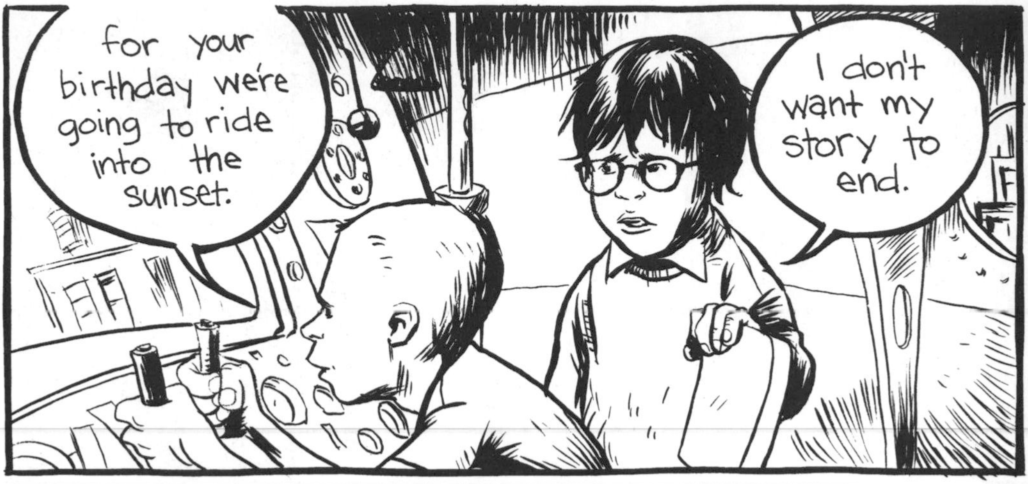
for your birthday we're going to ride into the sunset.
I don't want my story to end.

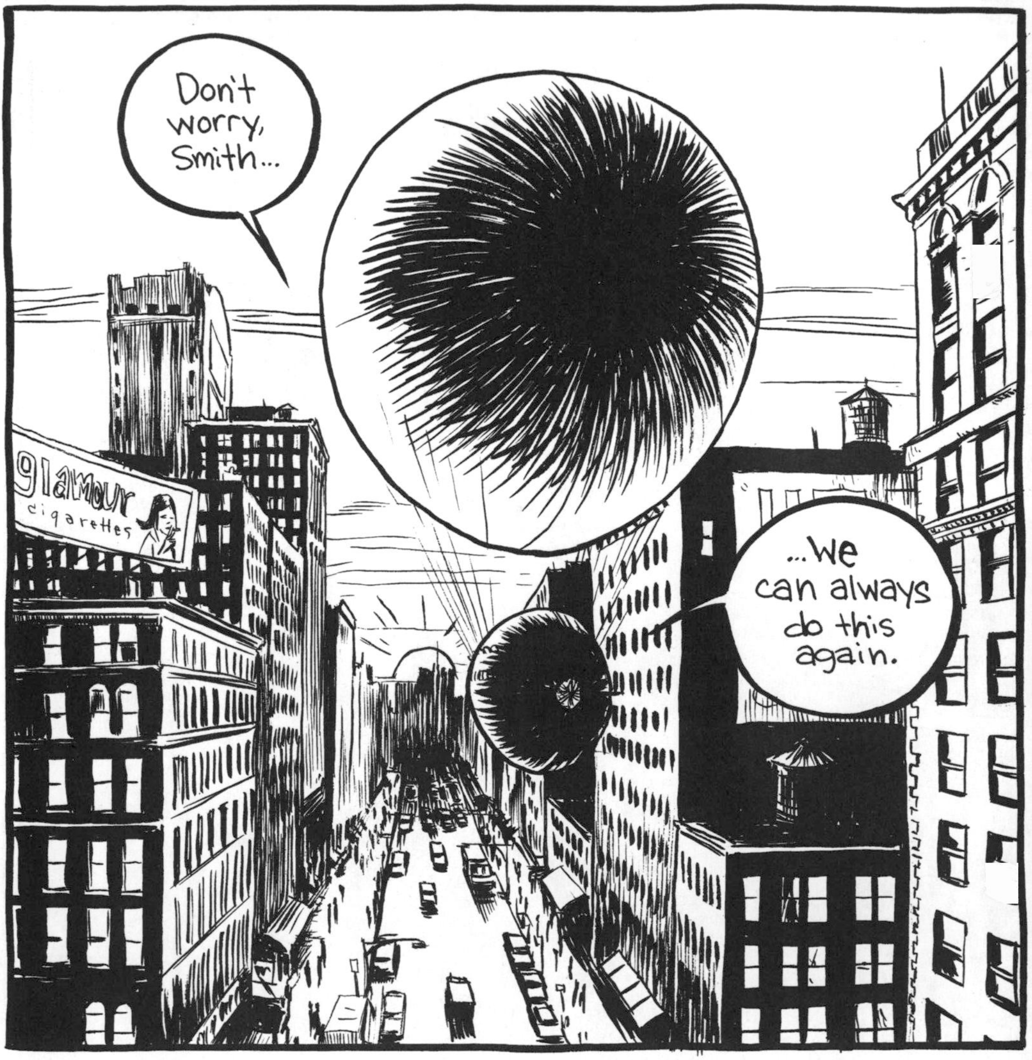
Don't worry, Smith...
glamour cigarettes
...we can always do this again.

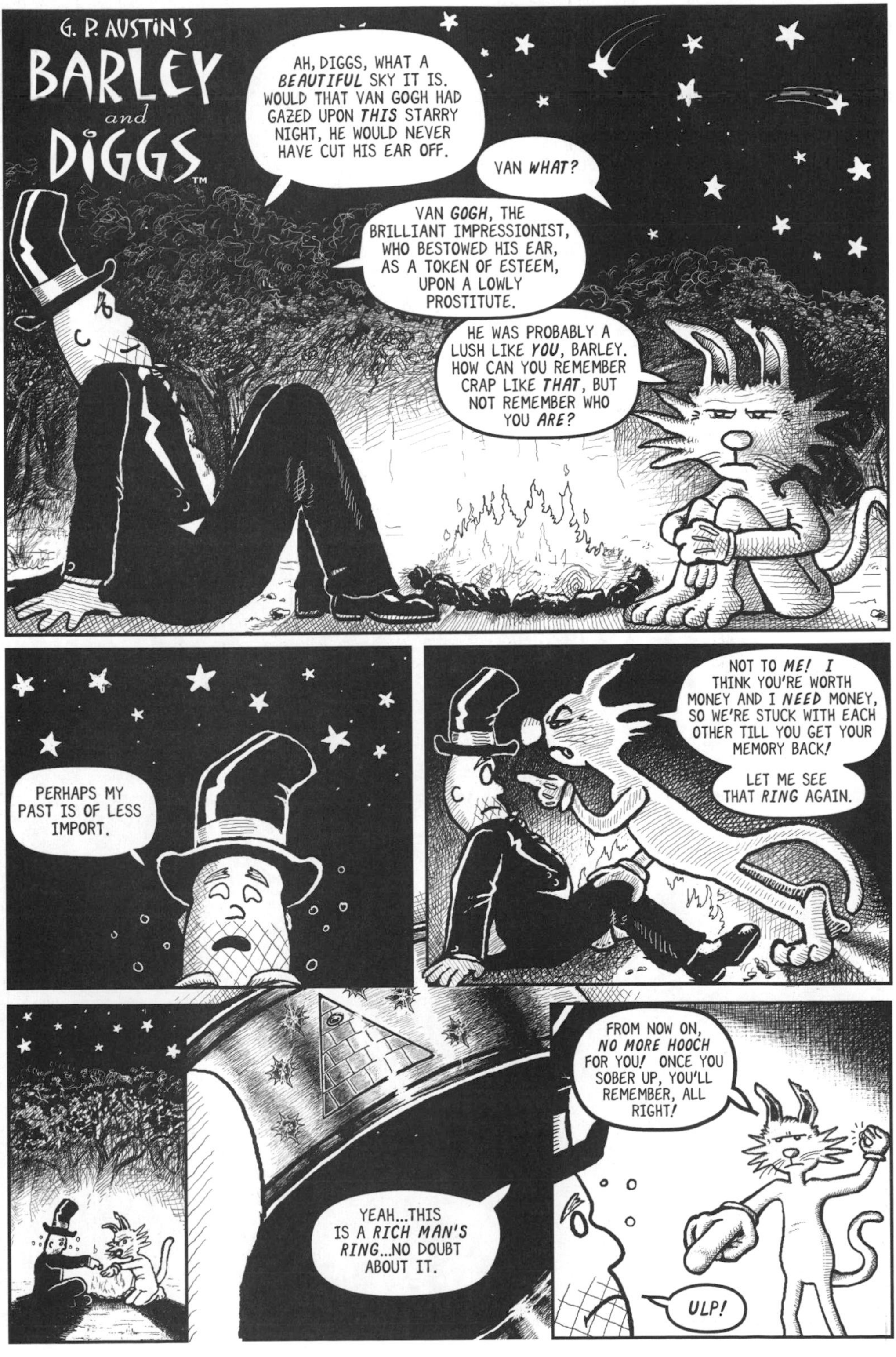
G. P. AUSTIN'S
BARLEY and DIGGS™
AH, DIGGS, WHAT A BEAUTIFUL SKY IT IS. WOULD THAT VAN GOGH HAD GAZED UPON THIS STARRY NIGHT, HE WOULD NEVER HAVE CUT HIS EAR OFF.
VAN WHAT?
VAN GOGH, THE BRILLIANT IMPRESSIONIST, WHO BESTOWED HIS EAR, AS A TOKEN OF ESTEEM, UPON A LOWLY PROSTITUTE.
HE WAS PROBABLY A LUSH LIKE YOU, BARLEY. HOW CAN YOU REMEMBER CRAP LIKE THAT, BUT NOT REMEMBER WHO YOU ARE?
PERHAPS MY PAST IS OF LESS IMPORT.
NOT TO ME! I THINK YOU'RE WORTH MONEY AND I NEED MONEY, SO WE'RE STUCK WITH EACH OTHER TILL YOU GET YOUR MEMORY BACK!
LET ME SEE THAT RING AGAIN.
YEAH...THIS IS A RICH MAN'S RING...NO DOUBT ABOUT IT.
FROM NOW ON, NO MORE HOOCH FOR YOU! ONCE YOU SOBER UP, YOU'LL REMEMBER, ALL RIGHT!
ULP!

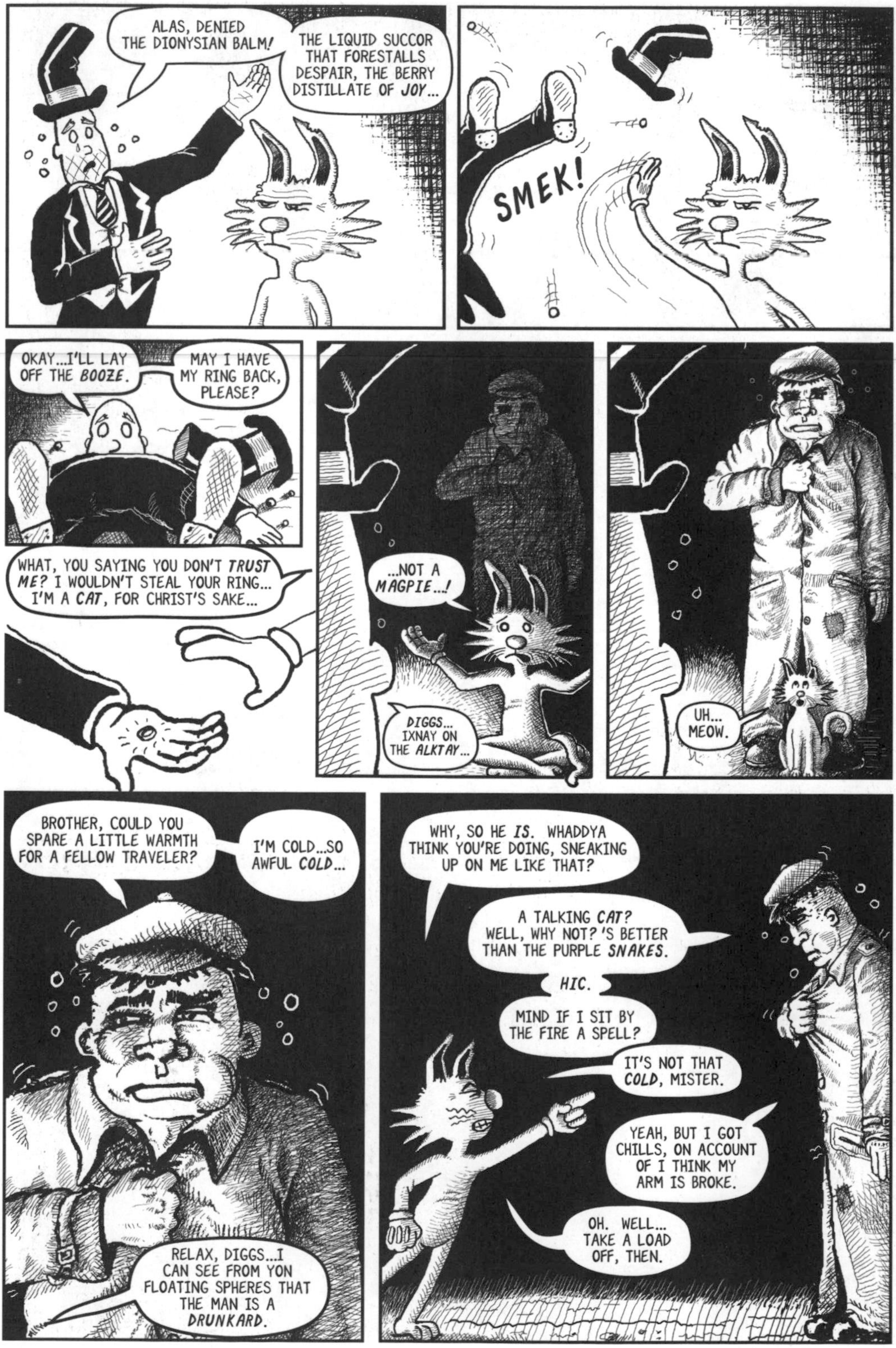
ALAS, DENIED THE DIONYSIAN BALM!
THE LIQUID SUCCOR THAT FORESTALLS DESPAIR, THE BERRY DISTILLATE OF JOY...
SMEK!
OKAY...I'LL LAY OFF THE BOOZE.
MAY I HAVE MY RING BACK, PLEASE?
WHAT, YOU SAYING YOU DON'T TRUST ME? I WOULDN'T STEAL YOUR RING... I'M A CAT, FOR CHRIST'S SAKE...
...NOT A MAGPIE...!
DIGGS... IXNAY ON THE ALKTAY...
UH... MEOW.
BROTHER, COULD YOU SPARE A LITTLE WARMTH FOR A FELLOW TRAVELER?
I'M COLD...SO AWFUL COLD...
RELAX, DIGGS...I CAN SEE FROM YON FLOATING SPHERES THAT THE MAN IS A DRUNKARD.
WHY, SO HE IS. WHADDYA THINK YOU'RE DOING, SNEAKING UP ON ME LIKE THAT?
A TALKING CAT? WELL, WHY NOT? 'S BETTER THAN THE PURPLE SNAKES.
HIC.
MIND IF I SIT BY THE FIRE A SPELL?
IT'S NOT THAT COLD, MISTER.
YEAH, BUT I GOT CHILLS, ON ACCOUNT OF I THINK MY ARM IS BROKE.
OH. WELL... TAKE A LOAD OFF, THEN.

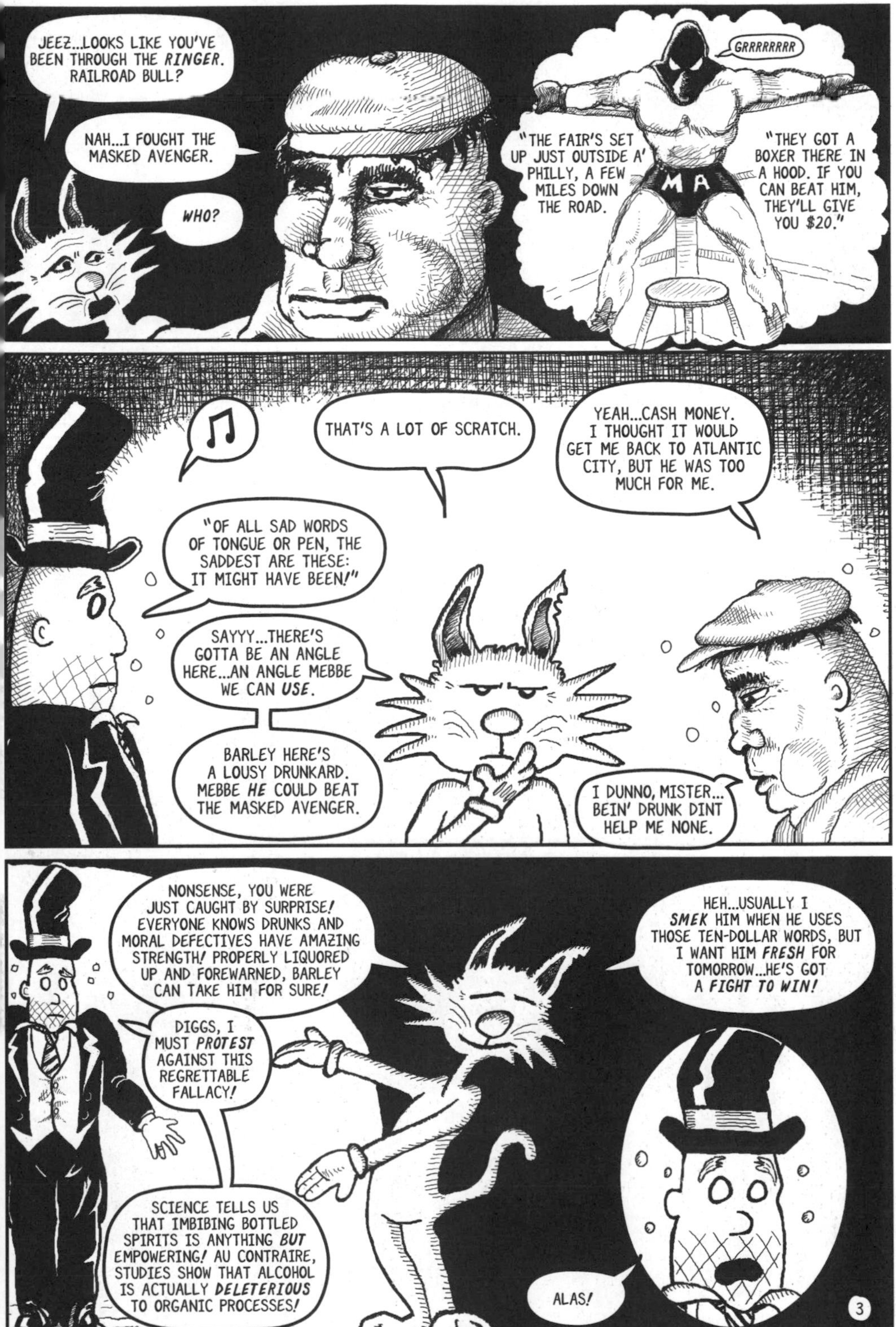
JEEZ...LOOKS LIKE YOU'VE BEEN THROUGH THE RINGER. RAILROAD BULL?
NAH...I FOUGHT THE MASKED AVENGER.
WHO?
GRRRRRRRR
"THE FAIR'S SET UP JUST OUTSIDE A' PHILLY, A FEW MILES DOWN THE ROAD.
"THEY GOT A BOXER THERE IN A HOOD. IF YOU CAN BEAT HIM, THEY'LL GIVE YOU $20."
MA
♫
THAT'S A LOT OF SCRATCH.
YEAH...CASH MONEY. I THOUGHT IT WOULD GET ME BACK TO ATLANTIC CITY, BUT HE WAS TOO MUCH FOR ME.
"OF ALL SAD WORDS OF TONGUE OR PEN, THE SADDEST ARE THESE: IT MIGHT HAVE BEEN!"
SAYYY...THERE'S GOTTA BE AN ANGLE HERE...AN ANGLE MEBBE WE CAN USE.
BARLEY HERE'S A LOUSY DRUNKARD. MEBBE HE COULD BEAT THE MASKED AVENGER.
I DUNNO, MISTER... BEIN' DRUNK DINT HELP ME NONE.
NONSENSE, YOU WERE JUST CAUGHT BY SURPRISE! EVERYONE KNOWS DRUNKS AND MORAL DEFECTIVES HAVE AMAZING STRENGTH! PROPERLY LIQUORED UP AND FOREWARNED, BARLEY CAN TAKE HIM FOR SURE!
DIGGS, I MUST PROTEST AGAINST THIS REGRETTABLE FALLACY!
SCIENCE TELLS US THAT IMBIBING BOTTLED SPIRITS IS ANYTHING BUT EMPOWERING! AU CONTRAIRE, STUDIES SHOW THAT ALCOHOL IS ACTUALLY DELETERIOUS TO ORGANIC PROCESSES!
HEH...USUALLY I SMEK HIM WHEN HE USES THOSE TEN-DOLLAR WORDS, BUT I WANT HIM FRESH FOR TOMORROW...HE'S GOT A FIGHT TO WIN!
ALAS!
3

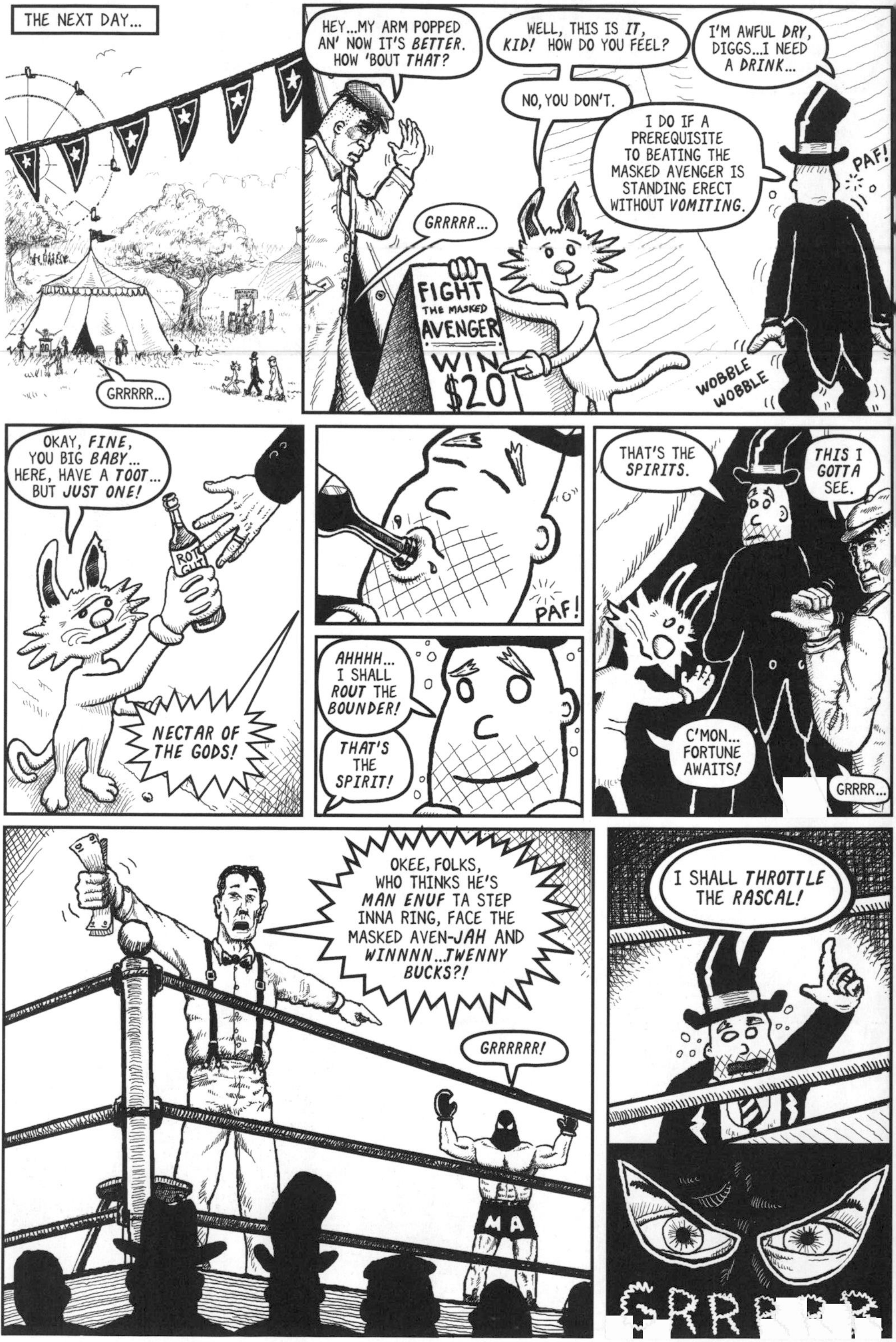
THE NEXT DAY...
GRRRRR...
HEY...MY ARM POPPED AN' NOW IT'S BETTER. HOW 'BOUT THAT?
WELL, THIS IS IT, KID! HOW DO YOU FEEL?
NO, YOU DON'T.
I'M AWFUL DRY, DIGGS...I NEED A DRINK...
I DO IF A PREREQUISITE TO BEATING THE MASKED AVENGER IS STANDING ERECT WITHOUT VOMITING.
PAF!
GRRRRR...
FIGHT THE MASKED AVENGER WIN $20
WOBBLE WOBBLE
OKAY, FINE, YOU BIG BABY... HERE, HAVE A TOOT... BUT JUST ONE!
ROT GUT
NECTAR OF THE GODS!
PAF!
AHHHH... I SHALL ROUT THE BOUNDER!
THAT'S THE SPIRIT!
THAT'S THE SPIRITS.
THIS I GOTTA SEE.
C'MON... FORTUNE AWAITS!
GRRRR...
OKEE, FOLKS, WHO THINKS HE'S MAN ENUF TA STEP INNA RING, FACE THE MASKED AVEN-JAH AND WINNNN...TWENNY BUCKS?!
GRRRRRR!
MA
I SHALL THROTTLE THE RASCAL!
GRRR

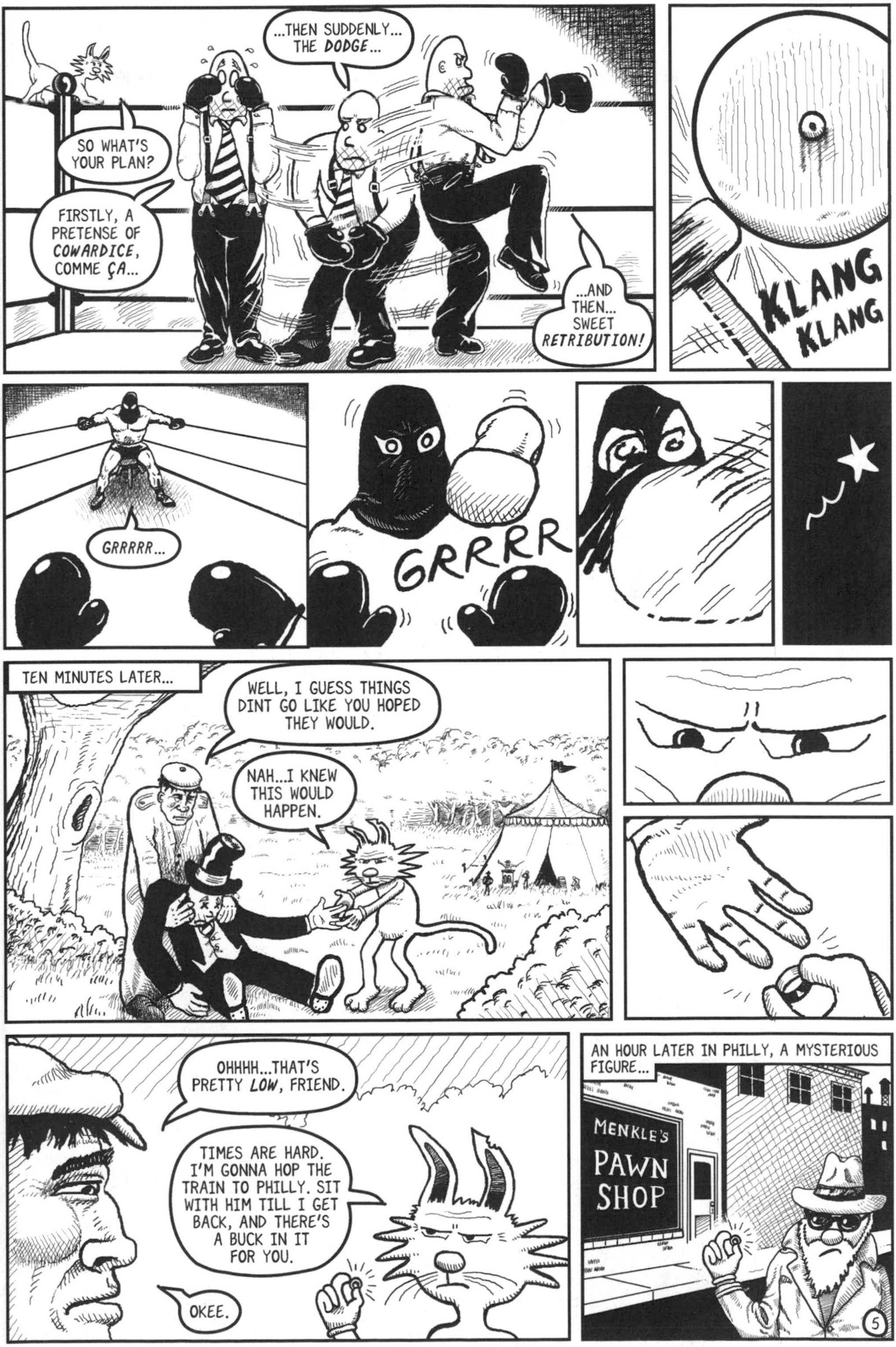
SO WHAT'S YOUR PLAN?
FIRSTLY, A PRETENSE OF COWARDICE, COMME ÇA...
...THEN SUDDENLY... THE DODGE...
...AND THEN... SWEET RETRIBUTION!
KLANG KLANG
GRRRRR...
GRRRR
TEN MINUTES LATER...
WELL, I GUESS THINGS DINT GO LIKE YOU HOPED THEY WOULD.
NAH...I KNEW THIS WOULD HAPPEN.
OHHHH...THAT'S PRETTY LOW, FRIEND.
TIMES ARE HARD. I'M GONNA HOP THE TRAIN TO PHILLY. SIT WITH HIM TILL I GET BACK, AND THERE'S A BUCK IN IT FOR YOU.
OKEE.
AN HOUR LATER IN PHILLY, A MYSTERIOUS FIGURE...
MENKLE'S PAWN SHOP
5

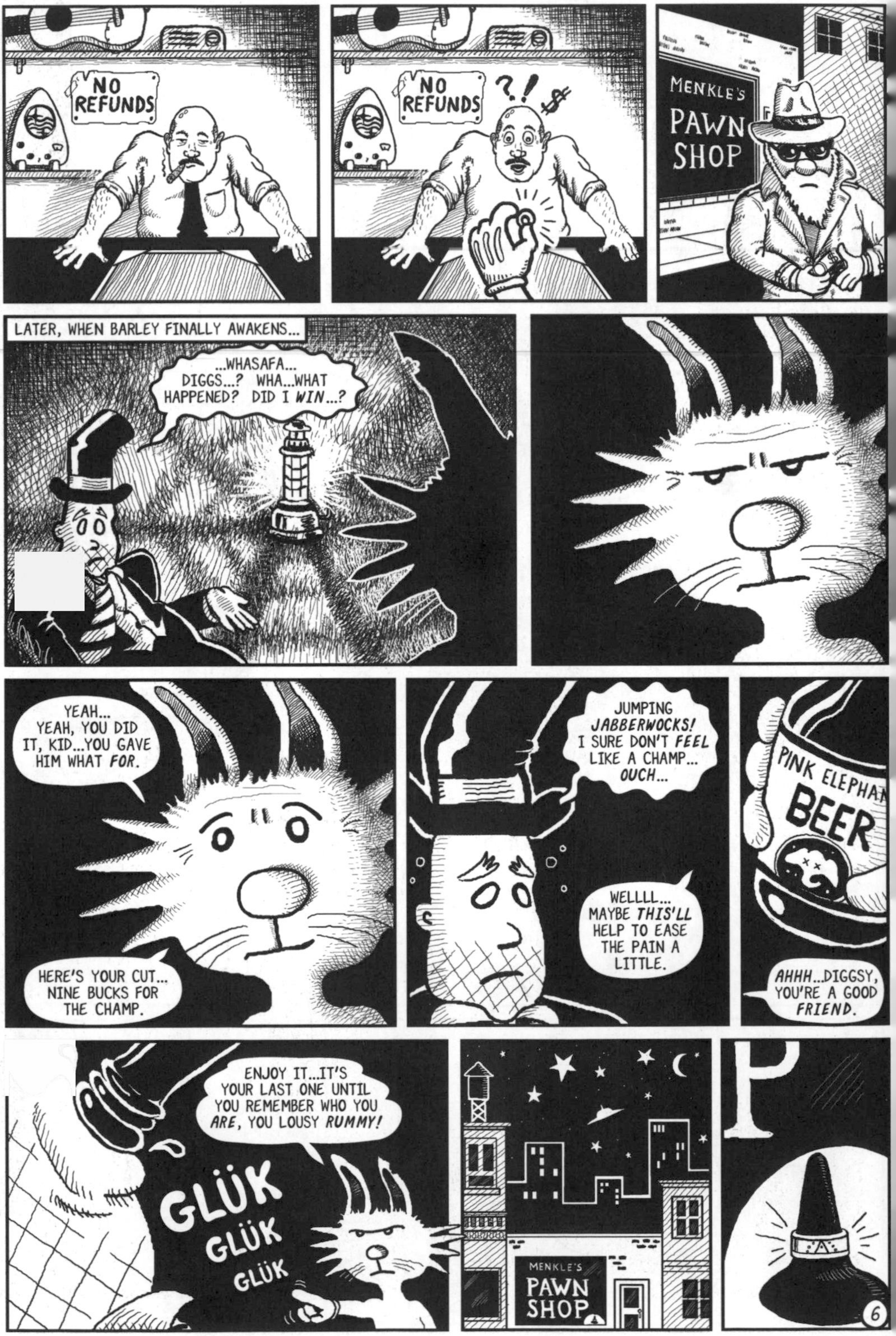
NO REFUNDS
NO REFUNDS
?!
$
MENKLE'S PAWN SHOP
LATER, WHEN BARLEY FINALLY AWAKENS...
...WHASAFA... DIGGS...? WHA...WHAT HAPPENED? DID I *WIN*...?
YEAH... YEAH, YOU DID IT, KID...YOU GAVE HIM WHAT *FOR*.
HERE'S YOUR CUT... NINE BUCKS FOR THE CHAMP.
JUMPING *JABBERWOCKS!* I SURE DON'T *FEEL* LIKE A CHAMP... *OUCH*...
WELLLL... MAYBE *THIS'LL* HELP TO EASE THE PAIN A LITTLE.
PINK ELEPHA BEER
AHHH...DIGGSY, YOU'RE A GOOD *FRIEND*.
ENJOY IT...IT'S YOUR LAST ONE UNTIL YOU REMEMBER WHO YOU *ARE*, YOU LOUSY *RUMMY!*
GLÜK GLÜK GLÜK
MENKLE'S PAWN SHOP
6

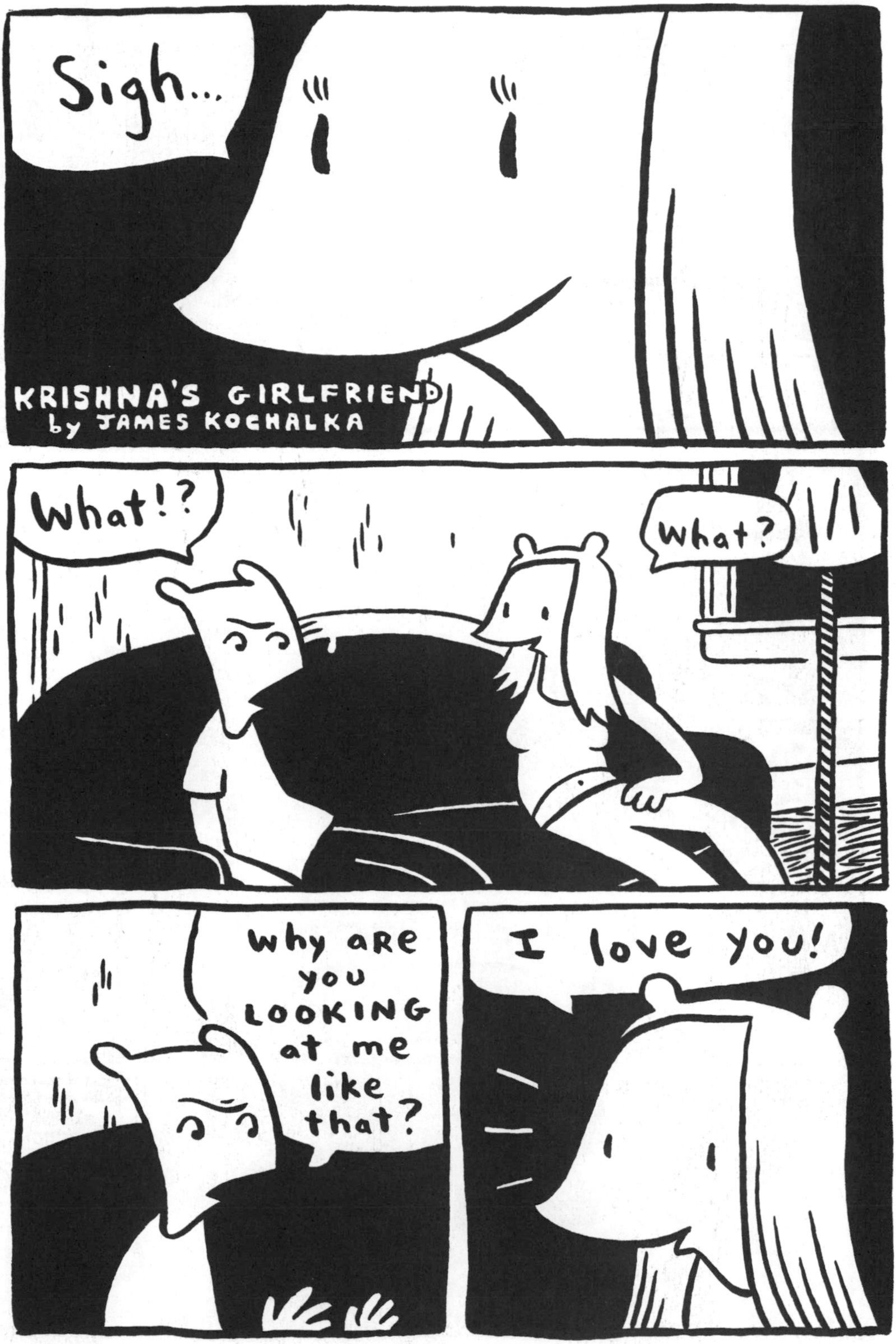
Sigh...
KRISHNA'S GIRLFRIEND
by JAMES KOCHALKA
What!?
What?
why are you LOOKING at me like that?
I love you!

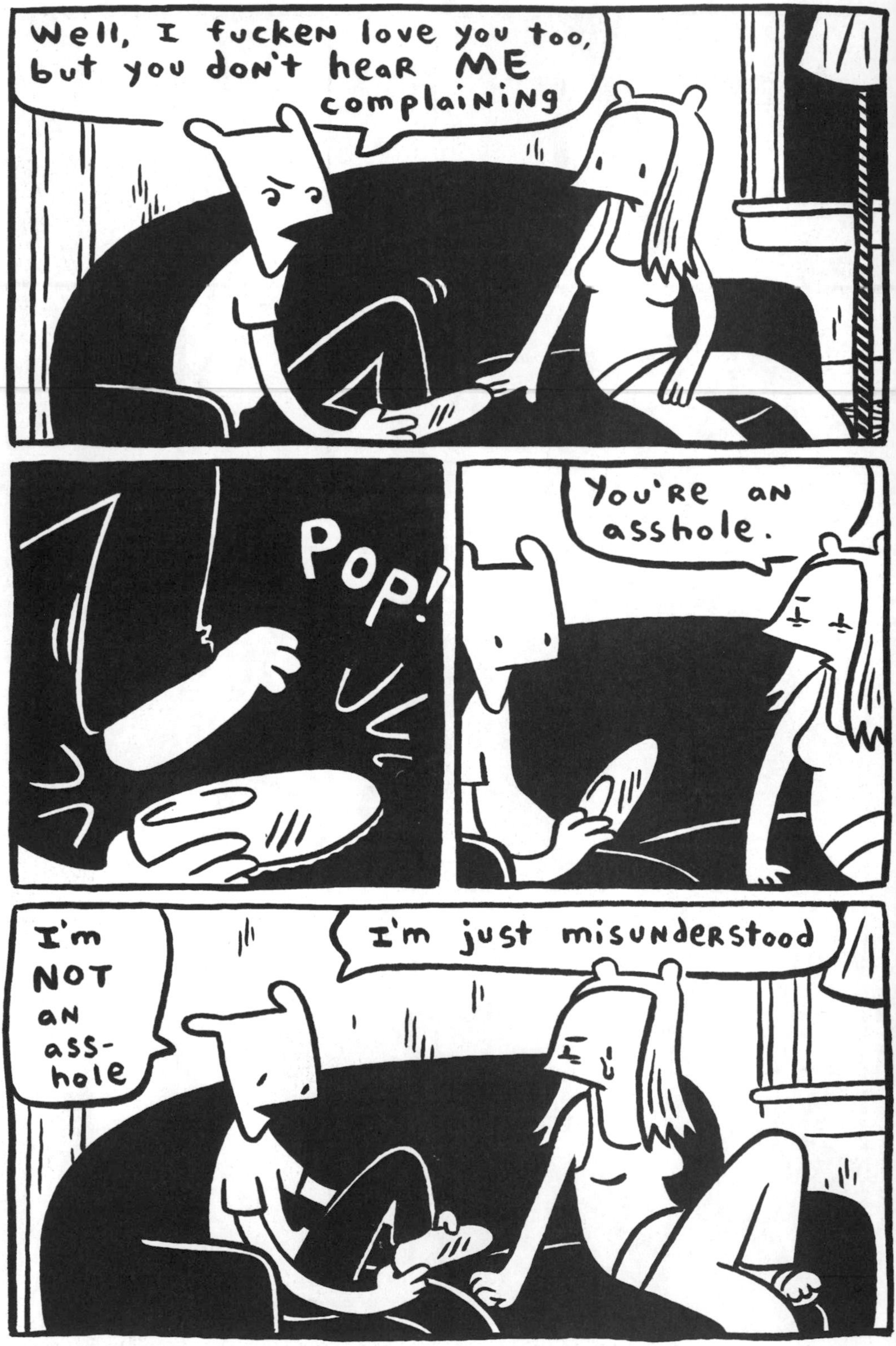
Well, I fucken love you too, but you don't hear ME complaining
POP!
You're an asshole.
I'm NOT an ass-hole
I'm just misunderstood

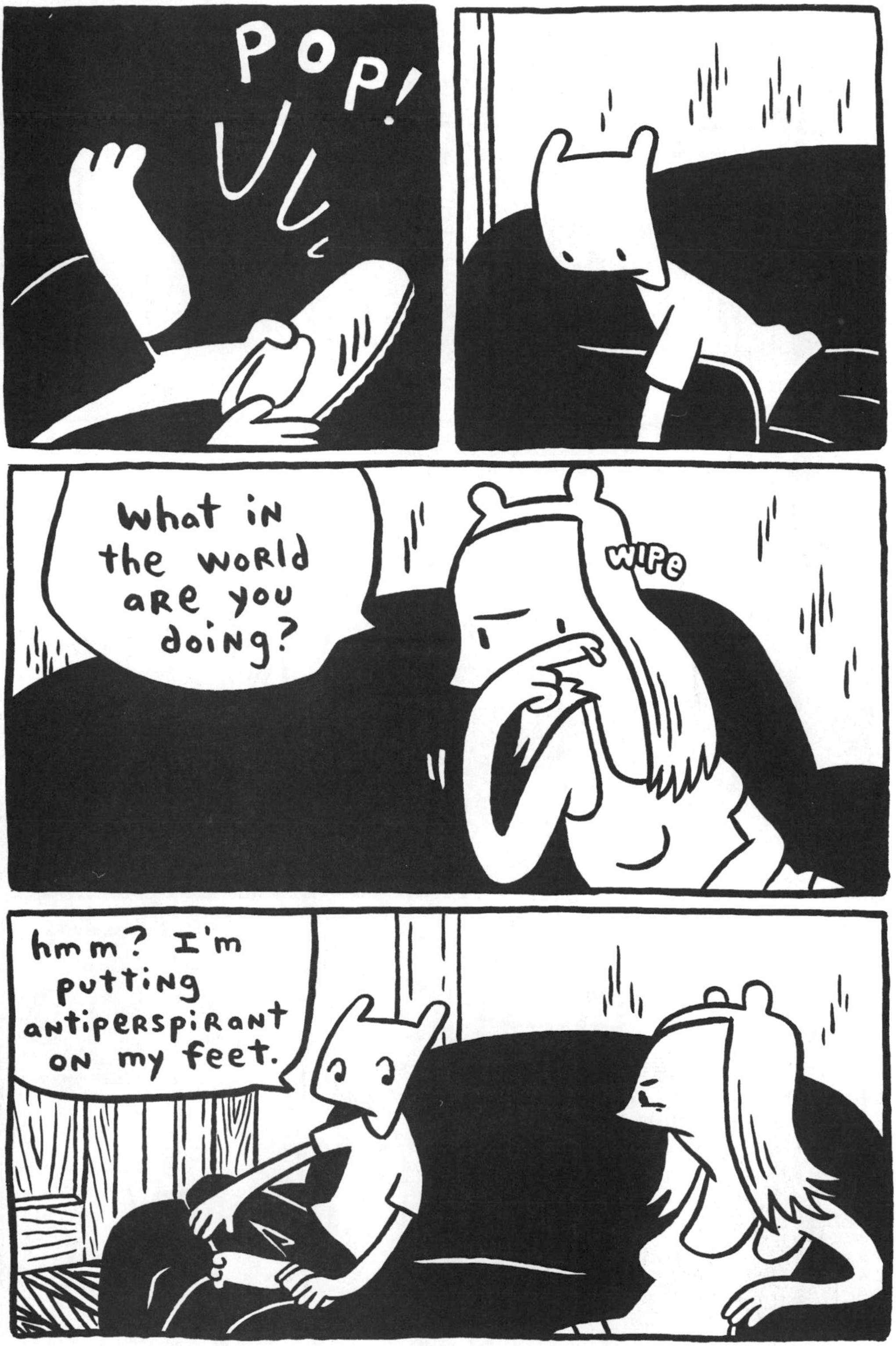
POP!
What in the world are you doing?
WIPE
hmm? I'm putting antiperspirant on my feet.

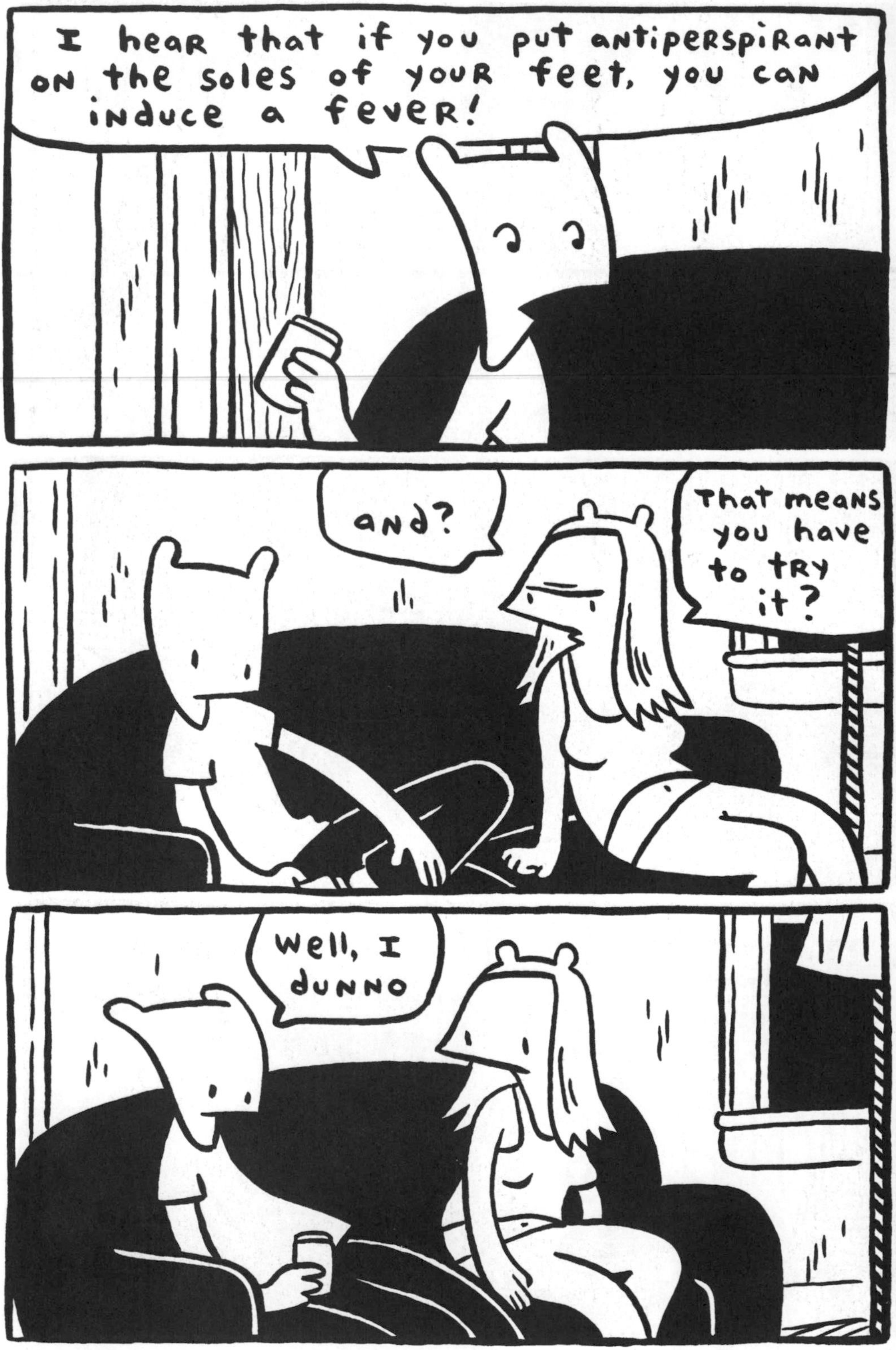

I hear that if you put antiperspirant on the soles of your feet, you can induce a fever!
and?
That means you have to try it?
well, I dunno

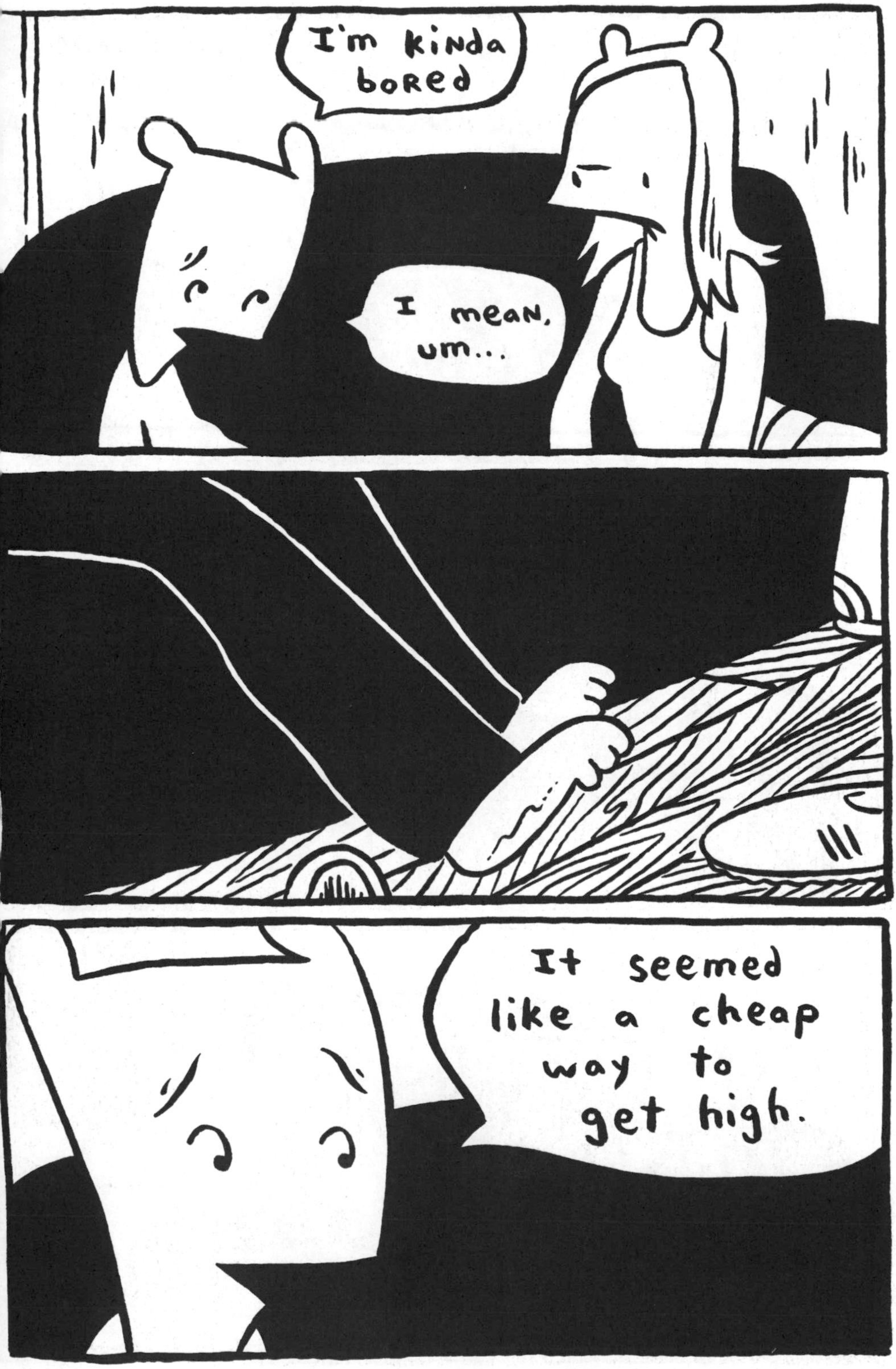
I'm kinda bored
I mean, um...
It seemed like a cheap way to get high.

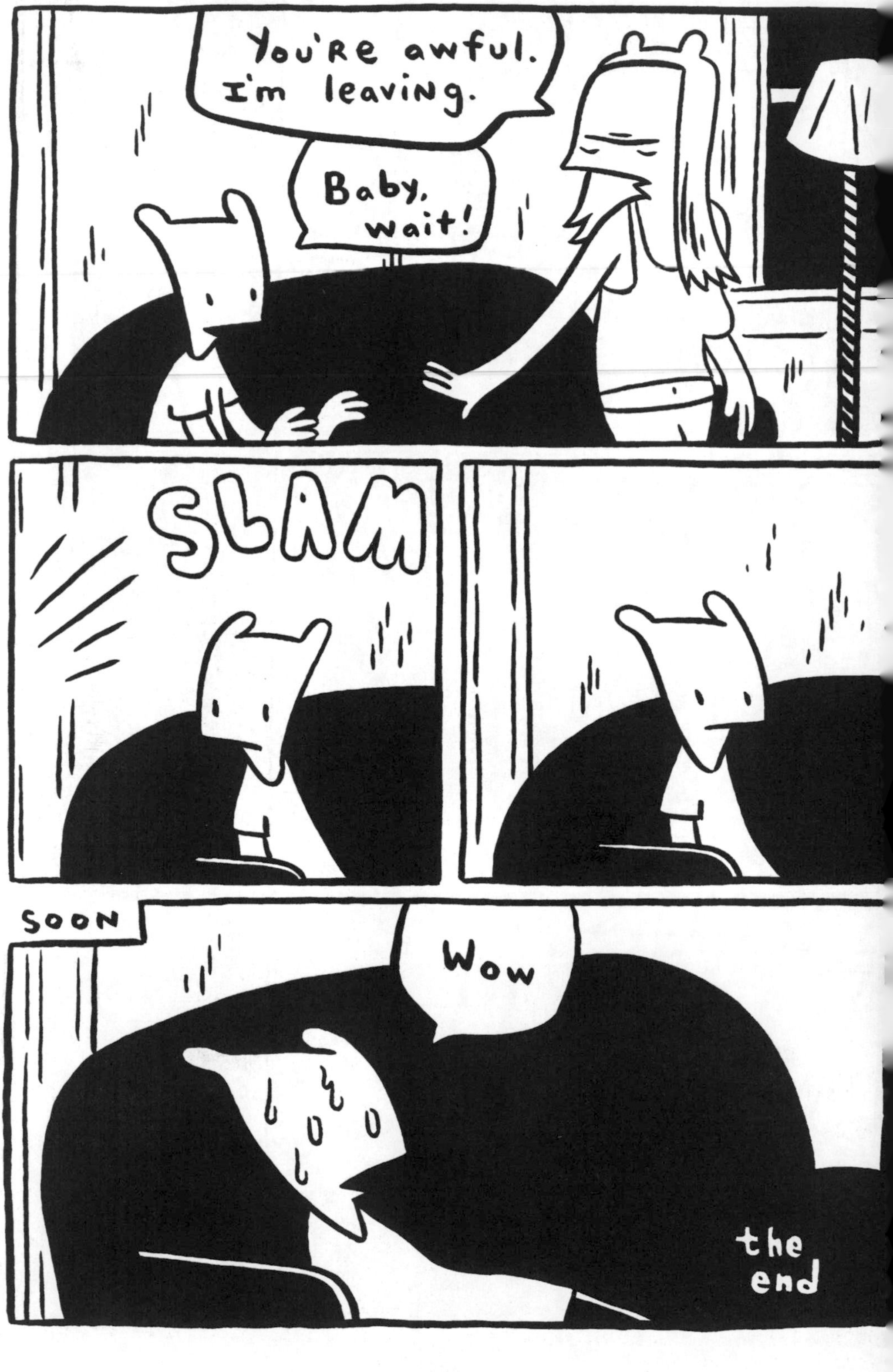
You're awful. I'm leaving.
Baby, wait!
SLAM
SOON
Wow
the end

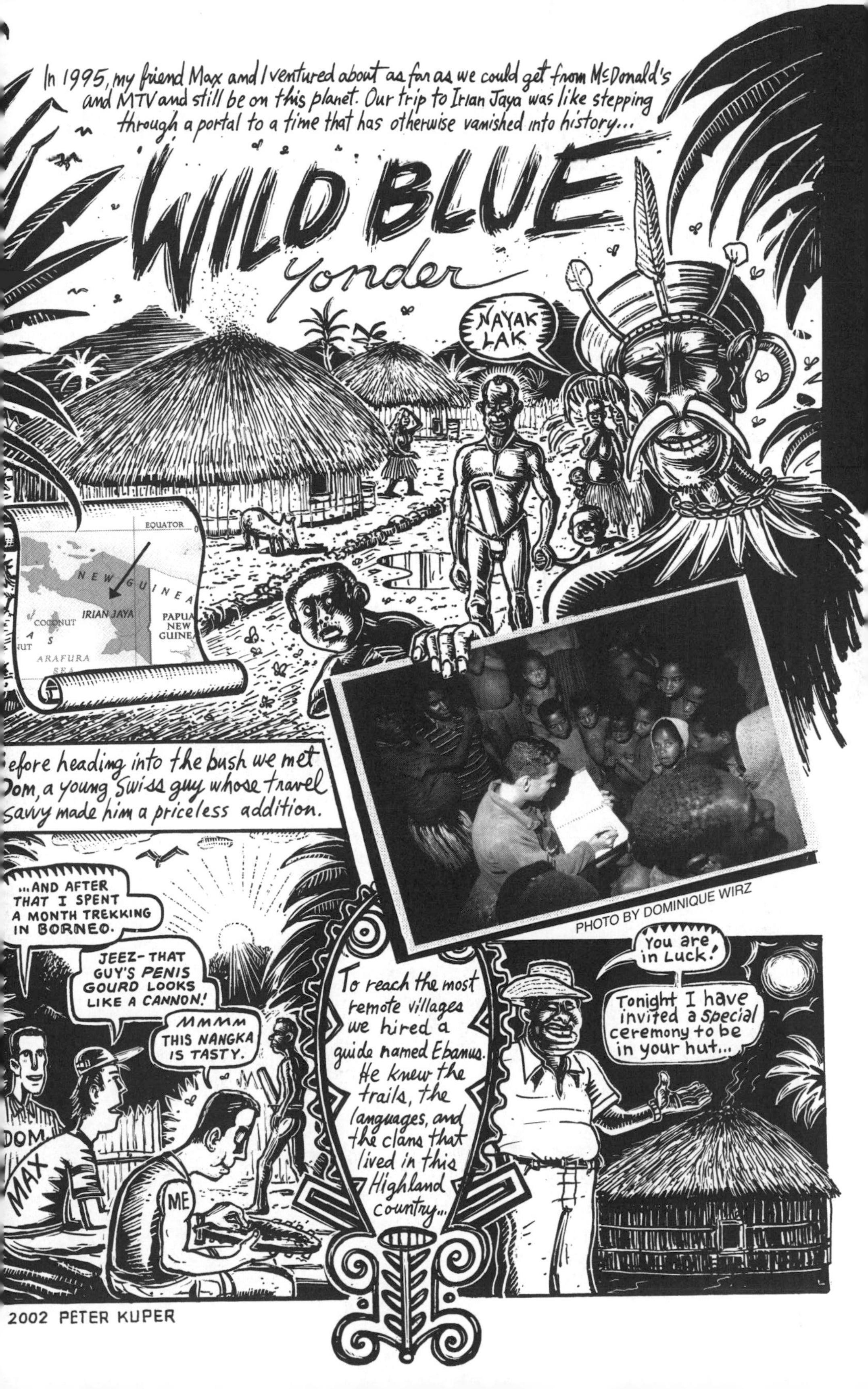
In 1995, my friend Max and I ventured about as far as we could get from McDonald's and MTV and still be on this planet. Our trip to Irian Jaya was like stepping through a portal to a time that has otherwise vanished into history...
WILD BLUE
yonder
NAYAK LAK
EQUATOR
NEW GUINEA
IRIAN JAYA
PAPUA NEW GUINEA
ARAFURA SEA
efore heading into the bush we met Dom, a young Swiss guy whose travel savvy made him a priceless addition.
PHOTO BY DOMINIQUE WIRZ
...AND AFTER THAT I SPENT A MONTH TREKKING IN BORNEO.
JEEZ- THAT GUY'S PENIS GOURD LOOKS LIKE A CANNON!
MMMM THIS NANGKA IS TASTY.
DOM
MAX
ME
To reach the most remote villages we hired a guide named Ebamus. He knew the trails, the languages, and the clans that lived in this Highland country...
You are in Luck!
Tonight I have invited a special ceremony to be in your hut...
2002 PETER KUPER

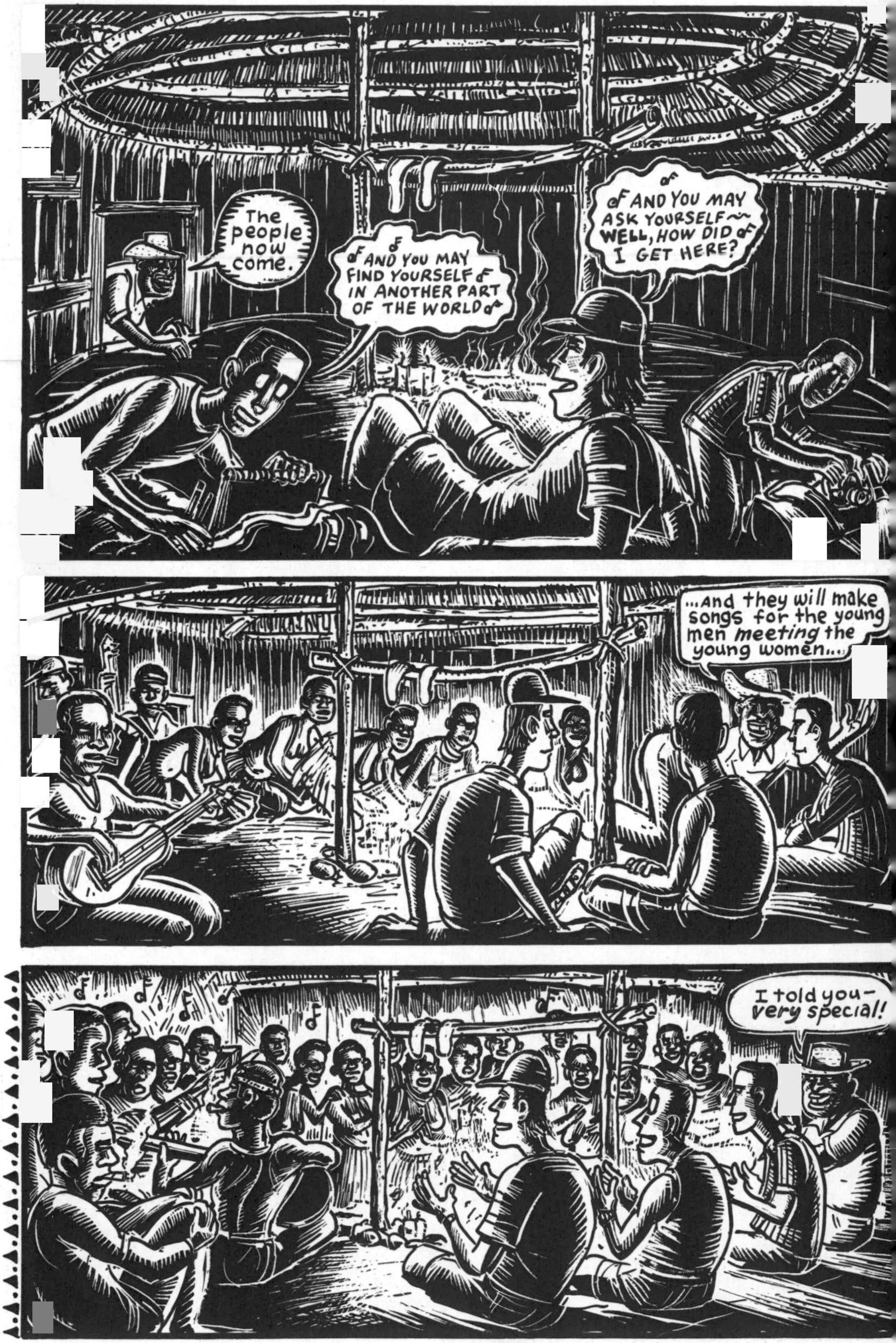
The people now come.
AND YOU MAY FIND YOURSELF IN ANOTHER PART OF THE WORLD
AND YOU MAY ASK YOURSELF ~~ WELL, HOW DID I GET HERE?
...And they will make songs for the young men *meeting* the young women...
I told you— *very* special!

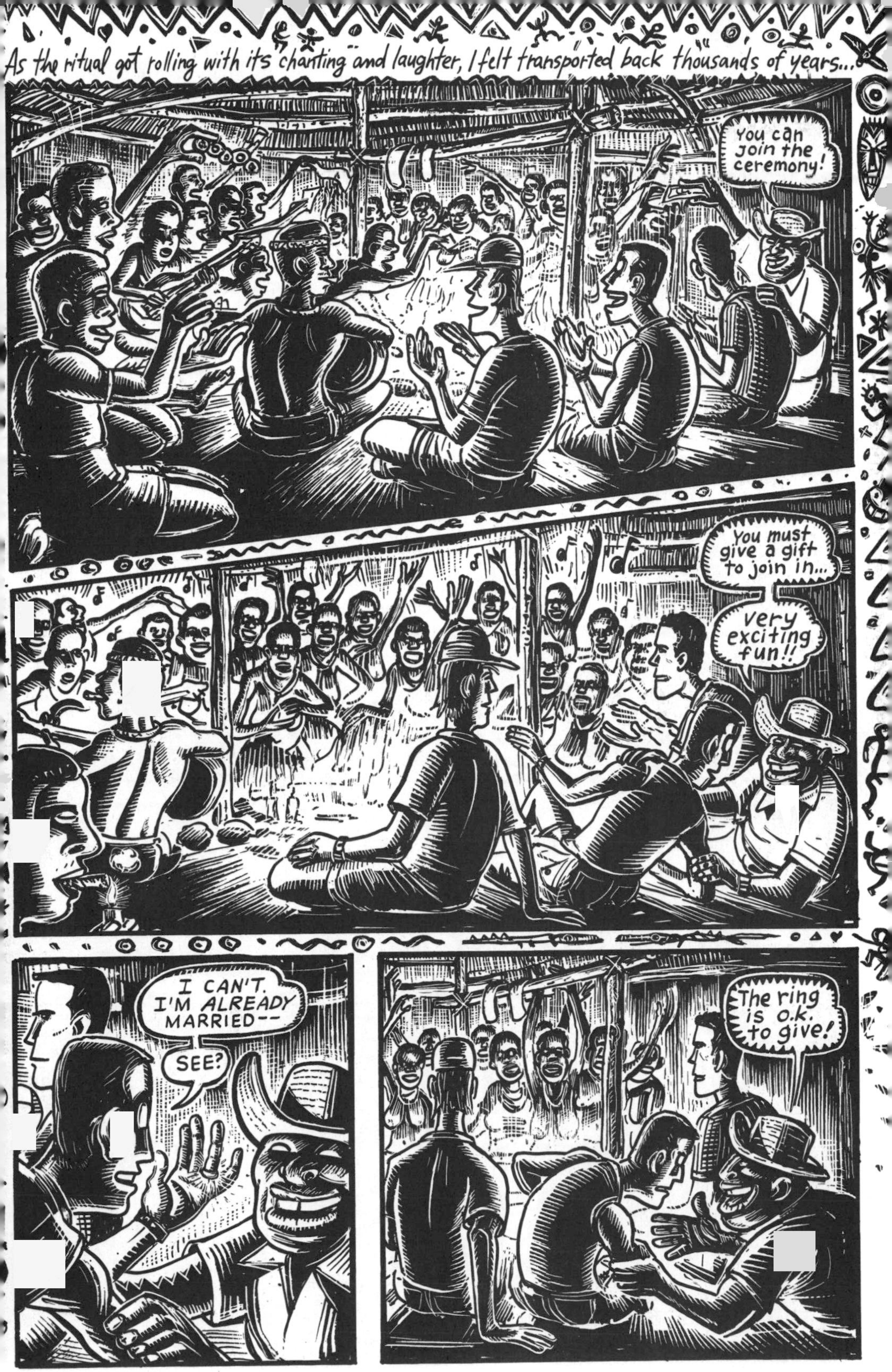
As the ritual got rolling with its "chanting" and laughter, I felt transported back thousands of years...
You can join the ceremony!
You must give a gift to join in...
very exciting fun!!
I CAN'T. I'M ALREADY MARRIED--
SEE?
The ring is o.k. to give!

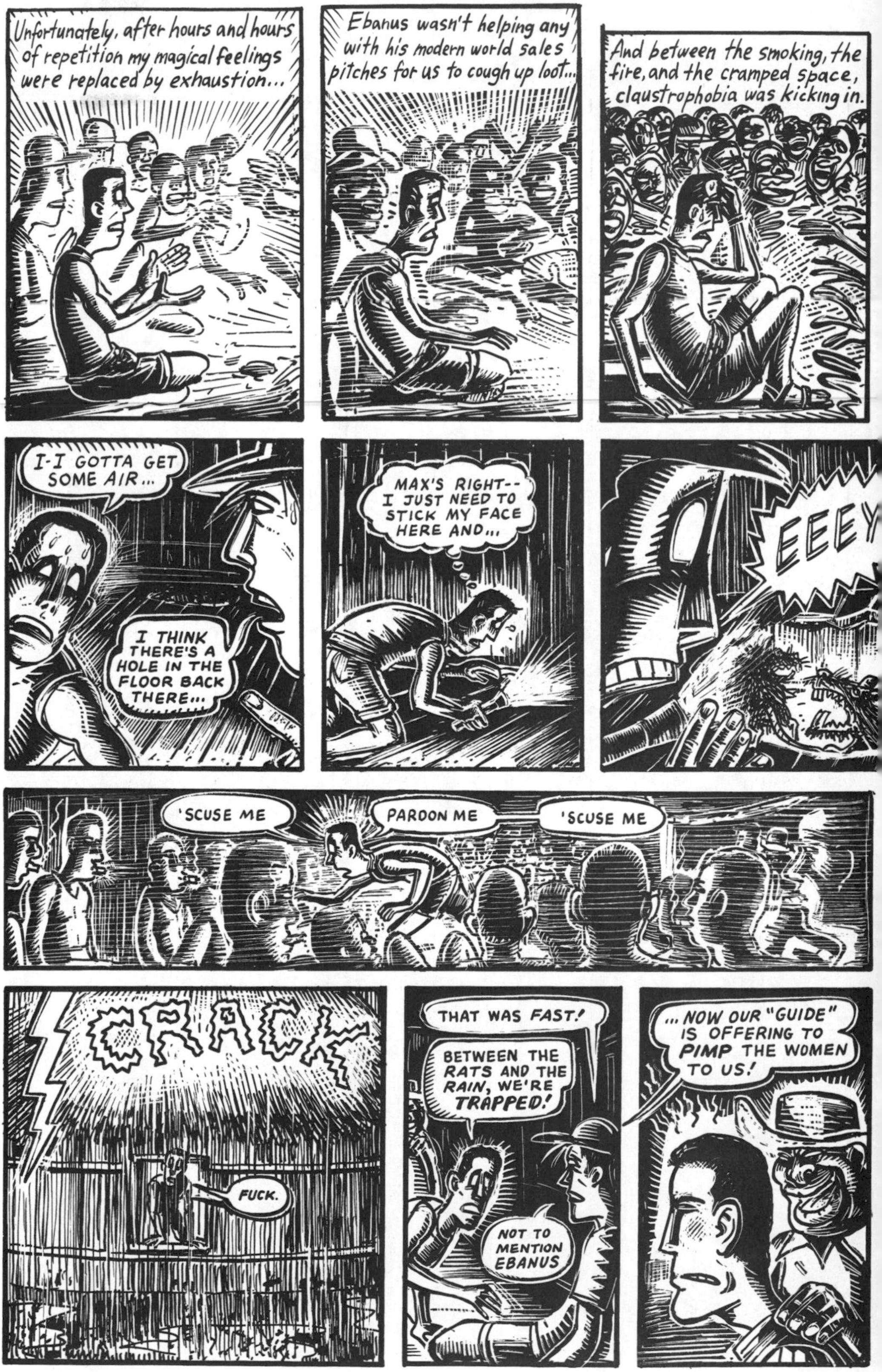
Unfortunately, after hours and hours of repetition my magical feelings were replaced by exhaustion...
Ebanus wasn't helping any with his modern world sales pitches for us to cough up loot...
And between the smoking, the fire, and the cramped space, claustrophobia was kicking in.
I-I GOTTA GET SOME AIR...
I THINK THERE'S A HOLE IN THE FLOOR BACK THERE...
MAX'S RIGHT-- I JUST NEED TO STICK MY FACE HERE AND...
EEEY
'SCUSE ME
PARDON ME
'SCUSE ME
CRACK
FUCK.
THAT WAS FAST!
BETWEEN THE RATS AND THE RAIN, WE'RE TRAPPED!
NOT TO MENTION EBANUS
...NOW OUR "GUIDE" IS OFFERING TO PIMP THE WOMEN TO US!

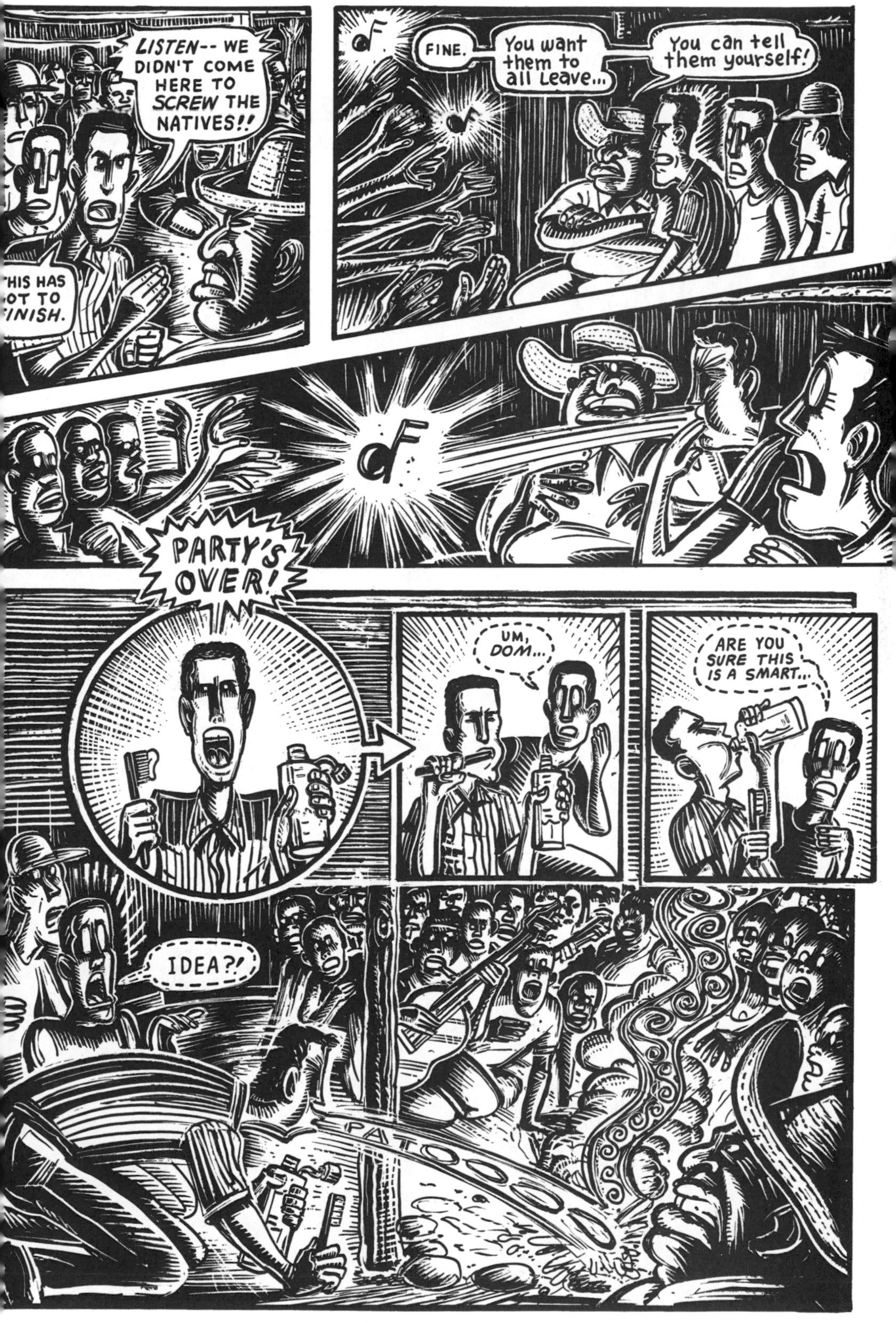
LISTEN-- WE DIDN'T COME HERE TO SCREW THE NATIVES!!
THIS HAS
OT TO
INISH.
FINE.
You want them to all Leave...
You can tell them yourself!
PARTY'S OVER!
UM, DOM...
ARE YOU SURE THIS IS A SMART...
IDEA?!
PATO

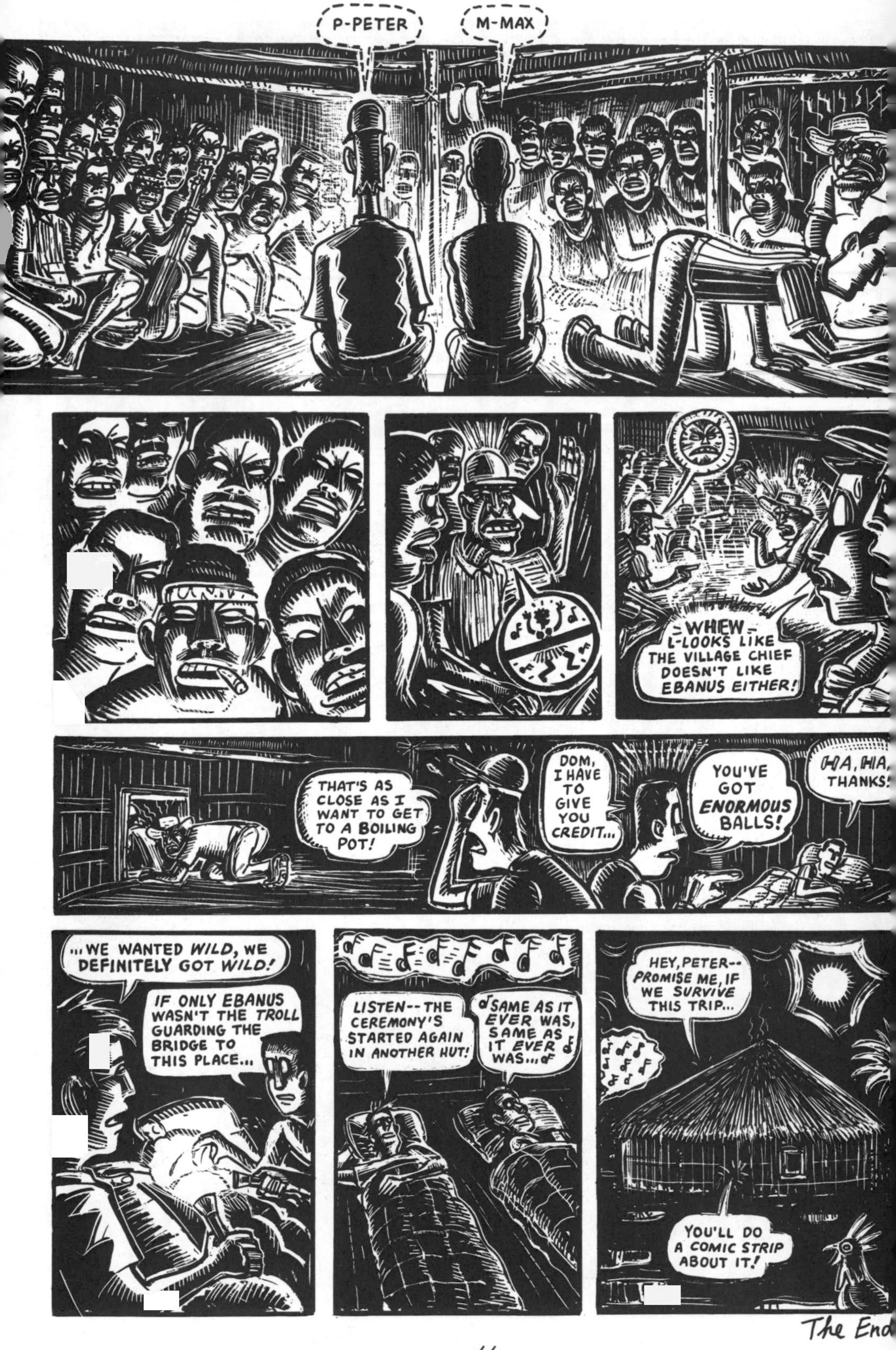
P-PETER
M-MAX
WHEW — L-LOOKS LIKE THE VILLAGE CHIEF DOESN'T LIKE EBANUS EITHER!
THAT'S AS CLOSE AS I WANT TO GET TO A BOILING POT!
DOM, I HAVE TO GIVE YOU CREDIT...
YOU'VE GOT ENORMOUS BALLS!
HA, HA, THANKS!
...WE WANTED WILD, WE DEFINITELY GOT WILD!
IF ONLY EBANUS WASN'T THE TROLL GUARDING THE BRIDGE TO THIS PLACE...
LISTEN--THE CEREMONY'S STARTED AGAIN IN ANOTHER HUT!
SAME AS IT EVER WAS, SAME AS IT EVER WAS...
HEY, PETER-- PROMISE ME, IF WE SURVIVE THIS TRIP...
YOU'LL DO A COMIC STRIP ABOUT IT!
The End

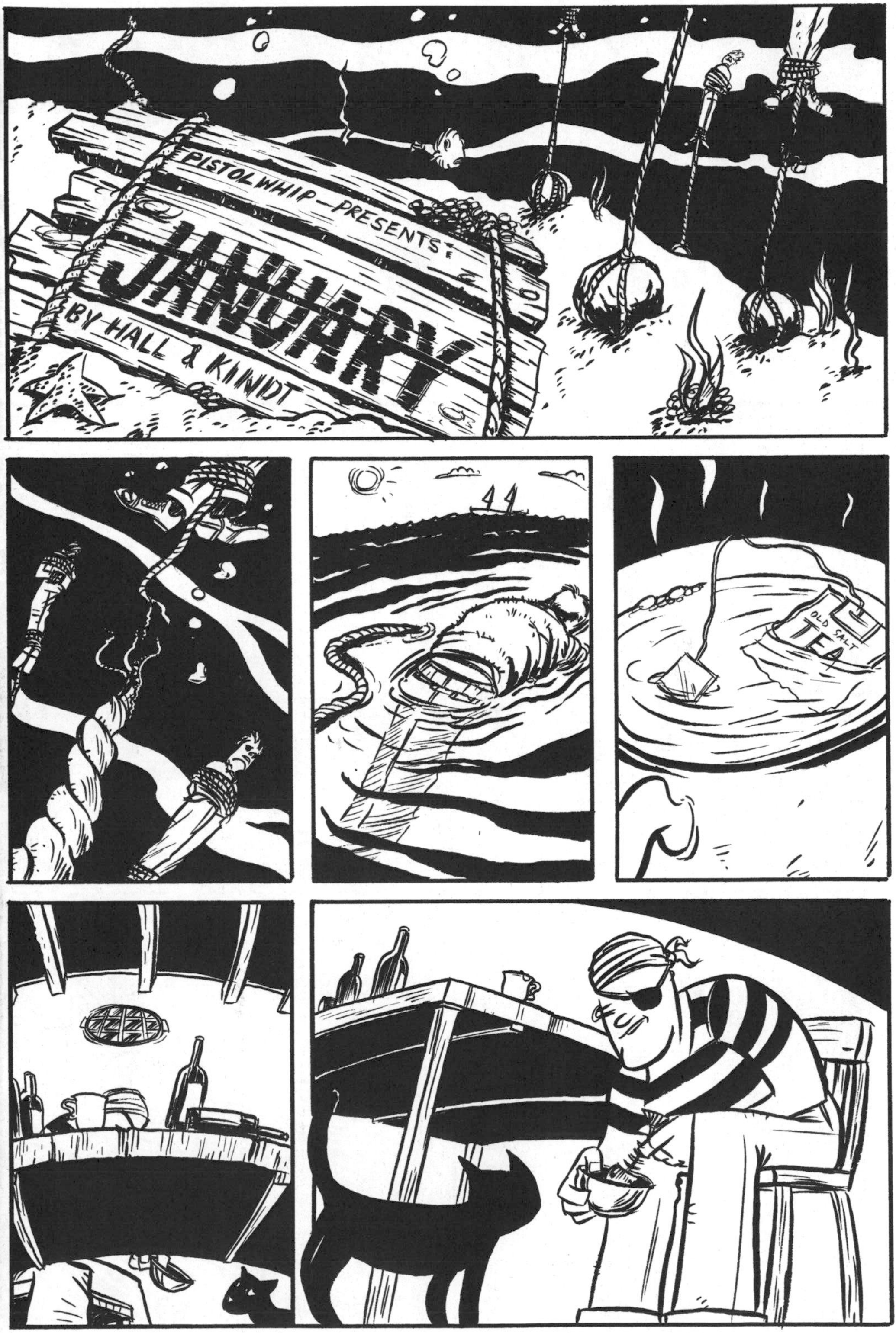
PISTOLWHIP PRESENTS:
JANUARY
BY HALL & KINDT
OLD SALT
TEA

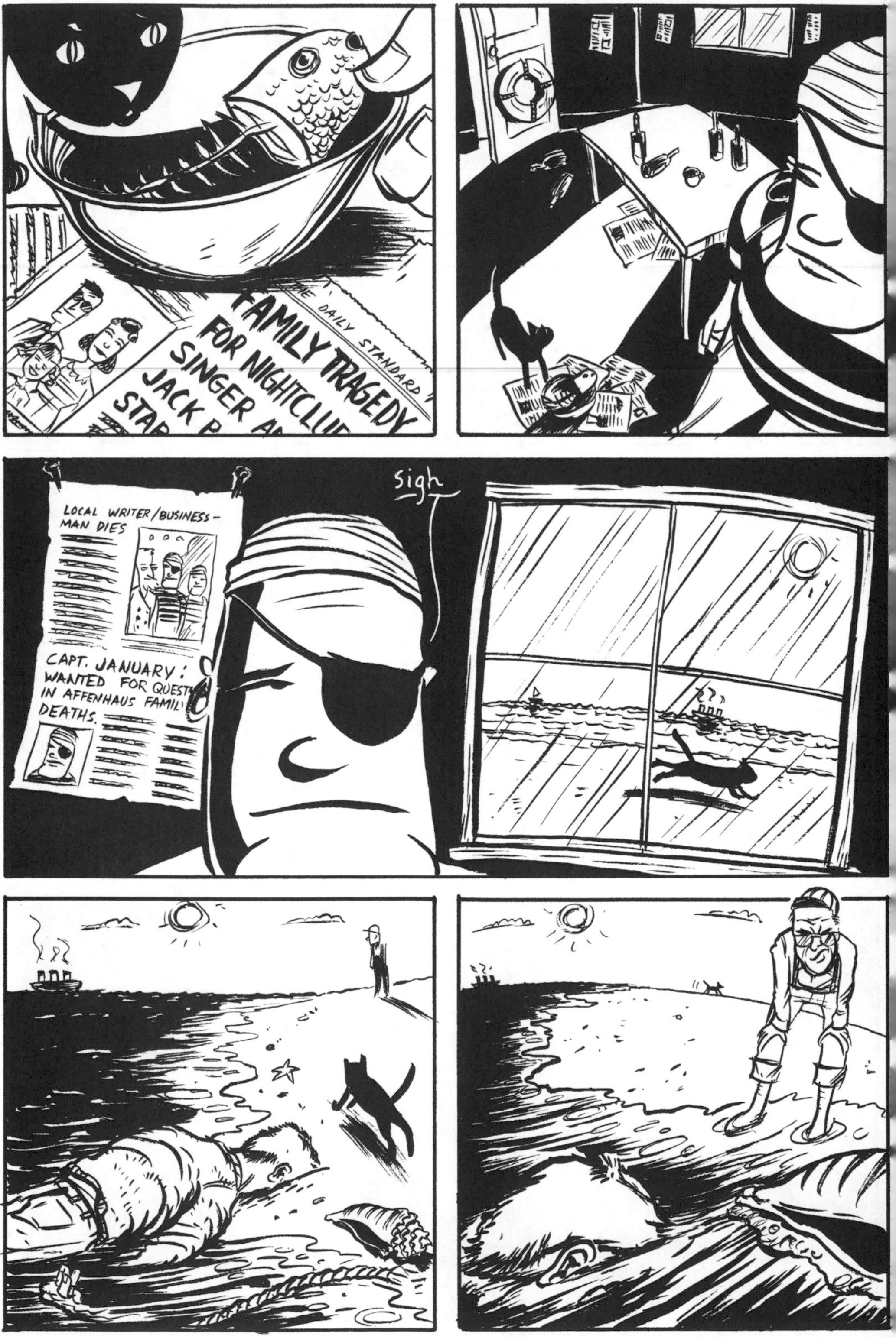
DAILY STANDARD
FAMILY TRAGEDY
FOR NIGHTCLU
SINGER AN
JACK B
STAR
LOCAL WRITER/BUSINESS-MAN DIES
CAPT. JANUARY: WANTED FOR QUEST IN AFFENHAUS FAMIL DEATHS.
Sigh

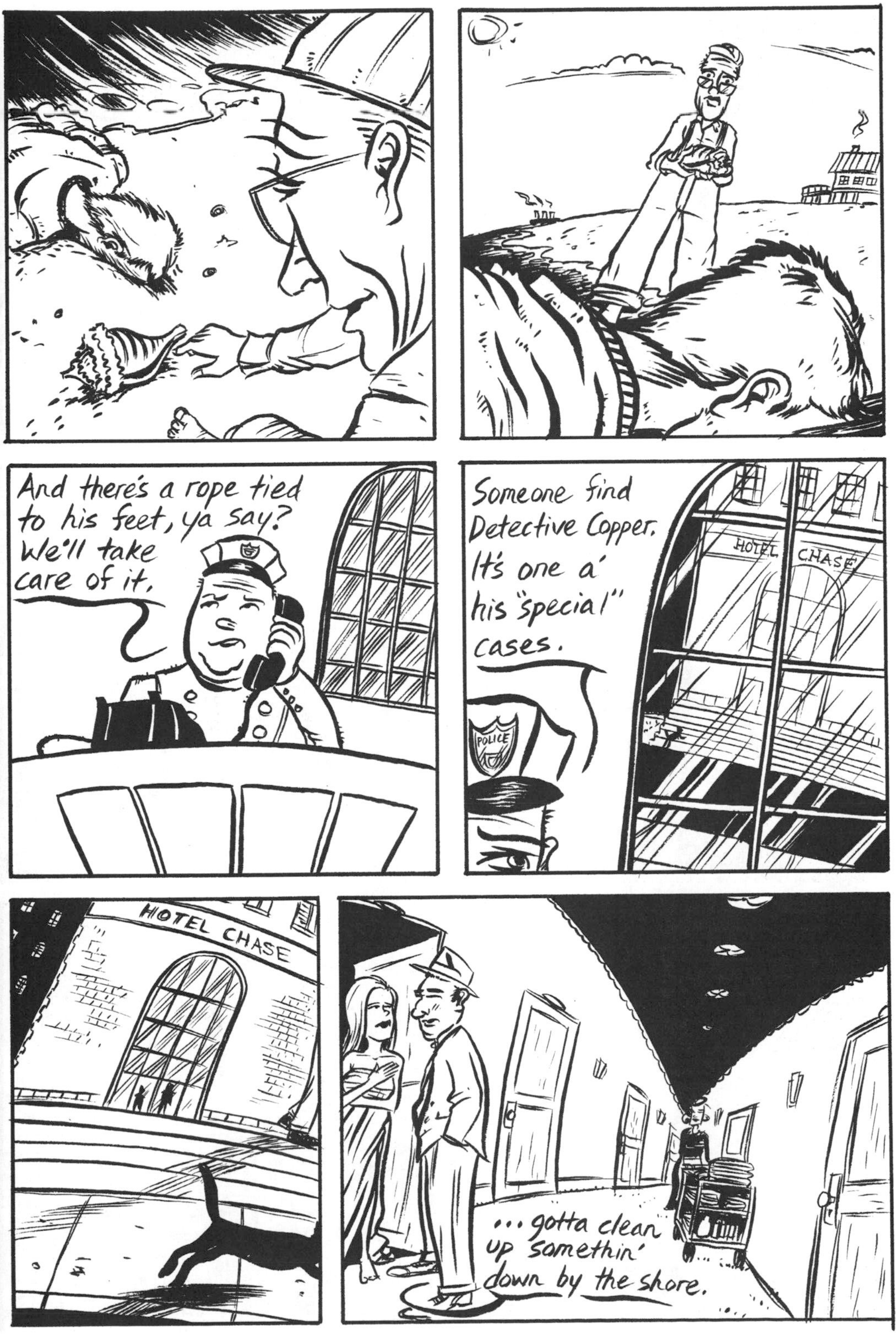
And there's a rope tied to his feet, ya say? We'll take care of it,
Someone find Detective Copper. It's one a' his "special" cases.
HOTEL CHASE
POLICE
HOTEL CHASE
...gotta clean up somethin' down by the shore.

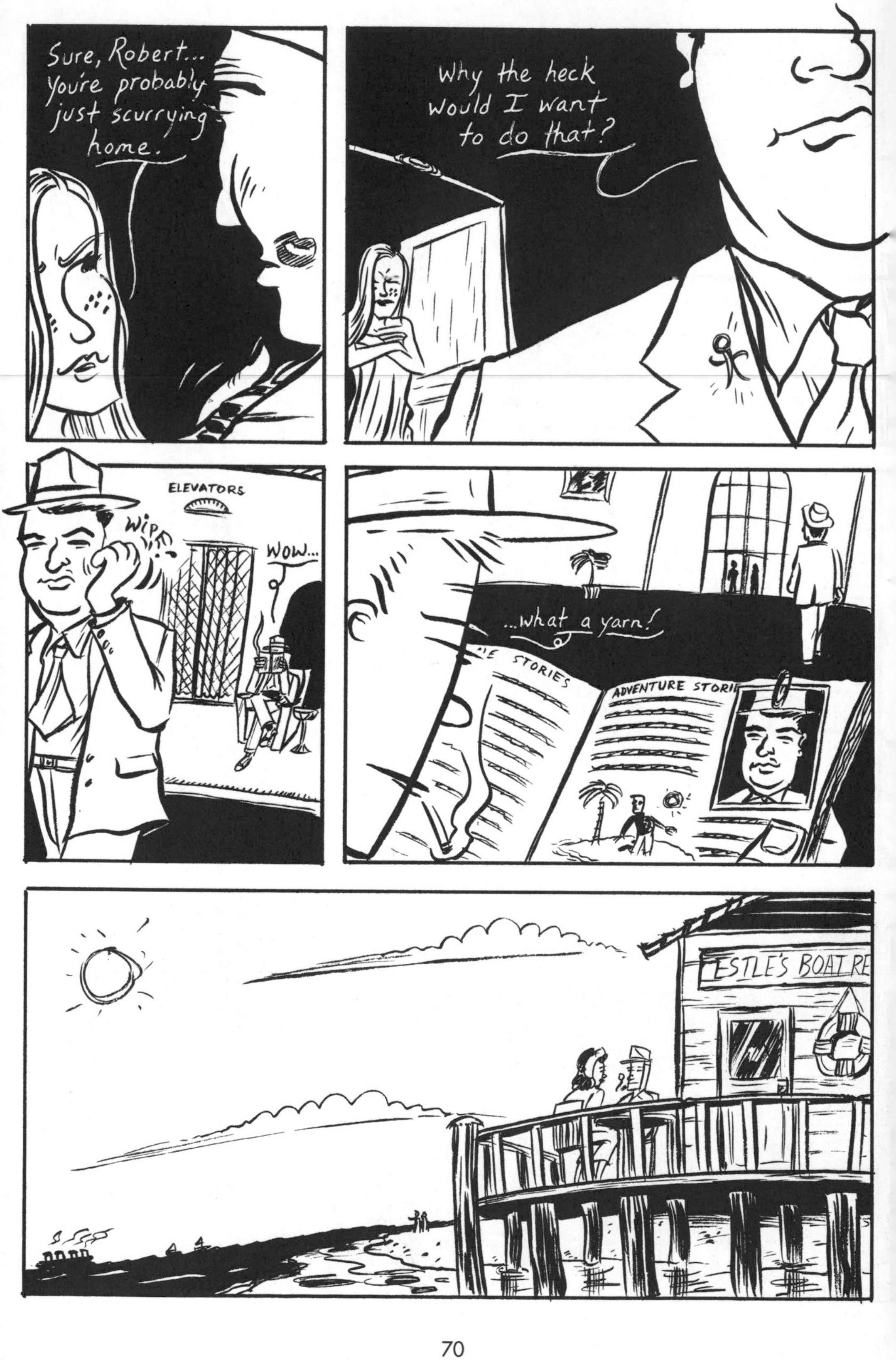
Sure, Robert... you're probably just scurrying home.
Why the heck would I want to do that?
ELEVATORS
WIPE
WOW...
...what a yarn!
STORIES
ADVENTURE STORI
ESTLE'S BOAT RE

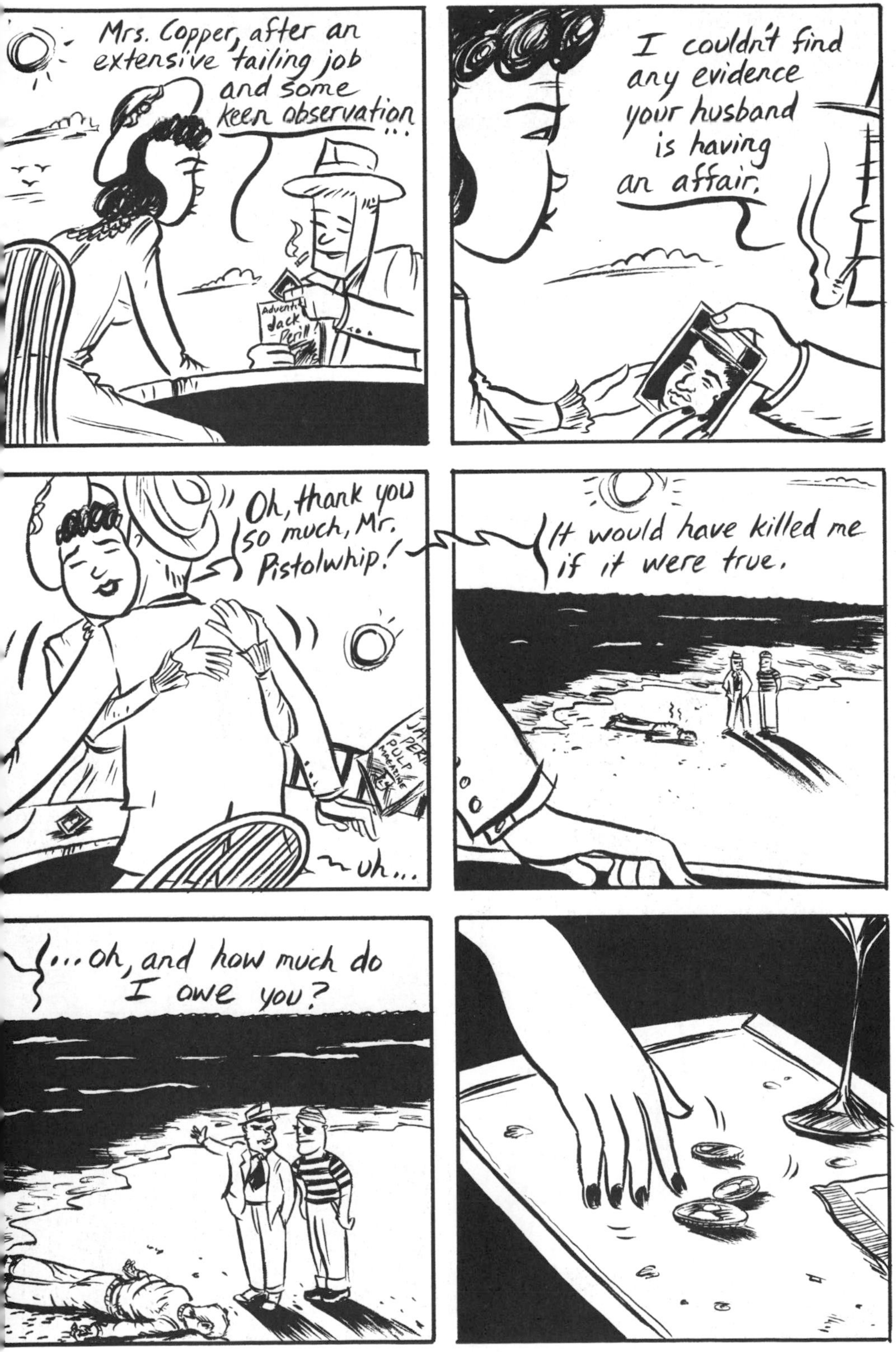
Mrs. Copper, after an extensive tailing job and some keen observation...
Adventures Jack Peril
I couldn't find any evidence your husband is having an affair.
Oh, thank you so much, Mr. Pistolwhip!
It would have killed me if it were true.
Jack Peril Pulp Magazine
uh...
...oh, and how much do I owe you?

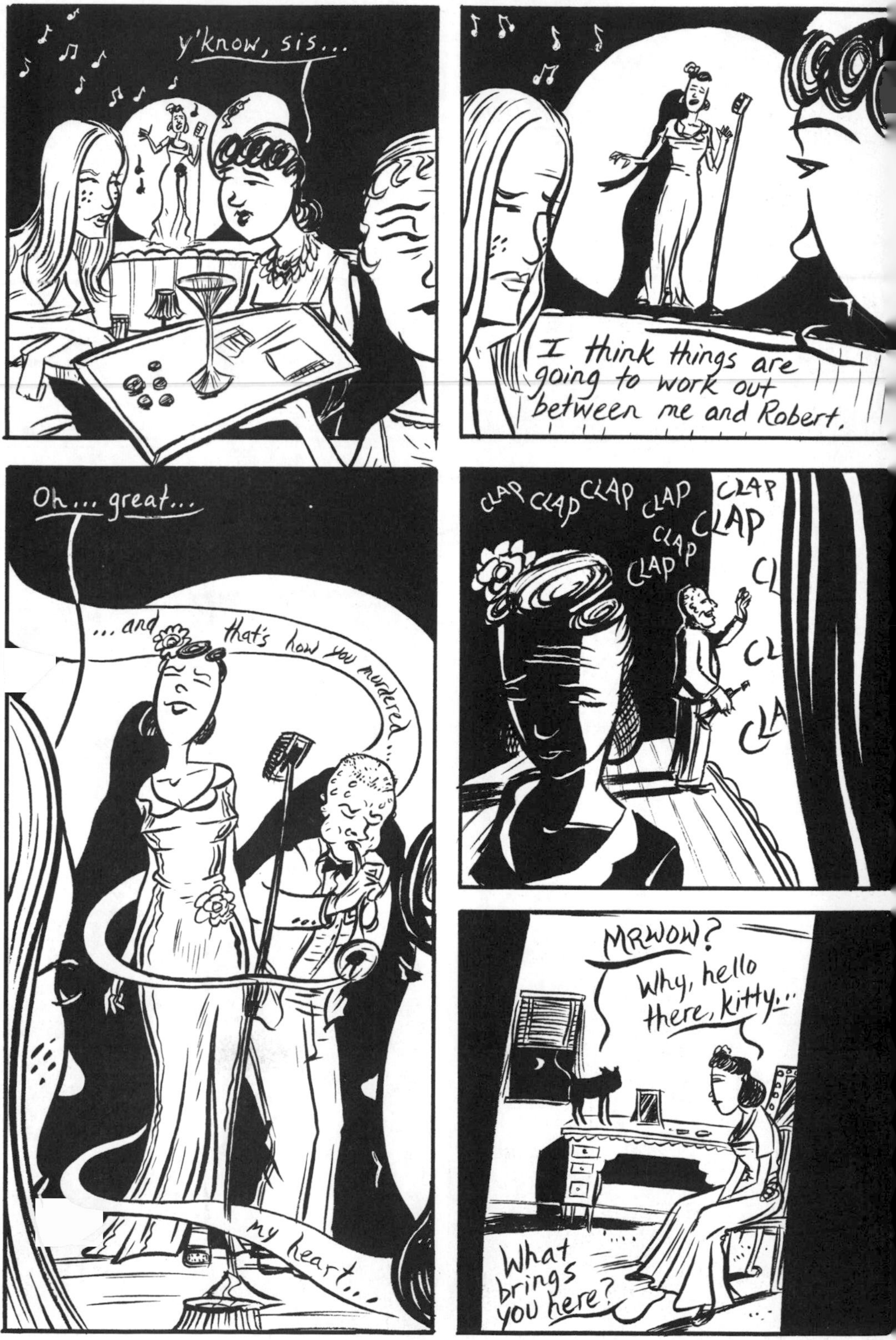
y'know, sis...
I think things are going to work out between me and Robert.
Oh... great...
...and that's how you murdered... my heart...
CLAP CLAP CLAP CLAP CLAP CLAP CLAP CLAP CLAP
MRWOW?
Why, hello there, kitty...
What brings you here?

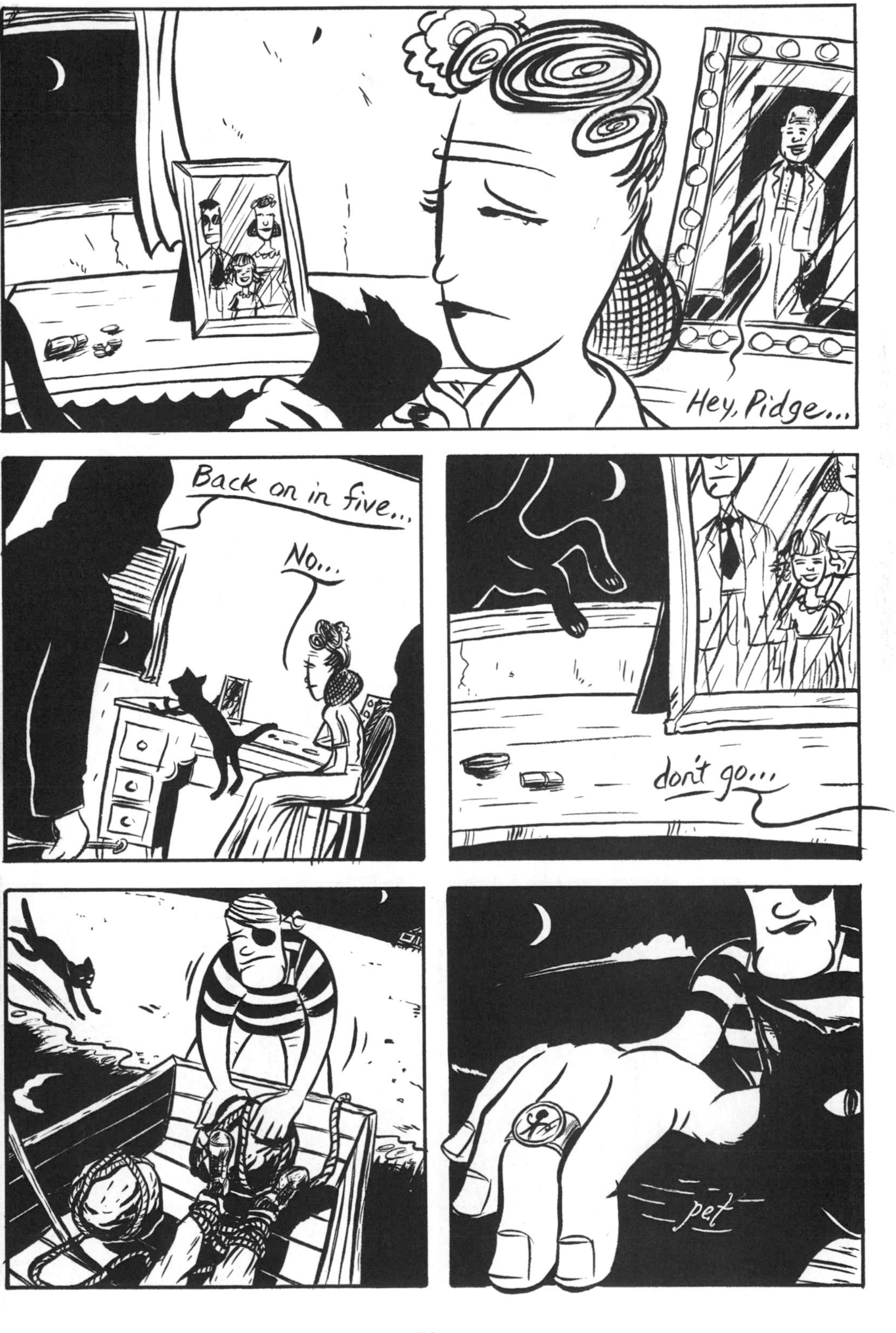
Hey, Pidge...
Back on in five...
No...
don't go...
pet

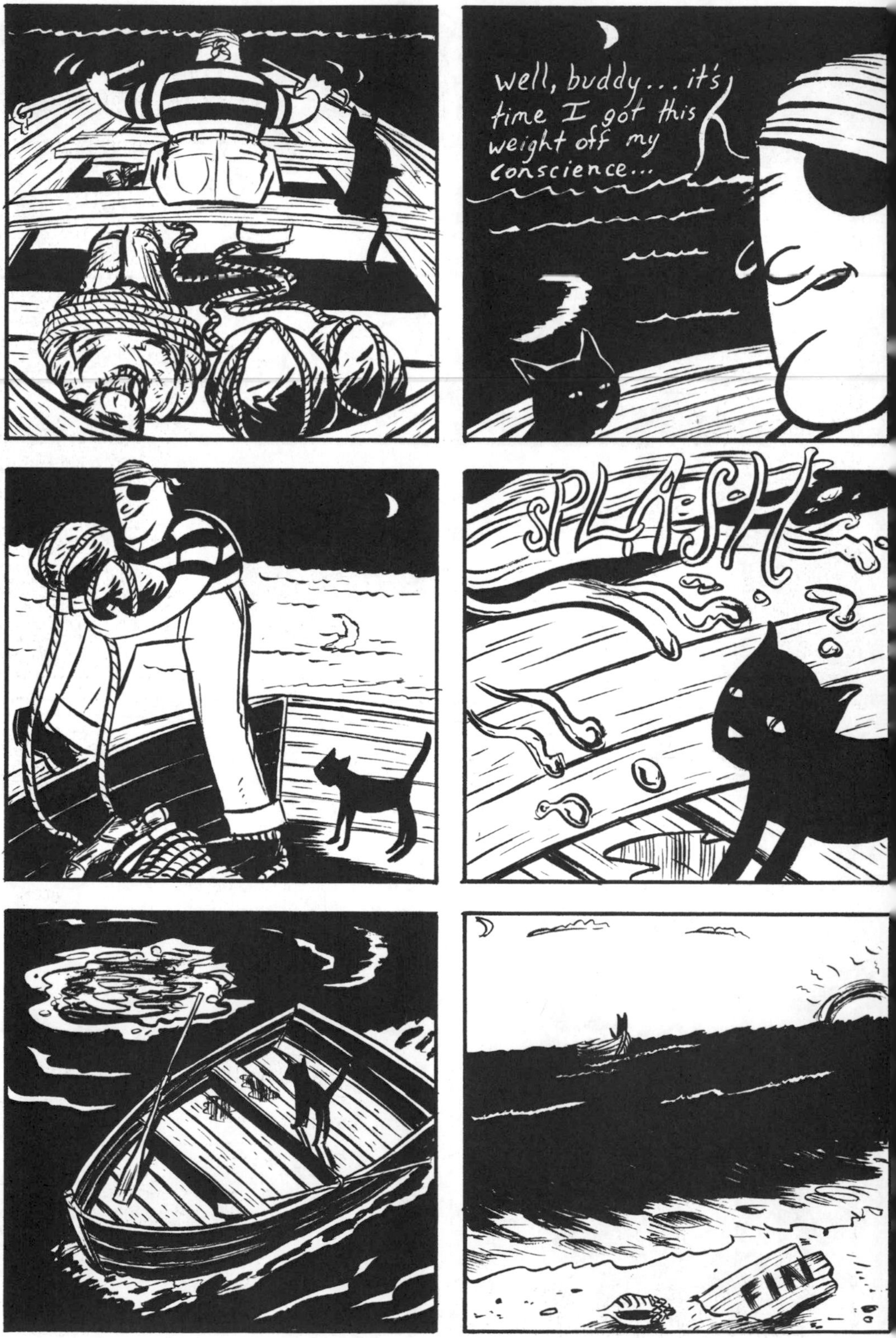
well, buddy... it's time I got this weight off my conscience...
SPLASH
FIN

PAPER AIRPLANES

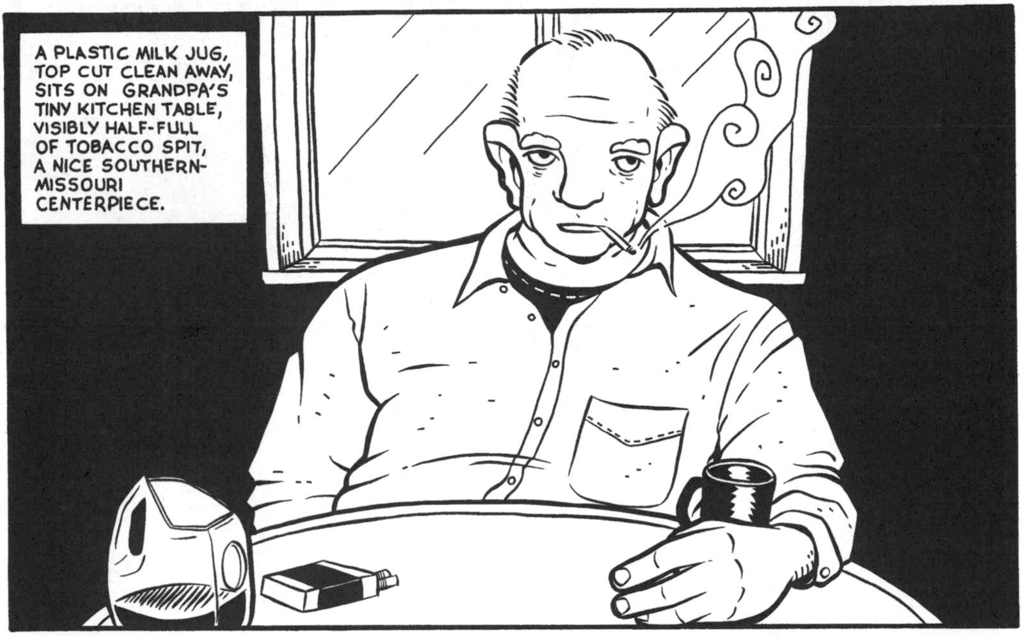
A PLASTIC MILK JUG, TOP CUT CLEAN AWAY, SITS ON GRANDPA'S TINY KITCHEN TABLE, VISIBLY HALF-FULL OF TOBACCO SPIT, A NICE SOUTHERN-MISSOURI CENTERPIECE.

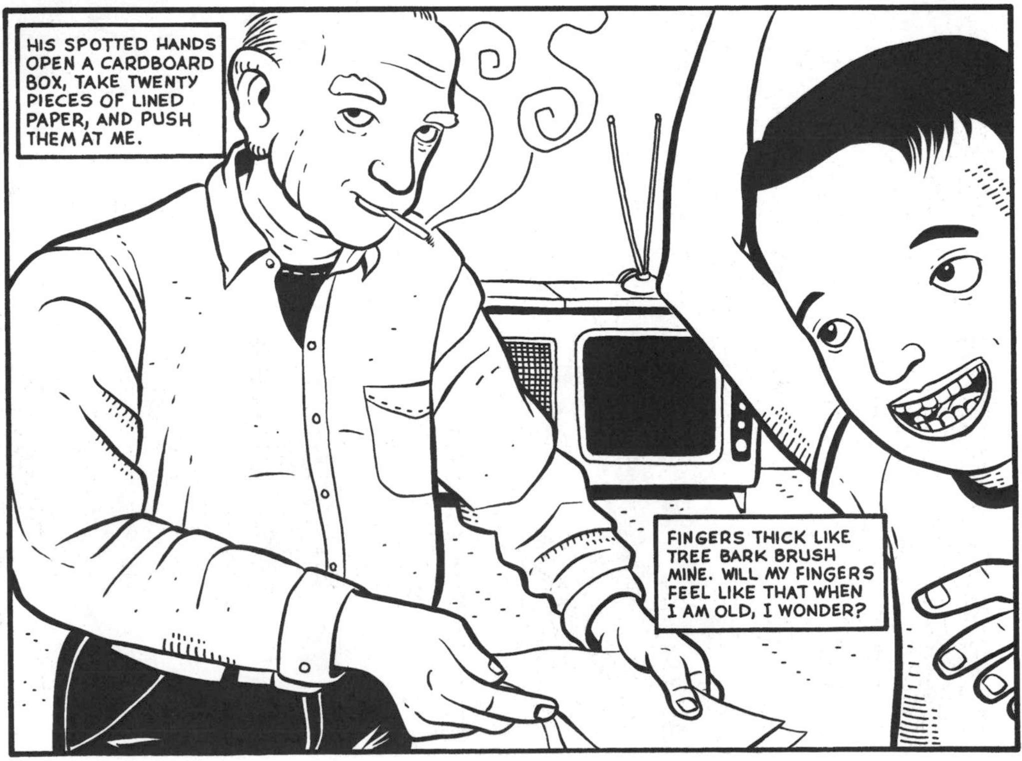
HIS SPOTTED HANDS OPEN A CARDBOARD BOX, TAKE TWENTY PIECES OF LINED PAPER, AND PUSH THEM AT ME.
FINGERS THICK LIKE TREE BARK BRUSH MINE. WILL MY FINGERS FEEL LIKE THAT WHEN I AM OLD, I WONDER?

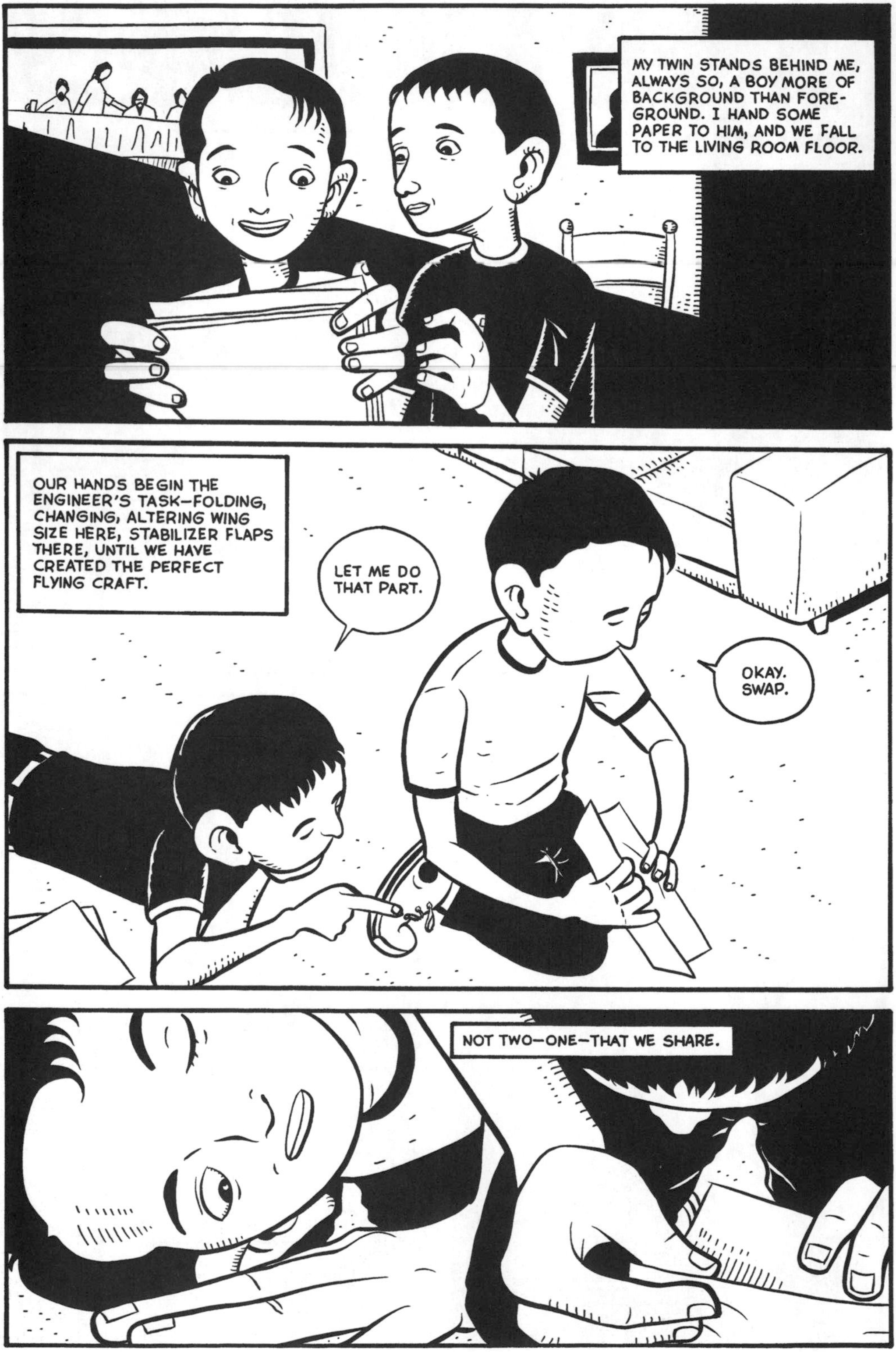
MY TWIN STANDS BEHIND ME, ALWAYS SO, A BOY MORE OF BACKGROUND THAN FOREGROUND. I HAND SOME PAPER TO HIM, AND WE FALL TO THE LIVING ROOM FLOOR.
OUR HANDS BEGIN THE ENGINEER'S TASK—FOLDING, CHANGING, ALTERING WING SIZE HERE, STABILIZER FLAPS THERE, UNTIL WE HAVE CREATED THE PERFECT FLYING CRAFT.
LET ME DO THAT PART.
OKAY. SWAP.
NOT TWO—ONE—THAT WE SHARE.

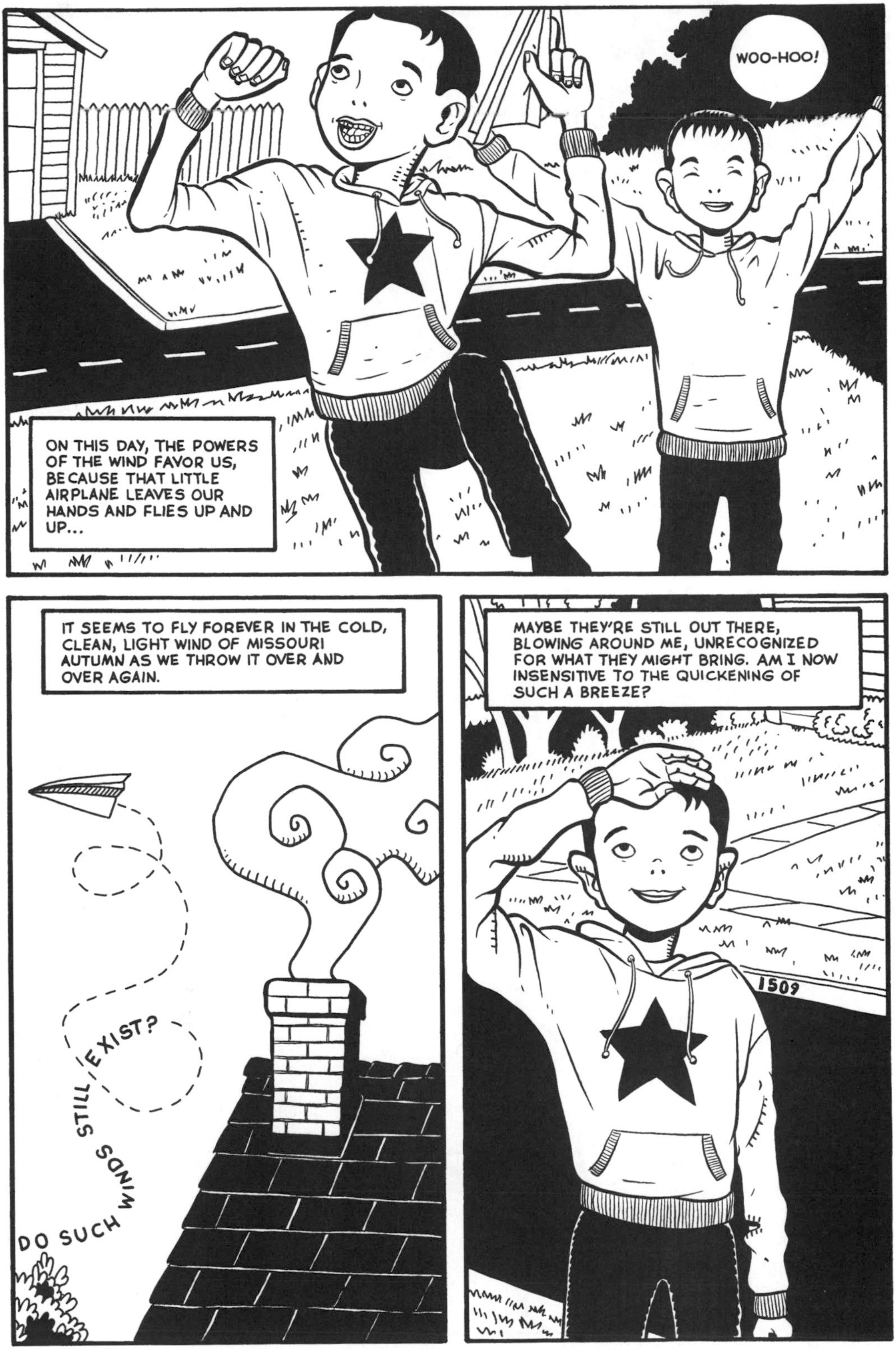
WOO-HOO!
ON THIS DAY, THE POWERS OF THE WIND FAVOR US, BECAUSE THAT LITTLE AIRPLANE LEAVES OUR HANDS AND FLIES UP AND UP...
IT SEEMS TO FLY FOREVER IN THE COLD, CLEAN, LIGHT WIND OF MISSOURI AUTUMN AS WE THROW IT OVER AND OVER AGAIN.
DO SUCH WINDS STILL EXIST?
MAYBE THEY'RE STILL OUT THERE, BLOWING AROUND ME, UNRECOGNIZED FOR WHAT THEY MIGHT BRING. AM I NOW INSENSITIVE TO THE QUICKENING OF SUCH A BREEZE?
1509

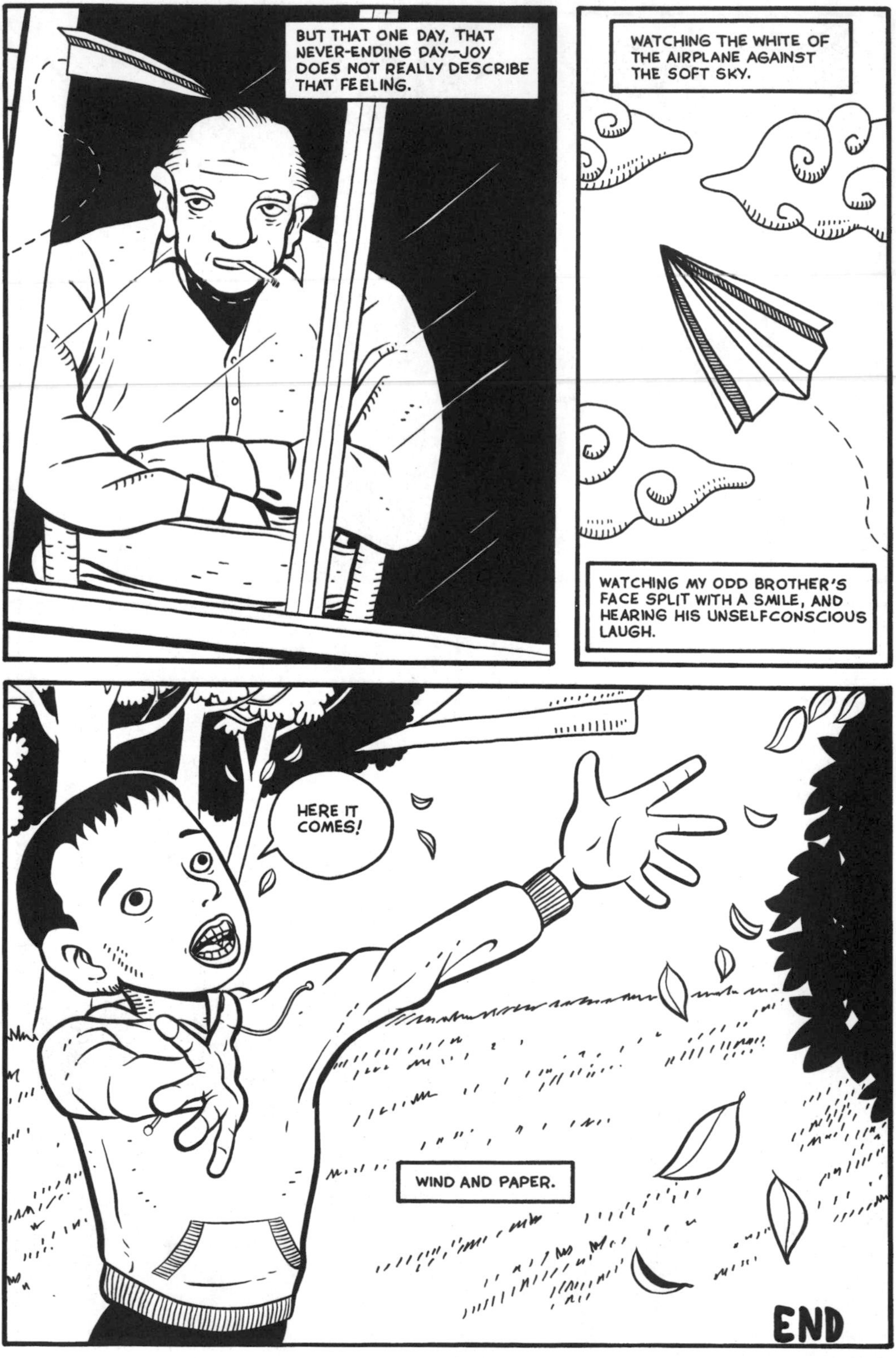
BUT THAT ONE DAY, THAT NEVER-ENDING DAY—JOY DOES NOT REALLY DESCRIBE THAT FEELING.
WATCHING THE WHITE OF THE AIRPLANE AGAINST THE SOFT SKY.
WATCHING MY ODD BROTHER'S FACE SPLIT WITH A SMILE, AND HEARING HIS UNSELFCONSCIOUS LAUGH.
HERE IT COMES!
WIND AND PAPER.
END

TONY MILLIONAIRE'S SOCK MONKEY™

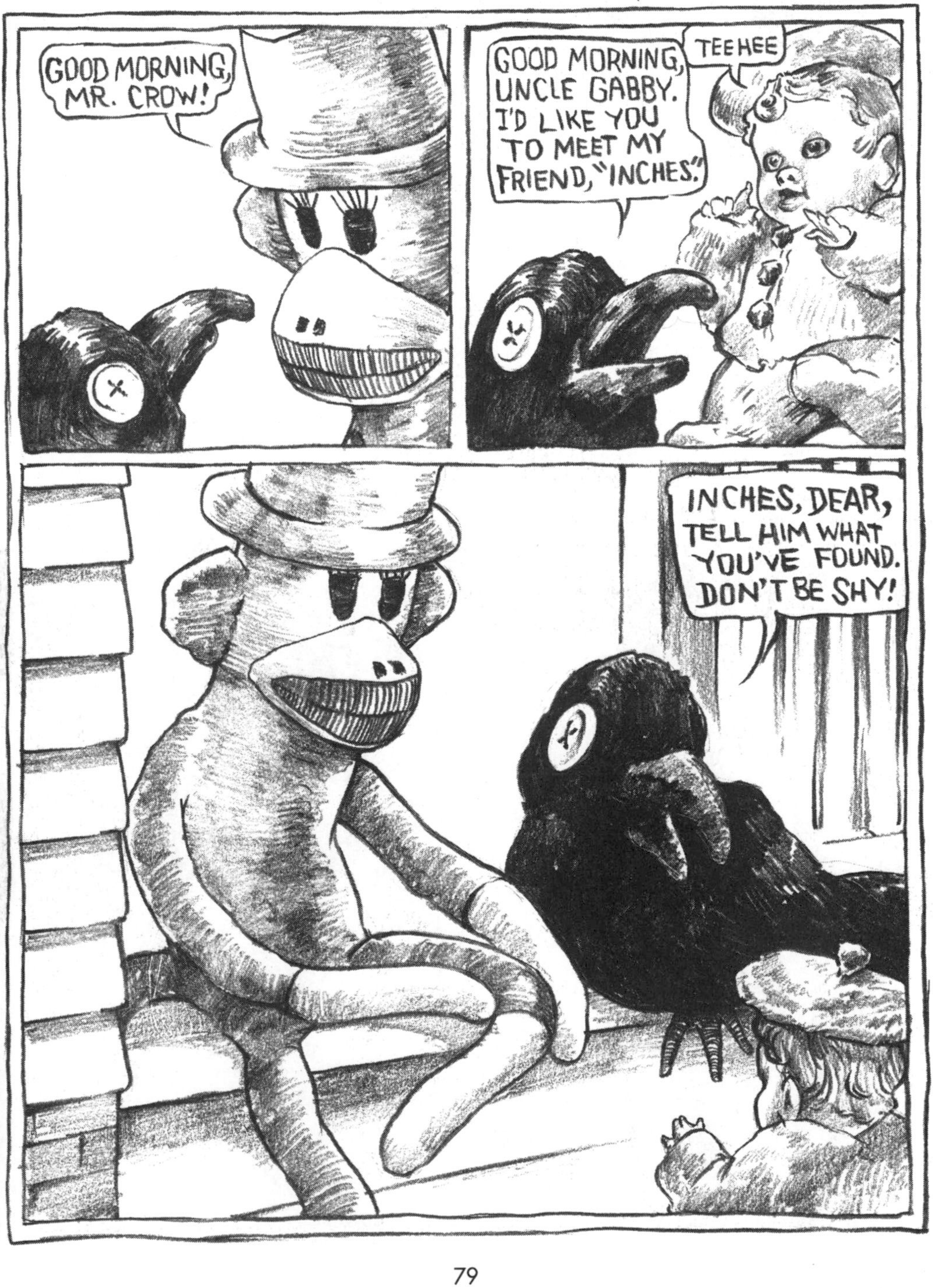
GOOD MORNING, MR. CROW!
GOOD MORNING, UNCLE GABBY. I'D LIKE YOU TO MEET MY FRIEND, "INCHES."
TEE HEE
INCHES, DEAR, TELL HIM WHAT YOU'VE FOUND. DON'T BE SHY!

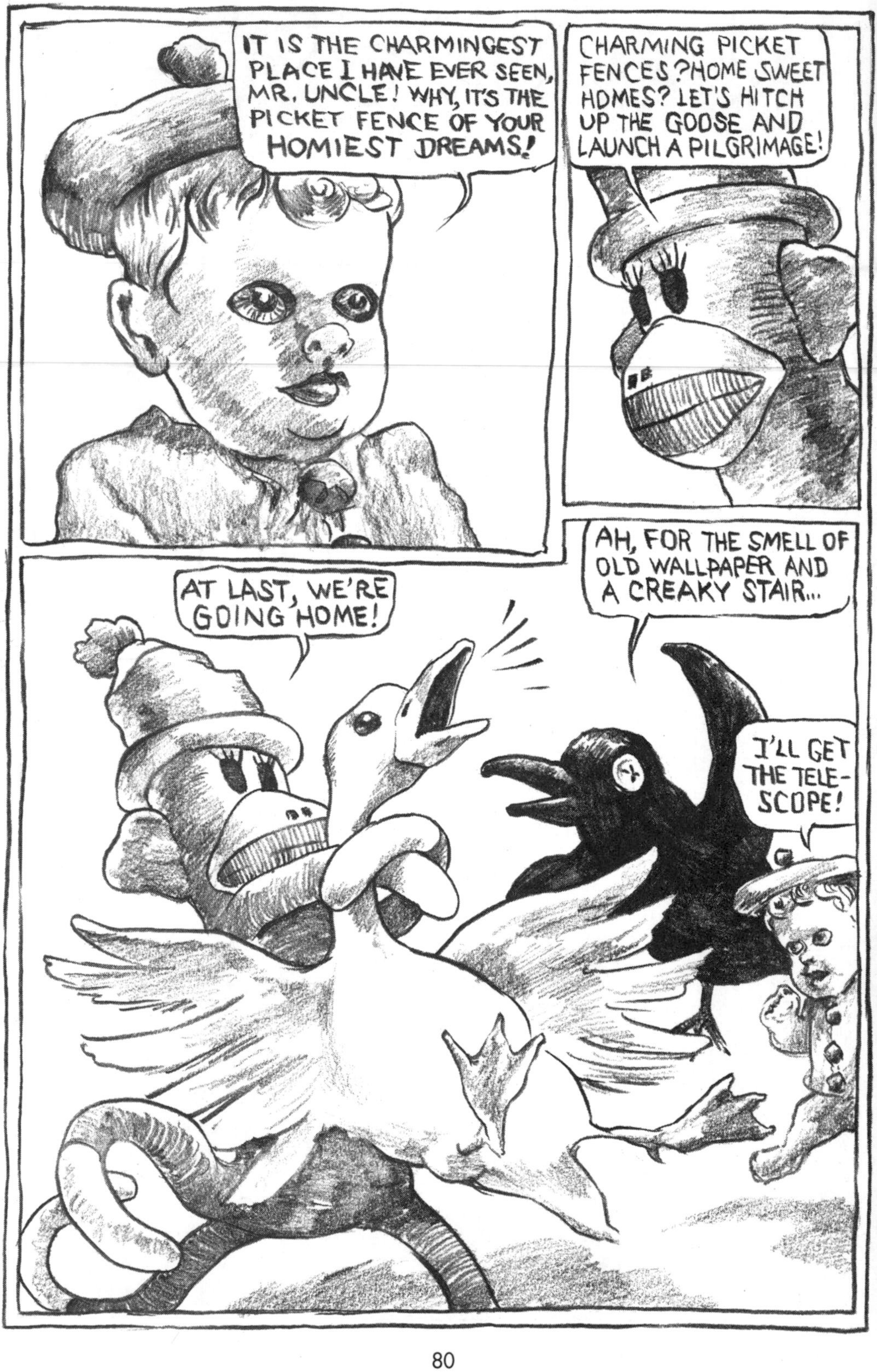
IT IS THE CHARMINGEST PLACE I HAVE EVER SEEN, MR. UNCLE! WHY, IT'S THE PICKET FENCE OF YOUR HOMIEST DREAMS!
CHARMING PICKET FENCES? HOME SWEET HOMES? LET'S HITCH UP THE GOOSE AND LAUNCH A PILGRIMAGE!
AT LAST, WE'RE GOING HOME!
AH, FOR THE SMELL OF OLD WALLPAPER AND A CREAKY STAIR...
I'LL GET THE TELE-SCOPE!

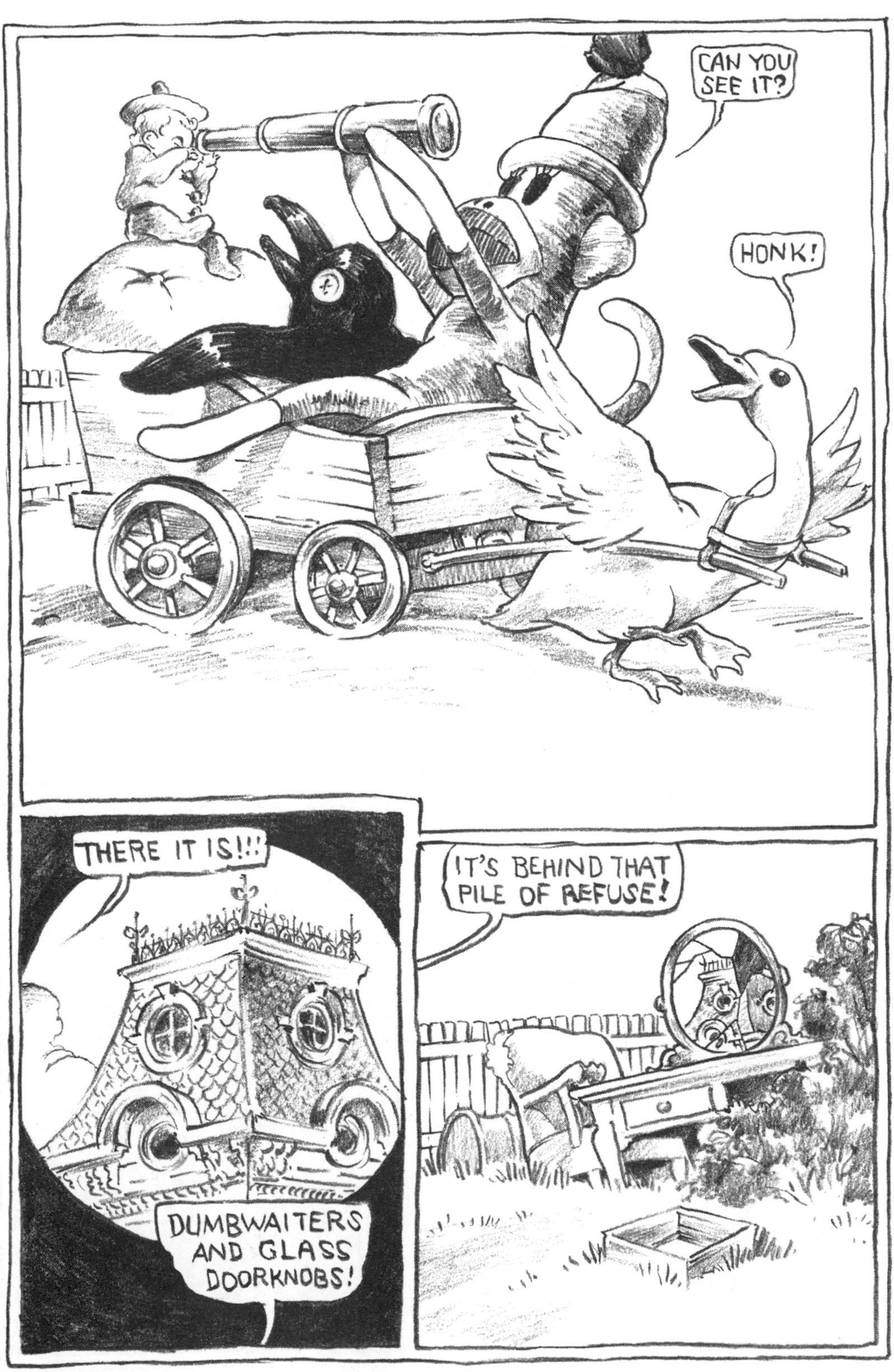
CAN YOU SEE IT?
HONK!
THERE IT IS!!!
DUMBWAITERS AND GLASS DOORKNOBS!
IT'S BEHIND THAT PILE OF REFUSE!

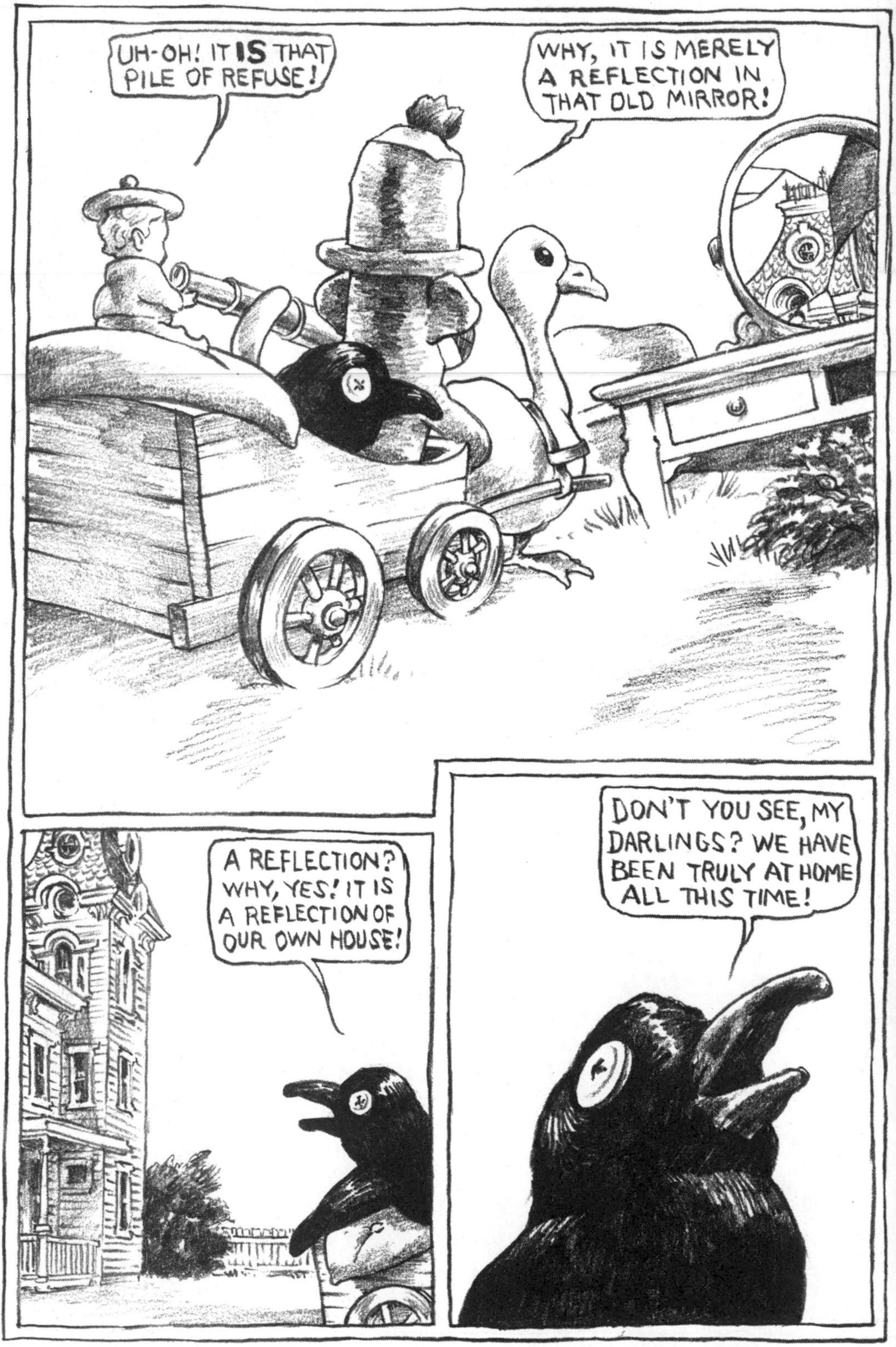
UH-OH! IT **IS** THAT PILE OF REFUSE!
WHY, IT IS MERELY A REFLECTION IN THAT OLD MIRROR!
A REFLECTION? WHY, YES! IT IS A REFLECTION OF OUR OWN HOUSE!
DON'T YOU SEE, MY DARLINGS? WE HAVE BEEN TRULY AT HOME ALL THIS TIME!

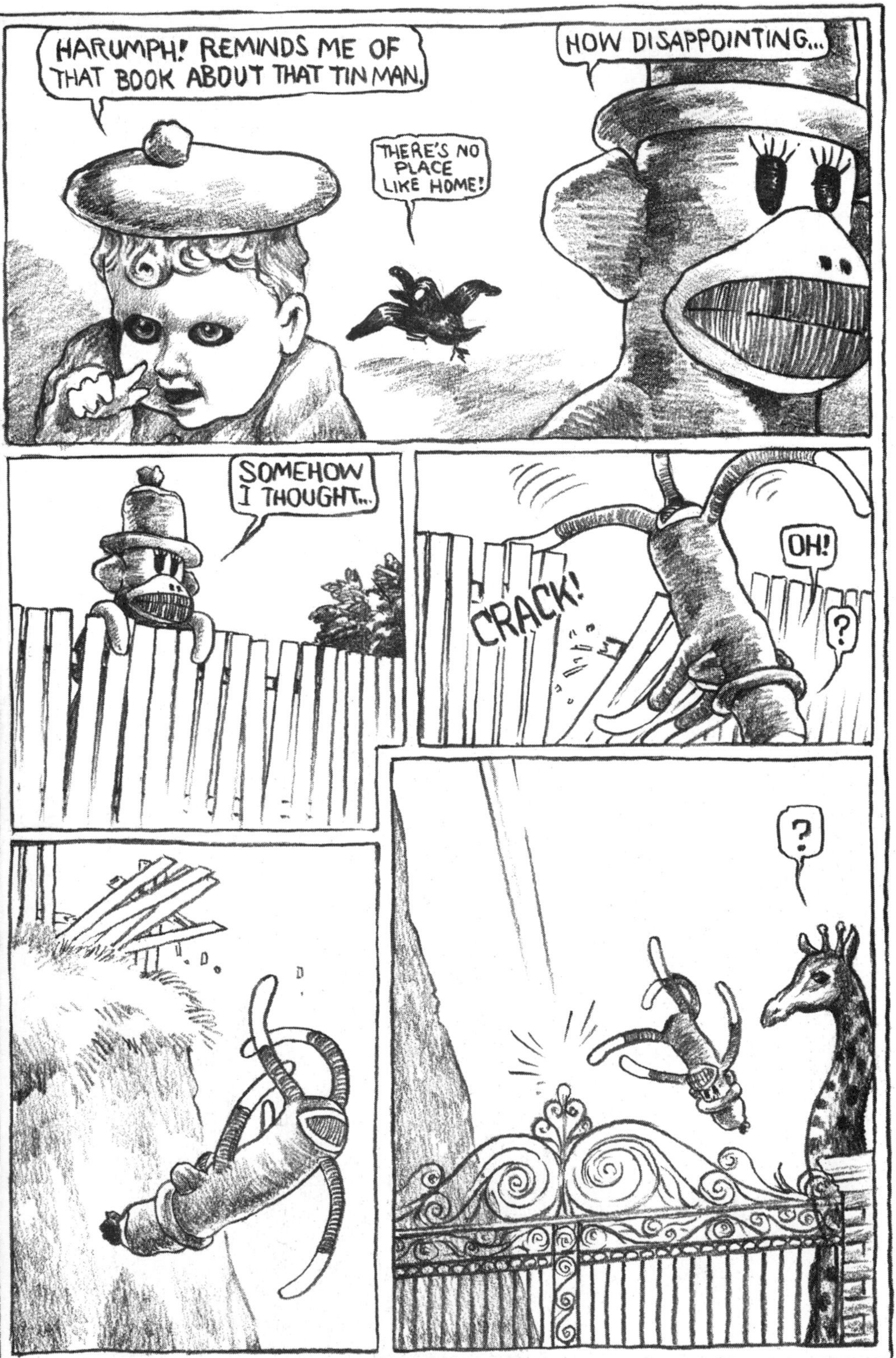
HARUMPH! REMINDS ME OF THAT BOOK ABOUT THAT TIN MAN.
THERE'S NO PLACE LIKE HOME!
HOW DISAPPOINTING...
SOMEHOW I THOUGHT...
CRACK!
OH!
?
?

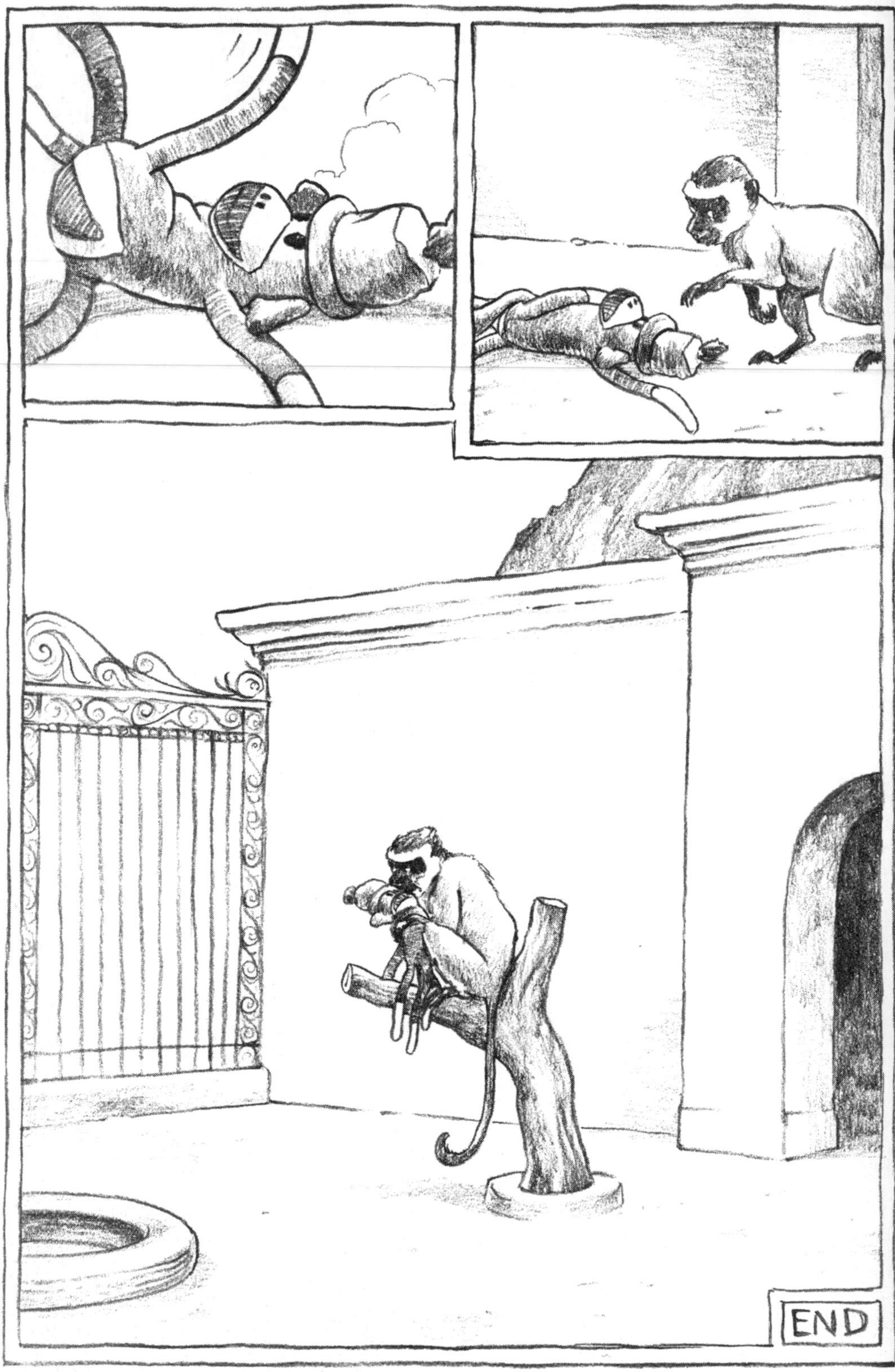
END

THE WAY IT'S GOING

STORY BY HARVEY PEKAR; ART BY JOE SACCO;

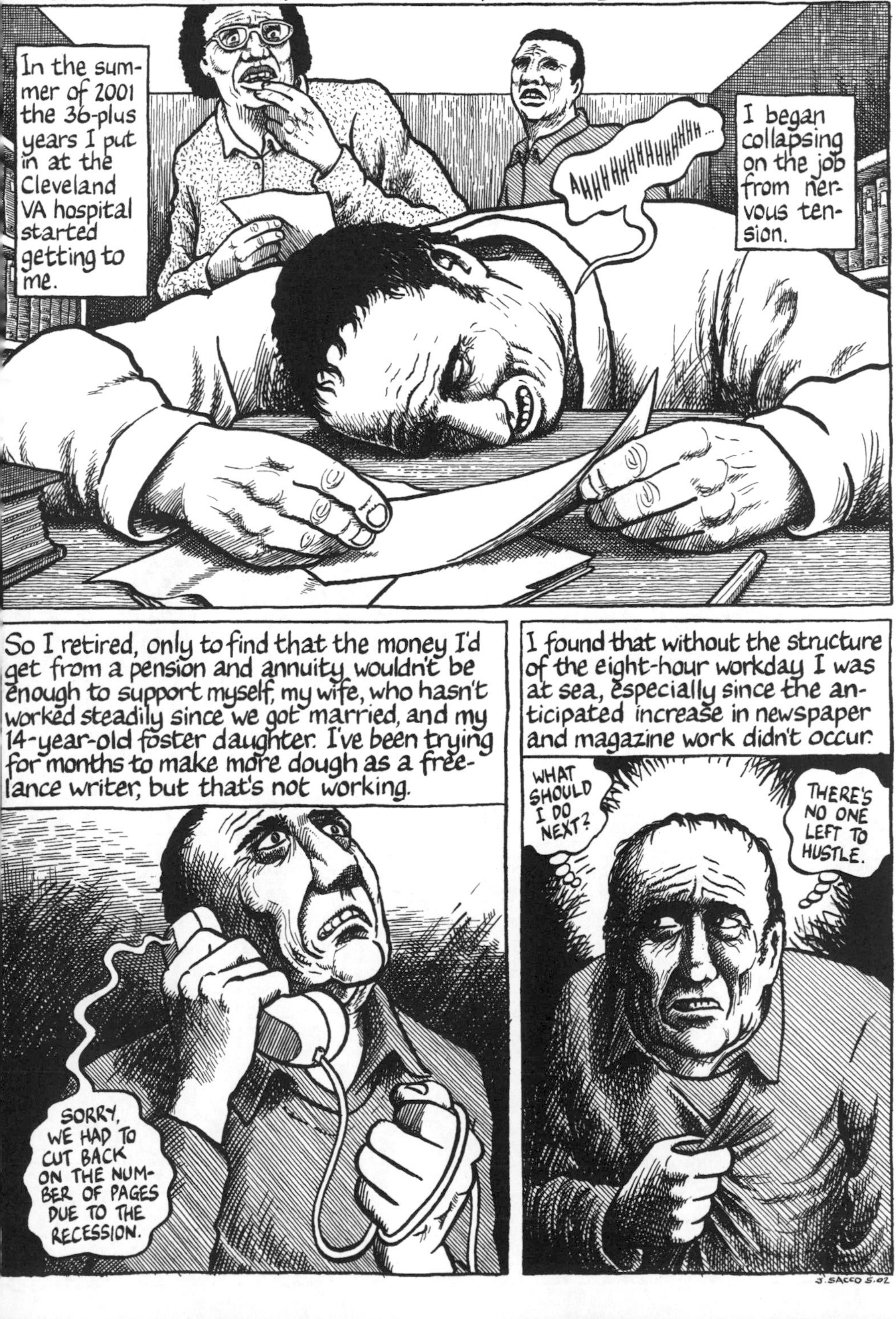
In the summer of 2001 the 36-plus years I put in at the Cleveland VA hospital started getting to me.
AHHHHHHHHHHHHHH...
I began collapsing on the job from nervous tension.
So I retired, only to find that the money I'd get from a pension and annuity wouldn't be enough to support myself, my wife, who hasn't worked steadily since we got married, and my 14-year-old foster daughter. I've been trying for months to make more dough as a freelance writer, but that's not working.
SORRY, WE HAD TO CUT BACK ON THE NUMBER OF PAGES DUE TO THE RECESSION.
I found that without the structure of the eight-hour workday I was at sea, especially since the anticipated increase in newspaper and magazine work didn't occur.
WHAT SHOULD I DO NEXT?
THERE'S NO ONE LEFT TO HUSTLE.
J. SACCO 5.02

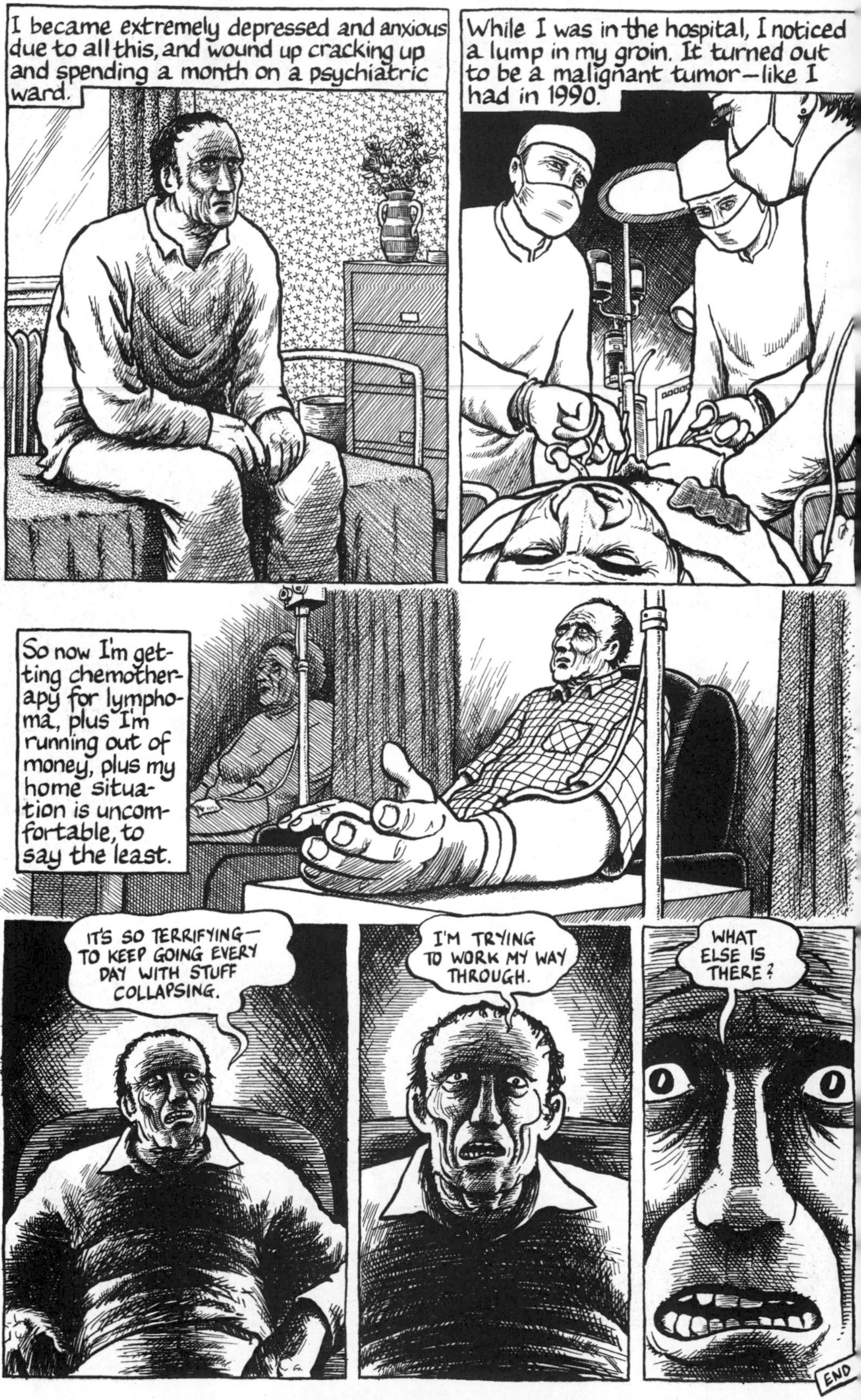
I became extremely depressed and anxious due to all this, and wound up cracking up and spending a month on a psychiatric ward.
While I was in the hospital, I noticed a lump in my groin. It turned out to be a malignant tumor—like I had in 1990.
So now I'm getting chemotherapy for lymphoma, plus I'm running out of money, plus my home situation is uncomfortable, to say the least.
IT'S SO TERRIFYING— TO KEEP GOING EVERY DAY WITH STUFF COLLAPSING.
I'M TRYING TO WORK MY WAY THROUGH.
WHAT ELSE IS THERE?
END

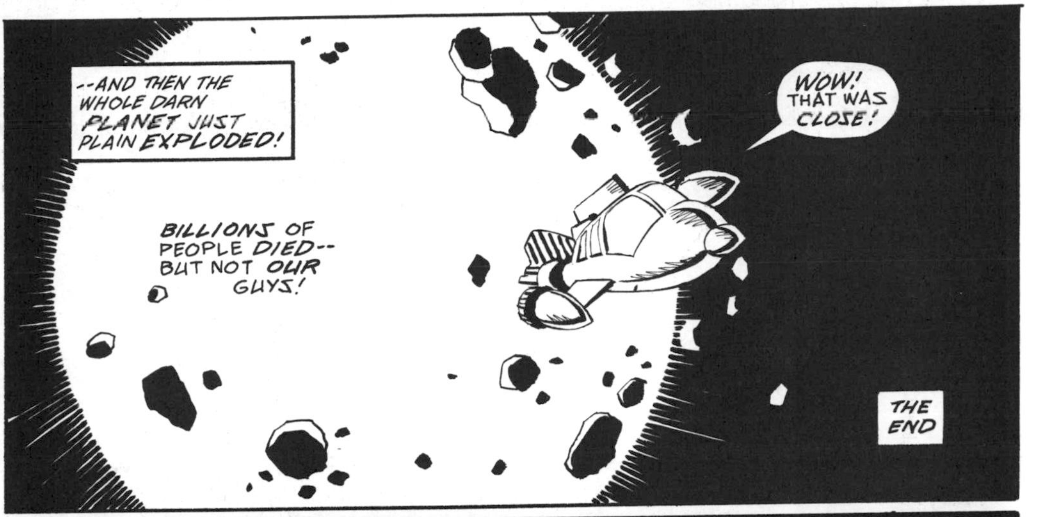
--AND THEN THE WHOLE DARN PLANET JUST PLAIN EXPLODED!
WOW! THAT WAS CLOSE!
BILLIONS OF PEOPLE DIED-- BUT NOT OUR GUYS!
THE END

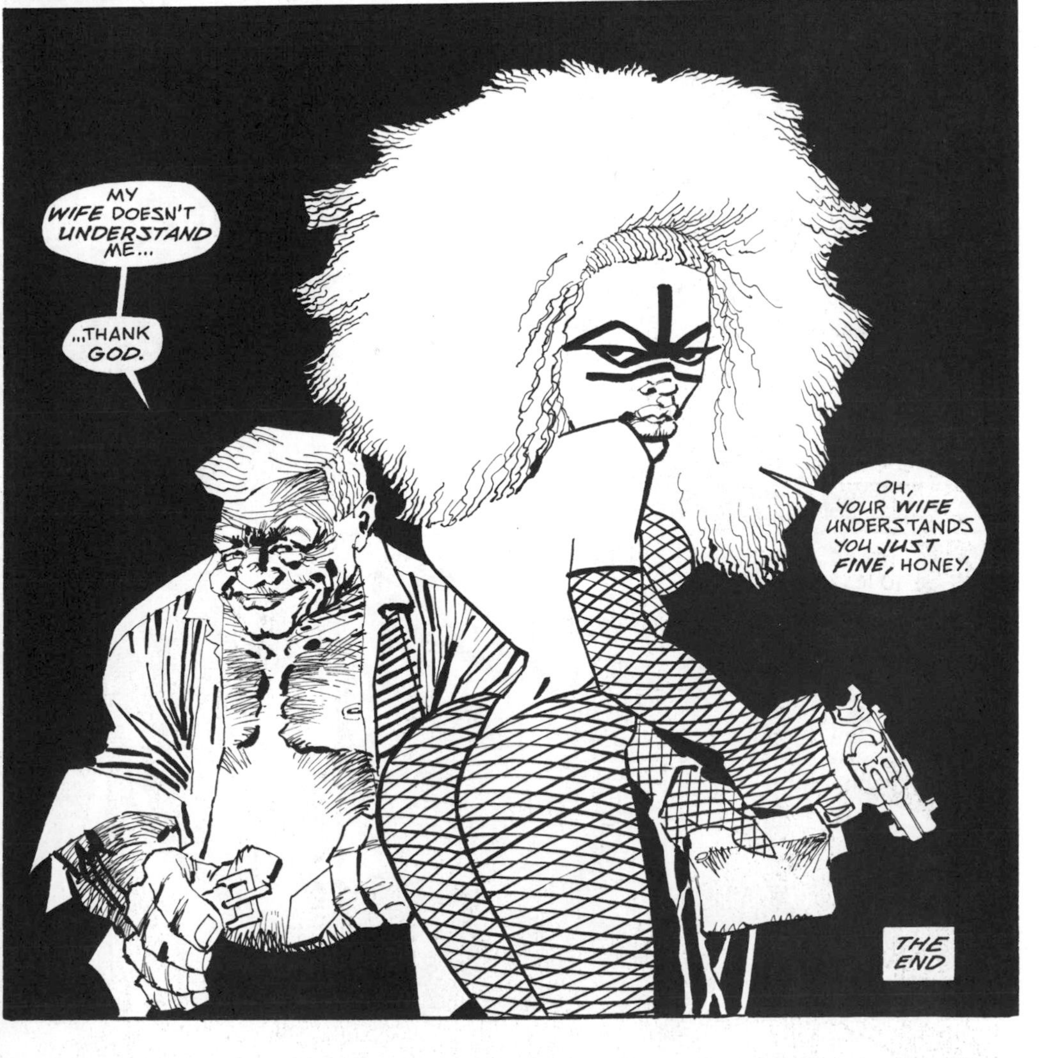
MY WIFE DOESN'T UNDERSTAND ME...
...THANK GOD.
OH, YOUR WIFE UNDERSTANDS YOU JUST FINE, HONEY.
THE END

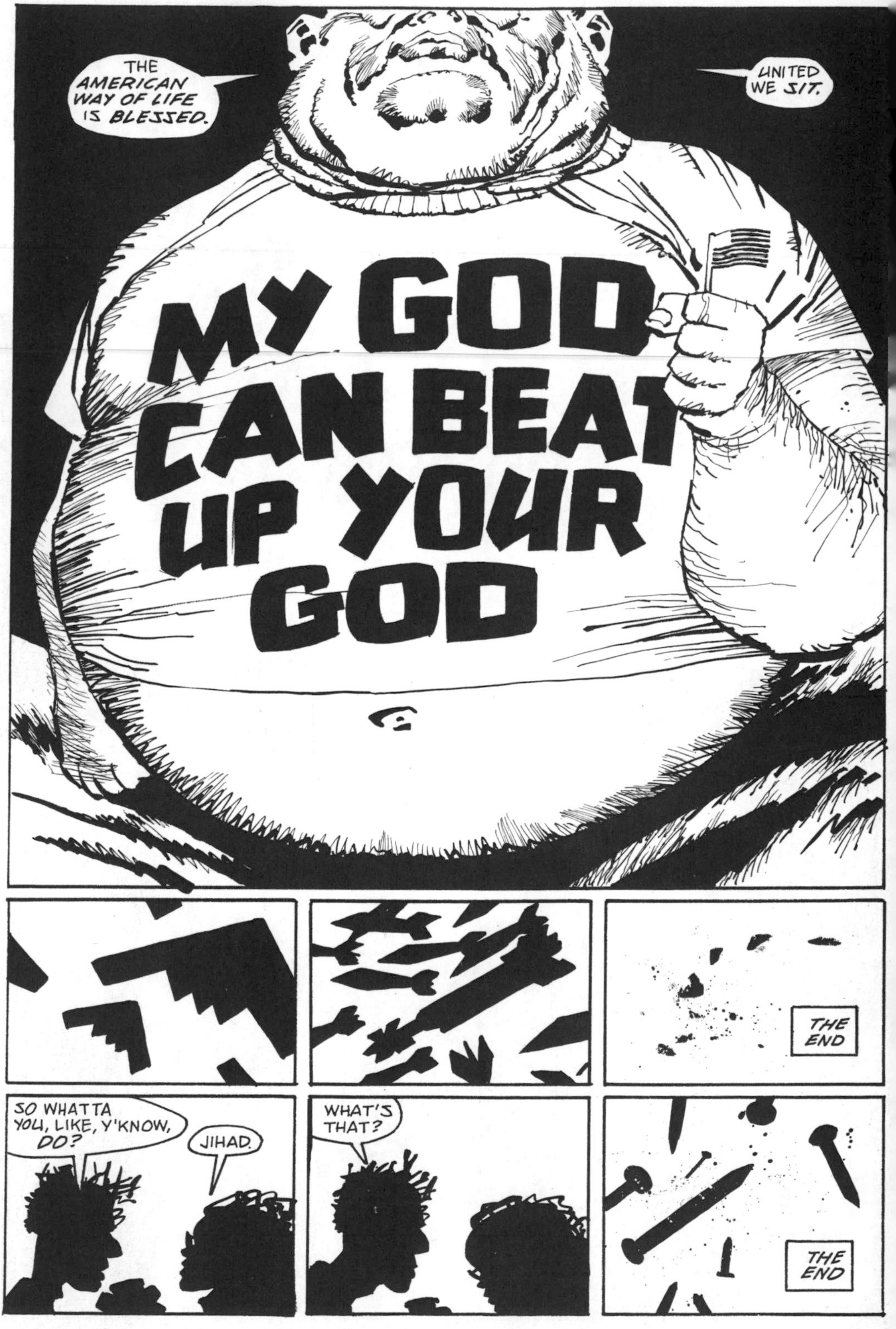
THE AMERICAN WAY OF LIFE IS BLESSED.
UNITED WE SIT.
MY GOD CAN BEAT UP YOUR GOD
THE END
SO WHATTA YOU, LIKE, Y'KNOW, DO?
JIHAD.
WHAT'S THAT?
THE END

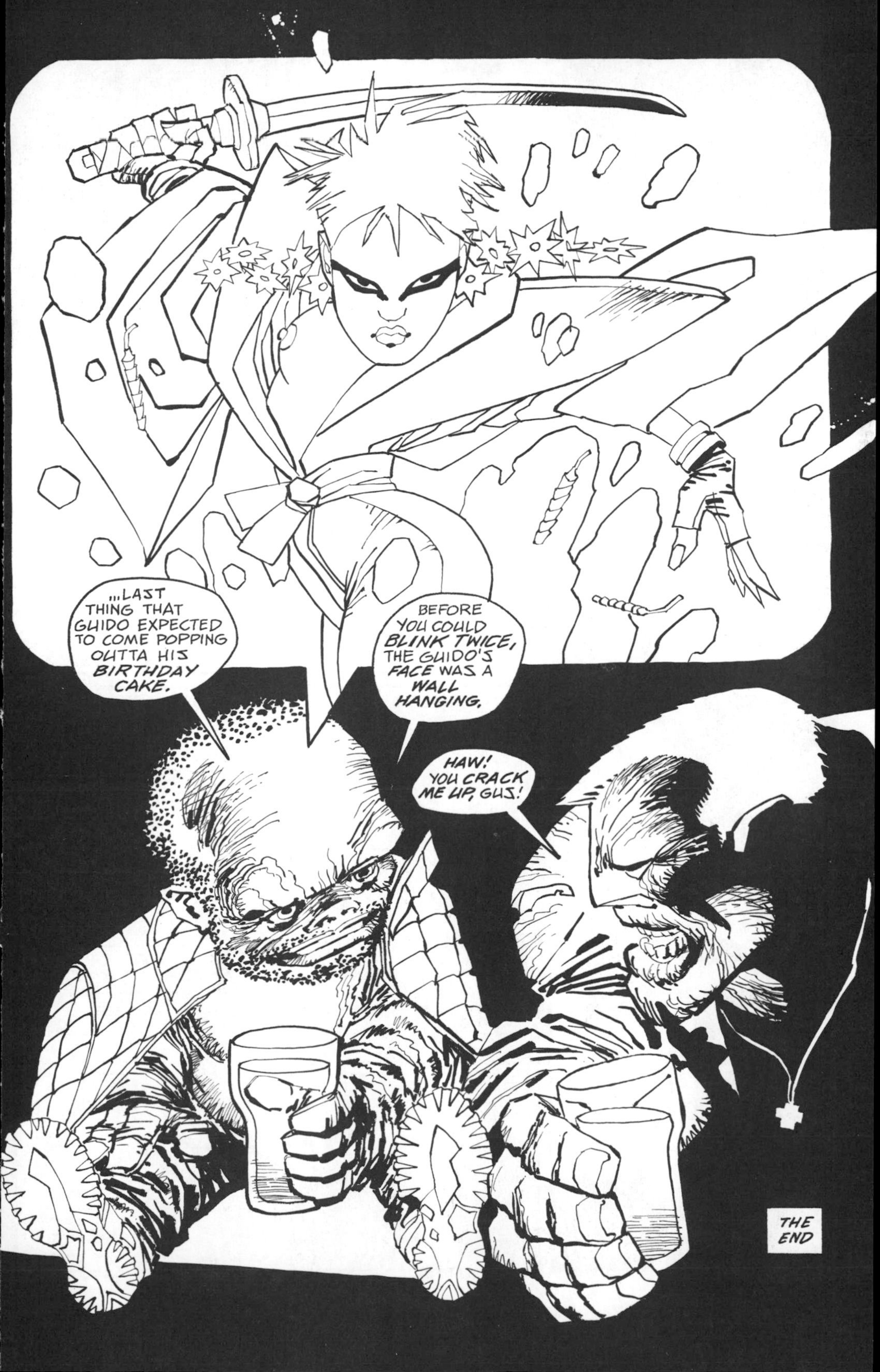
...LAST THING THAT GUIDO EXPECTED TO COME POPPING OUTTA HIS BIRTHDAY CAKE.
BEFORE YOU COULD BLINK TWICE, THE GUIDO'S FACE WAS A WALL HANGING.
HAW! YOU CRACK ME UP, GUS!
THE END

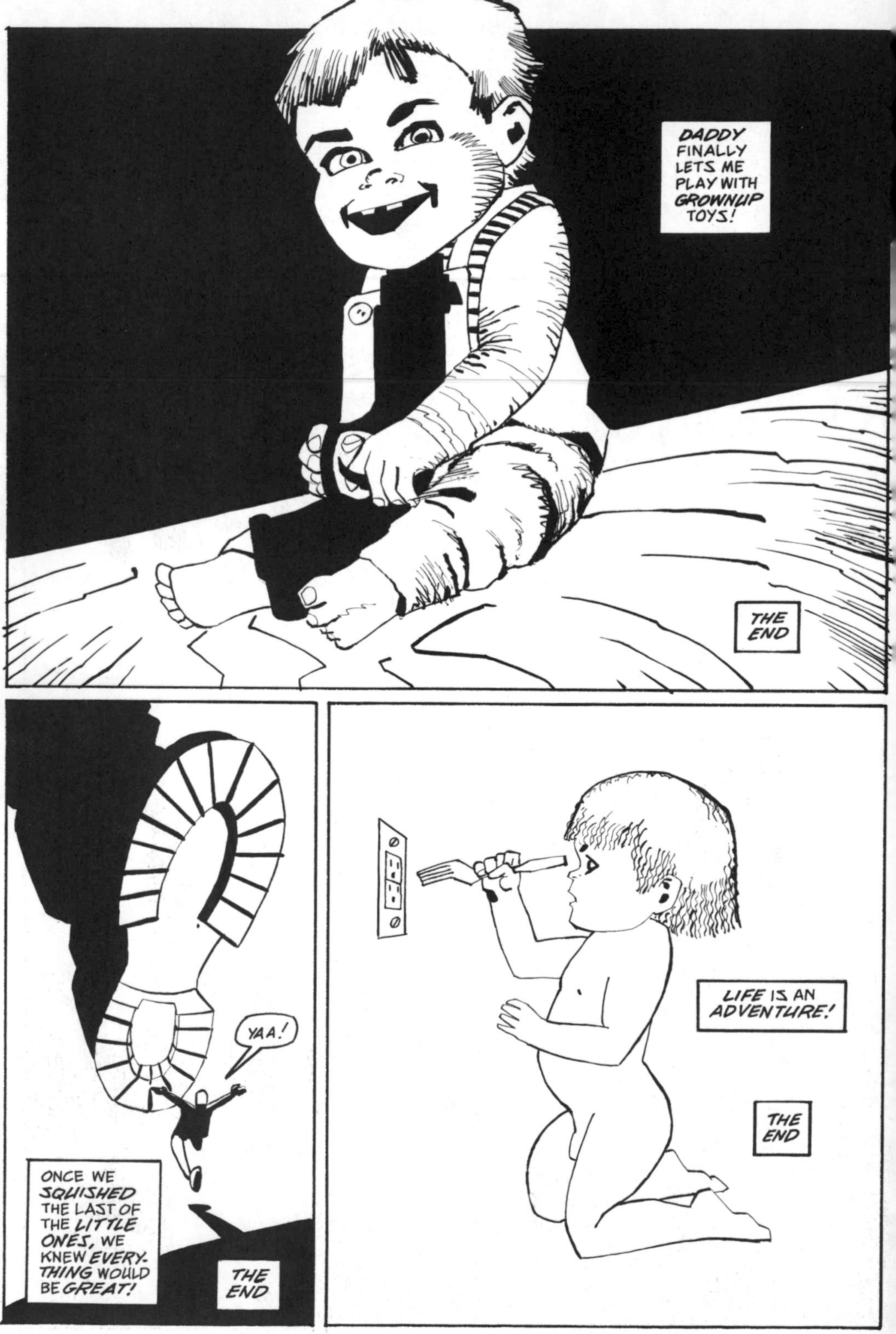
DADDY FINALLY LETS ME PLAY WITH GROWNUP TOYS!
THE END
YAA!
ONCE WE SQUISHED THE LAST OF THE LITTLE ONES, WE KNEW EVERYTHING WOULD BE GREAT!
THE END
LIFE IS AN ADVENTURE!
THE END

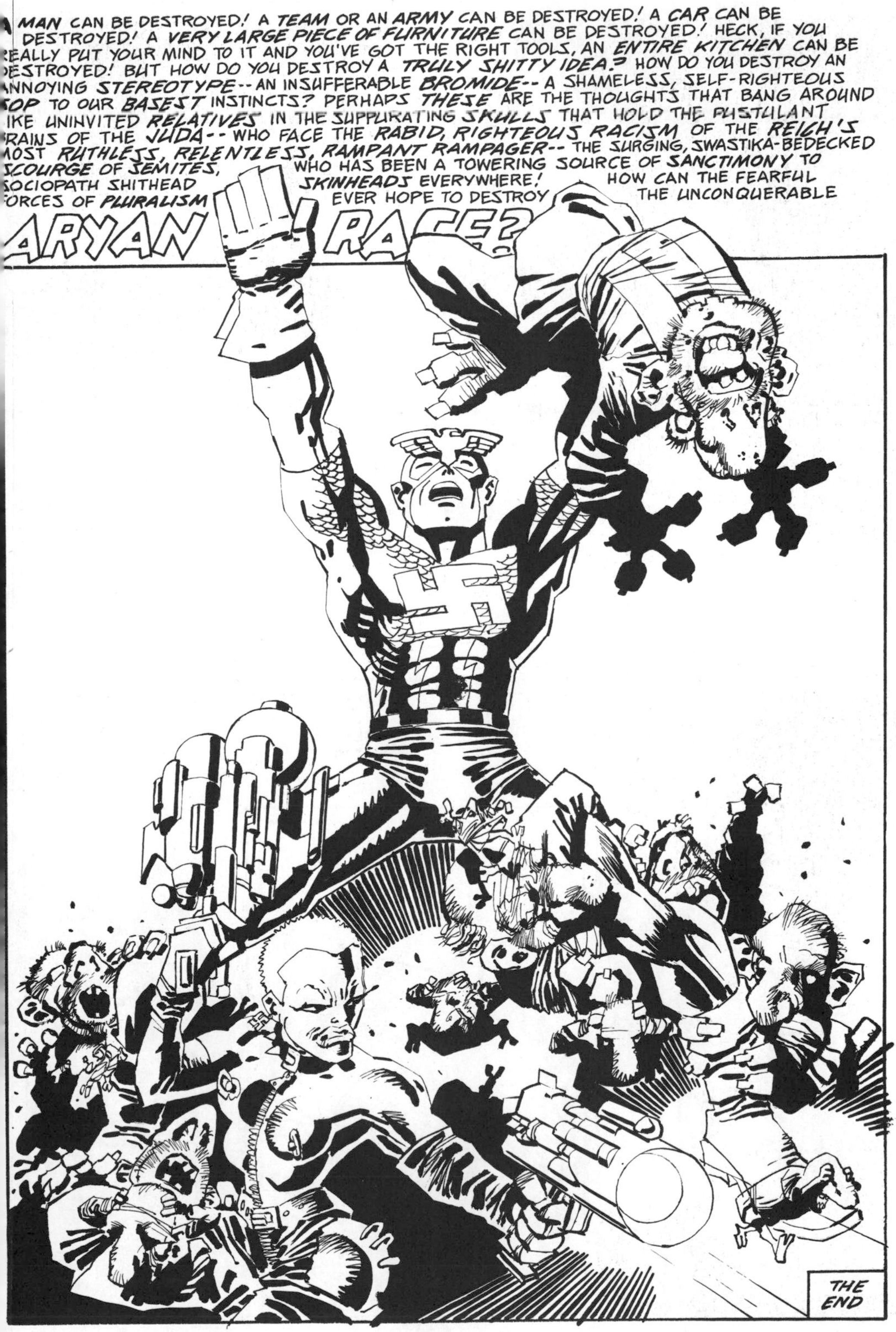
A MAN CAN BE DESTROYED! A TEAM OR AN ARMY CAN BE DESTROYED! A CAR CAN BE DESTROYED! A VERY LARGE PIECE OF FURNITURE CAN BE DESTROYED! HECK, IF YOU REALLY PUT YOUR MIND TO IT AND YOU'VE GOT THE RIGHT TOOLS, AN ENTIRE KITCHEN CAN BE DESTROYED! BUT HOW DO YOU DESTROY A TRULY SHITTY IDEA? HOW DO YOU DESTROY AN ANNOYING STEREOTYPE-- AN INSUFFERABLE BROMIDE-- A SHAMELESS, SELF-RIGHTEOUS SOP TO OUR BASEST INSTINCTS? PERHAPS THESE ARE THE THOUGHTS THAT BANG AROUND LIKE UNINVITED RELATIVES IN THE SUPPURATING SKULLS THAT HOLD THE PUSTULANT BRAINS OF THE JUDA-- WHO FACE THE RABID, RIGHTEOUS RACISM OF THE REICH'S MOST RUTHLESS, RELENTLESS, RAMPANT RAMPAGER-- THE SURGING, SWASTIKA-BEDECKED SCOURGE OF SEMITES, SOCIOPATH SHITHEAD WHO HAS BEEN A TOWERING SOURCE OF SANCTIMONY TO SKINHEADS EVERYWHERE! HOW CAN THE FEARFUL FORCES OF PLURALISM EVER HOPE TO DESTROY THE UNCONQUERABLE
ARYAN RACE?
THE END

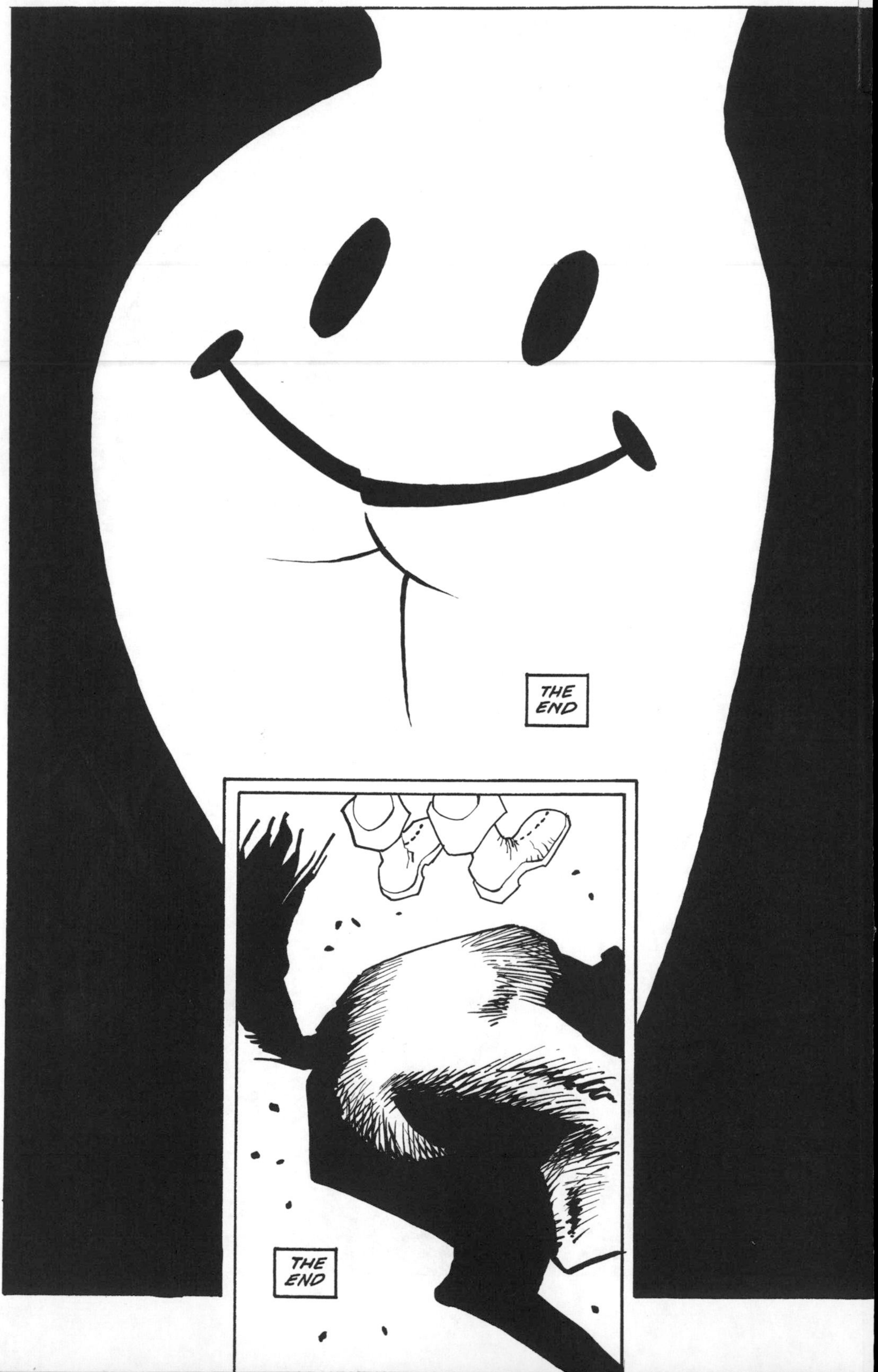
THE END
THE END

Afterword

In an age of irony — and especially in the wake of the terrifying events of September 11 — the concept of *happy endings* seems strangely archaic. For those of us who grew up in the middle of the previous century, raised on a Disney diet of Happily Ever After and Someday My Prince Will Come, I suspect we stopped believing in fairy tales just about the same time as "the day the music died."

With that in mind, I gave each of the artists in this year's Dark Horse Maverick anthology one single editorial mandate: to come up with a story that would somehow fit under the overarching umbrella of *Happy Endings*. Some artists interpreted that quite literally, others with tongue firmly embedded in cheek — still others chose to ponder the very idea itself. The results were unexpected, surprising — and in every case delightfully original, to this editor's eye.

I have to confess, however, that the title itself wasn't exactly original, as I shamelessly ripped off this volume's theme from Actus Independent Comics, an Israeli-based artists' collective who published their own anthology, *Happy End*, earlier this year. Those of you interested in the genesis of the book you hold in your hands — or just plain interested in more eclectic comics — are encouraged to seek out the Actus anthology, distributed by my good friends Chris Staros and Brett Warnock of Top Shelf Productions.

In this age of irony, faith in one's dreams is too often replaced by skepticism, or even cynicism. Curiously, as I grow older, I find my eyes becoming less jaundiced, my heart more willing than ever to believe. While Happily Ever After may be too grandiose or outrageous a notion, small happinesses arrive on a daily basis. This book is one of those, for me. I hope you feel the same.

Diana Schutz
Senior Editor

Creator Bios

Gilbert Austin is best known for his work in the computer game industry, where he wrote and/or directed such hits as *Harvester*, *Privateer*, *Strike Commander*, and *Wing Commander II*. His *Star Wars* parody "Glengarry Glen Darth" has been featured in numerous film festivals and can be seen on the internet at Ifilm.com. He is currently working on several comics projects, including a *Barley and Diggs* graphic novel.

Brian Michael Bendis doesn't really write every single comic on the racks; it only seems that way. A former Cleveland native recently transplanted to the Pacific Northwest, Bendis fought his way to the top of the comics heap with gritty and visceral books like *Torso* and *Jinx*. He currently writes the extremely successful *Ultimate Spider-Man* and *Alias* for Marvel Comics and is executive producer for the upcoming *Spider-Man* animated series on MTV.

Xeric Grant winning cartoonist **Farel Dalrymple** self-published his staggeringly beautiful book, *pop gun war* — a surreal tale of hope and redemption set against an urban landscape — until it was picked up recently by Absence of Ink Press. He currently lives in Brooklyn and has been nominated for this year's Russ Manning Award for Most Promising Newcomer.

In the seven years he's been working in the comics industry, digital production artist **Jason Hvam** has built a solid reputation and an impressive list of projects for himself, including *Usagi Yojimbo* and *Grendel: The Devil Inside* for Dark Horse. He lives in Portland, Oregon, with his wife and newborn son.

Sam Kieth has almost done it all. He is the acclaimed creator of *The Maxx*, which spun off the very strange and equally popular animated series for MTV, and was involved with the creation of DC/Vertigo's wildly popular *Sandman* relaunch with writer Neil Gaiman. Kieth's most recent work includes *Four Women* for DC/Wildstorm, and a *Wolverine/Hulk* miniseries for Marvel Comics.

When **Matt Kindt & Jason Hall** met over the internet, they had no idea that their first collaboration would land them on *Time* magazine's Top 10 Graphic Novels of 2001, but that's exactly what their book, *Pistolwhip* — a slick, film noir-ish tale of passion, betrayal, and radio drama — did. They are currently hard at work on their follow-up: *Pistolwhip: The Yellow Menace*, to be released by Top Shelf Productions in December 2002.

When he's not cartooning, **James Kochalka** hits the road with his indy band *James Kochalka Superstar*. His work has appeared on Nickelodeon, the Sci-Fi Channel, and Spike & Mike's Twisted Animation. He lives in Vermont with his wife and his cat, where he's currently playing old video games and working on a sequel to his *Monkey vs. Robot* graphic novel.

Peter Kuper's work has appeared in, among others, *Time*, *Newsweek*, the New York *Times*, *Washington Post*, *The Village Voice*, and *MAD*, where he illustrates *Spy vs. Spy*. His *Eye of the Beholder* was the first comic strip to regularly appear in the New York *Times* and is now syndicated nationally to alternative papers. *Rolling Stone* named him Comic Book Artist of the Year in 1995, and he has won awards from American Illustration, Print, Society of Illustrators, and Communication Arts, among others.

Arizona-based cartoonist ***Jim Mahfood*** is the artist/writer behind such hits as *Grrl Scouts*, *Zombie Kid*, *Stupid Comics*, and *Voodoom* (a collaborative effort with artist Scott Morse). His upcoming projects include character design work for the new *Tony Hawk* animated cartoon, and a black-and-white Batman story written by Brian Azzarello. For more information, check out his website at 40ozcomics.com.

Katie Mignola lives in New York City with her mother and father, and recently completed the second grade. When she's not inspiring her father to branch out creatively, she also writes short stories of her own. "The Snake and the Magician" is her first published work.

Mike Mignola began working as a comic book artist in 1982, drawing "a little bit of everything for just about everybody." In 1993 he created his own character, Hellboy, for which he has won numerous industry awards, and which is soon to be made into a film. He has also worked as a designer/visual consultant for television and films, including Disney's *Atlantis* and New Line's *Blade 2*.

Frank Miller began his career in comics in the '70s, revitalizing Marvel's *Daredevil*. He then took his talents to DC Comics where he reinvented Batman in 1986 with *Batman: The Dark Knight Returns*. Its recent sequel, the wildly successful *Batman: The Dark Knight Strikes Again*, has broken all industry sales records. Miller's groundbreaking creator-owned *Sin City* series, now in its eleventh year, reintroduced crime fiction to the comic book medium and has won multiple Eisner and Harvey Awards.

Tony Millionaire is the mastermind behind the beautifully twisted syndicated comic strip *Maakies*, which has been turned into a series of animated shorts for *Saturday Night Live*, and is the creator of the Eisner Award winning *Sock Monkey* series at Dark Horse. He and his family live in California.

Bernie Mireault is the writer/artist of *The Jam*, a comic book with a satirical take on the life of a costumed vigilante. Over the last decade, he has produced 16 issues, including *Madman/Jam*, a two-issue collaboration with Michael Allred. Bernie's latest efforts have included *The Blair Witch Chronicles* for Oni Press, the *Dr. Robot Special* for Dark Horse Maverick, and *Fallout* from GT Labs.

Leland Myrick is the creator of the Ignatz and Harvey Award nominated series *Sweet*. He grew up in the Missouri sticks, but now lives in Pasadena, California, with his wife, his daughter, three cats, and two dogs. He is currently working on a new series about one man's quest to find home and love, and he believes that poetry and comics are the same thing at heart, just in different formats.

Michael Avon Oeming is the artist of two hugely popular Image titles: *Powers* and *Bluntman & Chronic*. He began his career inking for Innovation Comics at the age of 14, and has gone on to ink or draw various comics for Marvel, DC, and Dark Horse. With writer/partner Bryan J.L. Glass, Mike created *Ship of Fools*, a six-issue miniseries originally published by Caliber Press. Mike lives in New Jersey with his wife, son, and six small mutants.

Harvey Pekar is a Cleveland-based author with a keen eye for the heartbreakingly mundane of everyday life. He began his career at the age of 19, contributing articles and reviews to jazz magazines, and has since gone on to develop a cult following and win the hearts of literary critics everywhere with his autobiographical series *American Splendor*.

If you made a list of your current favorite ongoing comics, chances are **Clem Robins** is lettering most of them. Based in Norwood, Ohio, with his wife Lisa, Clem splits his time between lettering books like *Preacher*, *100 Bullets*, *Hellblazer*, and *The Filth* for DC/Vertigo and teaching Anatomy at the Art Academy of Cincinnati. His forthcoming book, *The Art of Figure Drawing*, will be published by Northlight Books later this year.

Best known for his stark journalistic and cartooning work, **Joe Sacco** has spent the last 15 years crisscrossing the globe and chronicling his experiences in political hot-spots, including the Middle East. His graphic novel, *Safe Area Gorazde* — an exploration of a small Muslim enclave in Bosnia from 1992 to 1995 — received major coverage from National Public Radio, *Time* magazine, The New York *Times*, and dozens of other publications.

Craig Thompson was born in 1975 and raised in a rural Wisconsin farming community. His first graphic novel, *Good-Bye, Chunky Rice*, debuted to much praise: winner of the Harvey award for Best New Talent, nominated for Eisner, Firecracker, and Ignatz awards, and hailed by *The Comics Journal* as one of the top five comics of 1999. Craig's latest comic book undertaking — the 500-page *Blankets* — explores his childhood and adolescence growing up in the isolated Midwest.

As a colorist and long-time collaborator with Frank Miller, **Lynn Varley** has received many awards both in and outside of the comics industry. Past credits include *Elektra Lives Again* for Marvel Comics, *Sin City: Hell and Back*, *300* (for which she won the Eisner, Harvey, and *CBG* awards for best coloring) for Dark Horse, and most recently *Batman: The Dark Knight Strikes Again*, the sequel to the critically acclaimed *Batman: The Dark Knight Returns* miniseries, which she also colored. She lives in New York City.